MW01141783

# MySQL Admin Cookbook

99 great recipes for mastering MySQL configuration and administration

**Daniel Schneller**

**Udo Schwedt**

PUBLISHING

BIRMINGHAM - MUMBAI

# MySQL Admin Cookbook

Copyright © 2010 Packt Publishing

All rights reserved. No part of this book may be reproduced, stored in a retrieval system, or transmitted in any form or by any means, without the prior written permission of the publisher, except in the case of brief quotations embedded in critical articles or reviews.

Every effort has been made in the preparation of this book to ensure the accuracy of the information presented. However, the information contained in this book is sold without warranty, either express or implied. Neither the authors, nor Packt Publishing and its dealers and distributors will be held liable for any damages caused or alleged to be caused directly or indirectly by this book.

Packt Publishing has endeavored to provide trademark information about all of the companies and products mentioned in this book by the appropriate use of capitals. However, Packt Publishing cannot guarantee the accuracy of this information.

First published: March 2010

Production Reference: 1080310

Published by Packt Publishing Ltd.
32 Lincoln Road
Olton
Birmingham, B27 6PA, UK.

ISBN 978-1-847197-96-2

www.packtpub.com

Cover Image by Vinayak Chittar (vinayak.chittar@gmail.com)

# Credits

**Authors**
Daniel Schneller
Udo Schwedt

**Reviewers**
Kai Seidler
Marc Delisle

**Acquisition Editor**
Sarah Cullington

**Development Editor**
Reshma Sundaresan

**Technical Editors**
Pallavi Kachare
Bhupali Khule
Aaron Rosario

**Copy Editor**
Lakshmi Menon

**Editorial Team Leader**
Akshara Aware

**Indexer**
Rekha Nair

**Project Team Leader**
Lata Basantani

**Project Coordinator**
Shubhanjan Chatterjee

**Proofreader**
Chris Smith

**Graphics**
Geetanjali Sawant

**Production Coordinator**
Melwyn Arun D'sa

**Cover Work**
Melwyn Arun D'sa

# About the Authors

**Daniel Schneller** works as a software developer, database administrator, and general IT professional for an independent software vendor in the retail sector. After successfully graduating from the University of Cooperative Education in Heidenheim, Germany with a degree in Business Computer Science, he started his career as a professional software developer, focused on the Microsoft technology stack. In 2002, he started focusing on enterprise-level Java development and has since gained extensive knowledge and experience implementing large scale systems based on Java EE and relational databases, especially MySQL since version 4.0.

Currently, he is mostly involved with the ongoing development of framework-level functionality, including customization and extension of an ORM-based persistence layer. He is involved in different open source projects such as FindBugs, Eclipse, and Checkstyle, and infrequently blogs about Java, MySQL, Windows, Linux, and other insanities at `http://www.danielschneller.com`.

When I first was asked by Packt Publishing whether I would be interested in writing a book about MySQL on Christmas Eve 2008 little did I know how much work, stress, but also what a lot of fun I was headed for.

Now, that the book is finally done I would like to thank those people without whom getting it done would have been impossible.

First of all, I'd like to thank Udo for agreeing to be my co-author. Without him, this whole thing would have taken a lot longer and would have been not half as useful as I believe it has turned out now.

I would also like to thank the team at Packt Publishing—most importantly for noticing and reading my blog, consequently contacting me to get the whole thing started—but also for taking care of schedules, providing support, guidance and feedback, and keeping us on track the whole way.

Last, but by no means least, I want to thank Jenny—for encouraging me to write a book in the first place, and then making sure I never ran out of tea, cookies, or motivation on the countless evenings I spent sitting in front of the keyboard instead of with her. I dedicate this book to her.

**Udo Schwedt** has over ten years of experience in the IT industry as a professional Java developer and software architect. He is head of the Java architecture team and deputy head of the Java development department at the IT service provider for Germany's market leader in the Do-It-Yourself sector.

He has been fascinated by computers since his childhood, and taught himself the basics of programming during his school years. After graduating from school, he began his studies at the RWTH Aachen, Germany, which he finished with a summa cum laude degree in computer science, minoring in psychology with a focus on software ergonomics.

Udo started his career as a professional C, C++, and Java developer in a software company that delivers leading solutions in the financial online transaction processing sector. In 2003, he joined his current employer as a Java framework developer for a large-scale international project, where he met Daniel. In the course of the project, he gained extensive experience in using MySQL in a professional context.

For both **Daniel** and **Udo**, the common project involved the design and implementation of a database infrastructure solution for a Java-based merchandise management software system with tens of thousands of clients. The evaluation of different database systems and the realization of the infrastructure made it necessary for them to delve into MySQL beyond the typical utilization scenarios. The resulting decentralized multi-platform environment based on more than 500 decentralized MySQL server instances with more than 5,500 replication slaves bears challenges not covered by the standard MySQL documentation.

To the Packt Publishing team: Thank you for critiques, encouragement, and organization.

To Daniel: Thank you so much for your confidence in me. I still feel honored you asked me to co-author this book—you should know better by now!

To my parents: Thank you for supporting me from the very start and ever since.

To Katharina, Johannah, and Frida: Thank you for your support and all your patience—I love you!

# About the Reviewers

**Kai Seidler** was born in Hamburg in 1970. He graduated from the Technical University of Berlin with a Diplom Informatiker degree (Master of Science equivalent) in Computer Science. In the 90s he created and managed Germany's biggest IRCnet server irc.fu-berlin.de, and co-managed one of the world's largest anonymous FTP server ftp.cs.tu-berlin.de. He professionally set up his first public web servers in 1993. From 1993 until 1998, he was member of Projektgruppe Kulturraum Internet, a research project on net culture and network organization. In 2002, he co-founded Apache Friends and created the multi-platform Apache web server bundle XAMPP. Around 2005, XAMPP became the most popular Apache stack worldwide. In 2006, his third book, *Das XAMPP-Handbuch*, was published by Addison Wesley.

Currently he's working as a Technology Evangelist for web-tier products at Sun Microsystems.

**Marc Delisle** is a member of the MySQL Developers Guild—which brings together community developers—because of his involvement with phpMyAdmin. He started to contribute to this popular MySQL web interface in December 1998, when he made the first multi-language version. He has been actively involved with this software project since May 2001 as a developer and project administrator.

Marc has worked since 1980 at Cegep de Sherbrooke, Québec, Canada, as an application programmer and network manager. He has also been teaching networking, security, and PHP/MySQL application development. Marc lives in Sherbrooke with his wife and they enjoy spending time with their four children.

Marc authored the first ever Packt Publishing book, *Mastering phpMyAdmin for Effective MySQL Management*, and its revised editions. He also wrote *Creating your MySQL Database: Practical Design Tips and Techniques*, again with Packt Publishing.

I would like to thank the fine team at Packt for their support in reviewing this book.

# Table of Contents

# Preface

MySQL is the most popular open-source database and is also known for its easy set up feature. However, proper configuration beyond the default settings is still a challenge, along with some other day-to-day maintenance tasks such as backup and restoring, performance tuning, and server monitoring.

This book provides both step-by-step recipes and relevant background information on these topics and more. It covers everything from basic to advanced aspects of MySQL administration and configuration. All recipes are based on real-world experience and were derived from proven solutions used in an enterprise environment.

## What this book covers

Chapter 1, *Replication*: In this chapter, you will see how to set up MySQL replication, useful for load balancing, online backups, and fail-over scenarios. Advanced replication scenarios using the blackhole engine and streaming slave deployment are discussed beyond the basic topics.

Chapter 2, *Indexing*: You will be shown how to create, drop, and modify indexes, perhaps the most important means of optimizing your MySQL servers' performance. Fulltext indexing, clustered and non-clustered indexes are compared and presented with their respective strengths and typical use cases. Moreover, you will learn how to identify duplicate indexes, which can hinder your servers' performance.

Chapter 3, *Tools*: This chapter will get you acquainted with the MySQL Administrator and Query Browser GUI Tools as well as the MySQL command-line client and how to use it in concert with external scripts and tools. You will also see how to create custom diagrams for MySQL Administrator and share connection profiles between multiple computers.

Chapter 4, *Backing Up and Restoring MySQL Data*: In this chapter, we introduce the basic approaches to backing up your database and restoring data again. Advanced techniques like on-the-fly compression, point in time recovery, avoiding extended lock situations, backup in replication scenarios, and partial backup and restore are also covered.

Chapter 5, *Managing Data*: You will learn some tricks beyond the basic SQL commands, which enable you to delete data in a highly efficient manner and insert data based on existing database content, and how to import and export data to and from your database.

Chapter 6, *Monitoring and Analyzing a MySQL Installation*: We present approaches to monitoring table space usage, and how to use database metadata to your advantage. Typical performance bottlenecks and lock contention problems are discussed as well.

Chapter 7, *Configuring MySQL*: This chapter deals with MySQL configuration and how to best leverage available settings to their full potential. Table space management, pool sizing, and logging options are discussed along with platform-specific caveats and advanced installation scenarios, such as multiple instances on one server.

Chapter 8, *MySQL User Management*: Management of MySQL user accounts is discussed in detail throughout this chapter. Typical user roles with appropriate privileges and approaches to restricting access sensibly are proposed. You will also learn how to regain access to your database in case the administrative user credentials are lost.

Chapter 9, *Managing Schemas*: This chapter includes topics such as adding and removing columns to and from tables and choosing a suitable storage engine and character set for individual needs. Another recipe covers a technique to add a new primary key column to a table already filled with data. Ways to manage and automate database schema evolution, as part of a software life cycle are presented as well. And if you have always missed "ADD INDEX IF NOT EXISTS", you will find a solution to this, too.

Appendix, *Good to Know*: In this final part of the book you can find several things that can turn out useful in everyday situations, but did not fit the step-by-step recipe format naturally. Topics range from choosing character sets to getting the most out of 32 bit address space limitations.

# What you need for this book

This book was written using MySQL versions 5.0 and 5.1. Most recipes will work equally well on either on of these versions. Older versions might work as well, but have not been tested. You can download both versions of the MySQL server from `http://dev.mysql.com`. You will find references to programs and tools not included in the MySQL server distribution. These can be downloaded from their respective websites, named in the recipes. The "MySQL GUI Tools"—MySQL Administrator and MySQL Query Browser—which are referenced multiple times throughout the book—unfortunately have been declared End Of Life shortly before this book was finished. Currently, there is no functionally equivalent successor to these tools. "MySQL Workbench" is the new combined tool recommended on the MySQL website, but it does not offer all features required to apply many of the recipes in this book. We recommend you to download MySQL Administrator and MySQL Query Browser from the MySQL website's archive area where they are still available. You will find them by just using the links printed in this book.

# Who this book is for

This book is for ambitious MySQL users as well as professional data center database administrators. Beginners as well as experienced administrators will profit from this cookbook and get fresh ideas to improve their MySQL environments. Detailed background information will enable them to widen their MySQL horizon.

It does not cover SQL basics, how to install MySQL servers, or how to design a relational database schema. Readers are expected to have a basic understanding of the SQL language and database concepts in general.

# Conventions

In this book, you will find a number of styles of text that distinguish between different kinds of information. Here are some examples of these styles, and an explanation of their meaning.

Code words in text are shown as follows: "Only use qualified statements and `replicate-*-table` configuration options for intuitively predictable replication!"

A block of code is set as follows:

```
slave> create database sakila;
slave> use sakila;
slave> source /tmp/sakila_master.sql;
slave> CHANGE MASTER TO master_host='master.example.com', master_
port=3306, master_ user='repl', master_password='slavepass';
slave> START SLAVE;
```

When we wish to draw your attention to a particular part of a code block, the relevant lines or items are set in bold:

```
slave> SHOW SLAVE STATUS\G
*********************** 1. row ***********************
                    . . .
          Slave_IO_Running: Yes
         Slave_SQL_Running: Yes
                    . . .
```

**New terms** and **important words** are shown in bold. Words that you see on the screen, in menus or dialog boxes for example, appear in the text like this: "You will see the familiar messages about InnoDB filling up the data files and finally, the **Ready for connections** line".

Warnings or important notes appear in a box like this.

 Tips and tricks appear like this.

# Reader feedback

Feedback from our readers is always welcome. Let us know what you think about this book—what you liked or may have disliked. Reader feedback is important for us to develop titles that you really get the most out of.

To send us general feedback, simply send an e-mail to feedback@packtpub.com, and mention the book title via the subject of your message.

If there is a book that you need and would like to see us publish, please send us a note in the **SUGGEST A TITLE** form on www.packtpub.com or e-mail suggest@packtpub.com.

If there is a topic that you have expertise in and you are interested in either writing or contributing to a book on, see our author guide on www.packtpub.com/authors.

# Customer support

Now that you are the proud owner of a Packt book, we have a number of things to help you to get the most from your purchase.

 **Downloading the example code for the book**
Visit http://www.packtpub.com/files/code/7962_Code.zip to directly download the example code.

# Errata

Although we have taken every care to ensure the accuracy of our content, mistakes do happen. If you find a mistake in one of our books—maybe a mistake in the text or the code—we would be grateful if you would report this to us. By doing so, you can save other readers from frustration and help us improve subsequent versions of this book. If you find any errata, please report them by visiting http://www.packtpub.com/support, selecting your book, clicking on the **let us know** link, and entering the details of your errata. Once your errata are verified, your submission will be accepted and the errata will be uploaded on our website, or added to any list of existing errata, under the Errata section of that title. Any existing errata can be viewed by selecting your title from http://www.packtpub.com/support.

# Piracy

Piracy of copyright material on the Internet is an ongoing problem across all media. At Packt, we take the protection of our copyright and licenses very seriously. If you come across any illegal copies of our works, in any form, on the Internet, please provide us with the location address or website name immediately so that we can pursue a remedy.

Please contact us at copyright@packtpub.com with a link to the suspected pirated material.

We appreciate your help in protecting our authors, and our ability to bring you valuable content.

# Questions

You can contact us at questions@packtpub.com if you are having a problem with any aspect of the book, and we will do our best to address it.

# 1
# Replication

In this chapter, we will discuss:

- ► Setting up automatically updated slaves of a server based on a SQL dump
- ► Setting up automatically updated slaves of a selection of tables based on a SQL dump
- ► Setting up automatically updated slaves using data file copy
- ► Sharing read load across multiple machines
- ► Using replication to provide full-text indexing for InnoDB tables
- ► Estimating network and slave I/O load
- ► Limiting network and slave I/O load in heavy write scenarios using the blackhole storage engine
- ► Setting up slaves via network streaming
- ► Skipping problematic queries
- ► Checking if servers are in sync
- ► Avoiding duplicate server IDs
- ► Setting up slaves to report custom information about themselves to the master

## Introduction

Replication is an interesting feature of MySQL that can be used for a variety of purposes. It can help to balance server load across multiple machines, ease backups, provide a workaround for the lack of fulltext search capabilities in InnoDB, and much more.

The basic idea behind replication is to reflect the contents of one database server (this can include all databases, only some of them, or even just a few tables) to more than one instance. Usually, those instances will be running on separate machines, even though this is not technically necessary.

Traditionally, MySQL replication is based on the surprisingly simple idea of repeating the execution of all statements issued that can modify data—not SELECT—against a single *master* machine on other machines as well. Provided all secondary *slave* machines had identical data contents when the replication process began, they should automatically remain in sync. This is called **Statement Based Replication (SBR)**.

With MySQL 5.1, **Row Based Replication (RBR***)* was added as an alternative method for replication, targeting some of the deficiences SBR brings with it. While at first glance it may seem superior (and more reliable), it is not a silver bullet—the pain points of RBR are simply different from those of SBR.

Even though there are certain use cases for RBR, all recipes in this chapter will be using Statement Based Replication.

While MySQL makes replication generally easy to use, it is still important to understand what happens internally to be able to know the limitations and consequences of the actions and decisions you will have to make. We assume you already have a basic understanding of replication in general, but we will still go into a few important details.

## Statement Based Replication

SBR is based on a simple but effective principle: if two or more machines have the same set of data to begin with, they will remain identical if all of them execute the exact same SQL statements in the same order.

Executing all statements manually on multiple machines would be extremely tedious and impractical. SBR automates this process. In simple terms, it takes care of sending all the SQL statements that *change* data on one server (the master) to any number of additional instances (the slaves) over the network.

The slaves receiving this stream of modification statements execute them automatically, thereby effectively reproducing the changes the master machine made to its data originally. That way they will keep their local data files in sync with the master's.

One thing worth noting here is that the network connection between the master and its slave(s) need not be permanent. In case the link between a slave and its master fails, the slave will remember up to which point it had read the data last time and will continue from there once the network becomes available again.

In order to minimize the dependency on the network link, the slaves will retrieve the *binary logs* (*binlogs*) from the master as quickly as they can, storing them on their local disk in files called *relay logs*. This way, the connection, which might be some sort of dial-up link, can be terminated much sooner while executing the statements from the local *relay-log* asynchronously. The relay log is just a copy of the master's *binlog*.

The following image shows the overall architecture:

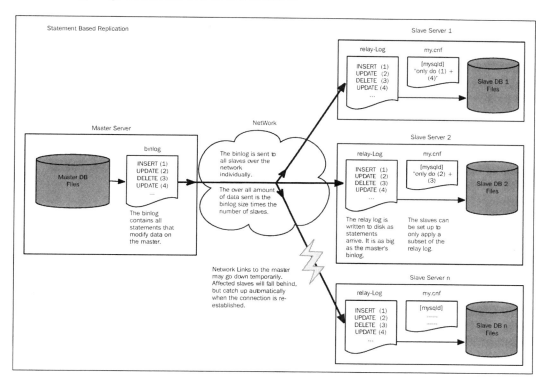

## Filtering

In the image you can see that each slave may have its individual configuration on whether it executes all the statements coming in from the master, or just a selection of those. This can be helpful when you have some slaves dedicated to special tasks, where they might not need all the information from the master.

All of the binary logs have to be sent to each slave, even though it might then decide to throw away most of them. Depending on the size of the binlogs, the number of slaves and the bandwidth of the connections in between, this can be a heavy burden on the network, especially if you are replicating via wide area networks.

Even though the general idea of transferring SQL statements over the wire is rather simple, there are lots of things that can go wrong, especially because MySQL offers some configuration options that are quite counter-intuitive and lead to hard-to-find problems.

For us, this has become a best practice:

"Only use qualified statements and `replicate-*-table` configuration options for intuitively predictable replication!"

What this means is that the only filtering rules that produce intuitive results are those based on the `replicate-do-table` and `replicate-ignore-table` configuration options. This includes those variants with wildcards, but specifically excludes the *all-database* options like `replicate-do-db` and `replicate-ignore-db`. These directives are applied on the slave side on all incoming relay logs.

The master-side `binlog-do-*` and `binlog-ignore-*` configuration directives influence which statements are sent to the binlog and which are not. We strongly recommend against using them, because apart from hard-to-predict results they will make the binlogs undesirable for server backup and restore. They are often of limited use anyway as they do not allow individual configurations per slave but apply to all of them.

For these reasons you will not find any use of these options in this book.

# Setting up automatically updated slaves of a server based on a SQL dump

In this recipe, we will show you how to prepare a dump file of a MySQL master server and use it to set up one or more replication slaves. These will automatically be updated with changes made on the master server over the network.

## Getting ready

You will need a running MySQL master database server that will act as the *replication master* and at least one more server to act as a *replication slave*. This needs to be a separate MySQL instance with its own data directory and configuration. It can reside on the same machine if you just want to try this out. In practice, a second machine is recommended because this technique's very goal is to distribute data across multiple pieces of hardware, not place an even higher burden on a single one.

For production systems you should pick a time to do this when there is a lighter load on the master machine, often during the night when there are less users accessing the system. Taking the SQL dump uses some extra resources, but unless your server is maxed out already, the performance impact usually is not a serious problem. Exactly how long the dump will take depends mostly on the amount of data and speed of the I/O subsystem.

You will need an administrative operating system account on the master and the slave servers to edit the MySQL server configuration files on both of them. Moreover, an administrative MySQL database user is required to set up replication.

We will just replicate a single database called `sakila` in this example.

**Replicating more than one database**

In case you want to replicate more than one schema, just add their names to the commands shown below. To replicate all of them, just leave out any database name from the command line.

## How to do it...

1. At the operating system level, connect to the master machine and open the MySQL configuration file with a text editor. Usually it is called `my.ini` on Windows and `my.cnf` on other operating systems.

2. On the master machine, make sure the following entries are present and add them to the `[mysqld]` section if not already there:

```
server-id=1000
log-bin=master-bin
```

If one or both entries already exist, do not change them but simply note their values. The `log-bin` setting need not have a value, but can stand alone as well.

3. Restart the master server if you need to modify the configuration.

4. Create a user account on the master that can be used by the slaves to connect:

```
master> grant replication slave on *.* to 'repl'@'%' identified by
'slavepass';
```

5. Using the `mysqldump` tool included in the default MySQL install, create the initial copy to set up the slave(s):

```
$ mysqldump -uUSER -pPASS --master-data --single-transaction
sakila > sakila_master.sql
```

6. Transfer the `sakila_master.sql` dump file to each slave you want to set up, for example, by using an external drive or network copy.

7. On the slave, make sure the following entries are present and add them to the `[mysqld]` section if not present:

```
server-id=1001
replicate-wild-do-table=sakila.%
```

When adding more than one slave, make sure the `server-id` setting is unique among master and all clients.

8. Restart the slave server.

9. Connect to the slave server and issue the following commands (assuming the data dump was stored in the `/tmp` directory):

```
slave> create database sakila;
slave> use sakila;
slave> source /tmp/sakila_master.sql;
slave> CHANGE MASTER TO master_host='master.example.com',
master_port=3306, master_ user='repl',
master_password='slavepass';
slave> START SLAVE;
```

10. Verify the slave is running with:

```
slave> SHOW SLAVE STATUS\G
************************* 1. row *************************
                . . .
        Slave_IO_Running: Yes
       Slave_SQL_Running: Yes
                . . .
```

## How it works...

Some of the instructions discussed in the previous section are to make sure that both master and slave are configured with different `server-id` settings. This is of paramount importance for a successful replication setup. If you fail to provide unique `server-id` values to all your server instances, you might see strange replication errors that are hard to debug.

Moreover, the master must be configured to write *binlogs*—a record of all statements manipulating data (this is what the slaves will receive).

 Before taking a full content dump of the `sakila` demo database, we create a user account for the slaves to use. This needs the REPLICATION SLAVE privilege.

Then a data dump is created with the `mysqldump` command line tool. Notice the provided parameters `--master-data` and `--single-transaction`. The former is needed to have `mysqldump` include information about the precise moment the dump was created in the resulting output. The latter parameter is important when using InnoDB tables, because only then will the dump be created based on a transactional snapshot of the data. Without it, statements changing data while the tool was running could lead to an inconsistent dump.

The output of the command is redirected to the `/tmp/sakila_master.sql` file. As the `sakila` database is not very big, you should not see any problems. However, if you apply this recipe to larger databases, make sure you send the data to a volume with sufficient free disk space—the SQL dump can become quite large. To save space here, you may optionally pipe the output through `gzip` or `bzip2` at the cost of a higher CPU load on both the master and the slaves, because they will need to unpack the dump before they can load it, of course.

If you open the uncompressed dump file with an editor, you will see a line with a CHANGE MASTER TO statement. This is what `--master-data` is for. Once the file is imported on a slave, it will know at which point in time (well, rather at which binlog position) this dump was taken. Everything that happened on the master after that needs to be replicated.

Finally, we configure that slave to use the credentials set up on the master before to connect and then start the replication. Notice that the CHANGE MASTER TO statement used for that does not include the information about the log positions or file names because that was already taken from the dump file just read in.

From here on the slave will go ahead and record all SQL statements sent from the master, store them in its relay logs, and then execute them against the local data set.

This recipe is very important because the following recipes are based on this! So in case you have not fully understood the above steps yet, we recommend you go through them again, before trying out more complicated setups.

## See also

▶  *Avoiding duplicate server IDs*

# Setting up automatically updated slaves of a selection of tables based on a SQL dump

Often you might not need to replicate everything, but only a subset of tables in a database. MySQL allows exercising fine-grained control over what to replicate and what to ignore. Unfortunately, the configuration settings are not as obvious as they might seem at first glance.

In this recipe, you will see how to replicate only a few select tables from a database.

## Getting ready

The setup for this recipe is the same as for the previous one, *Setting up automatically updated slaves of a server based on a SQL dump*. Only the configuration options on the slave need to be changed. So instead of repeating everything here, we just present the important differences.

## How to do it...

1. Follow the steps of the previous recipe up to the point where the `mysqldump` tool is used to extract the initial data set from the master. Use this command instead:

   ```
   $ mysqldump -uUSER -pPASS --master-data --single-transaction
   sakila address country city > sakila_master.sql
   ```

2. Go on with the steps of the previous recipe up to the point where it tells you to edit the slave machine's configuration. Change the configuration as follows instead in the `[mysqld]` section:

   ```
   server-id=1001
   replicate-wild-ignore-table=sakila.%
   replicate-do-table=sakila.address
   replicate-do-table=sakila.country
   replicate-do-table=sakila.city
   ```

3. Continue with the rest of the instructions as in the *Setting up automatically updated slaves of a server based on a SQL dump* recipe.

## How it works...

The SQL dump file taken on the master is limited to three tables: `address`, `country`, and `city`. The slave's configuration also tells it to only execute statements coming from the master that targets one of these three tables (`replicate-do-table` directives), while overtly ignoring any other changes in the `sakila` database (`replicate-wild-ignore-table`). Even though all other statements are still retrieved from the master and stored temporarily in the relay log files on the slave, only those with modifications to one of the three tables explicitly configured are actually run. The rest are discarded.

You can choose any subset of tables, but you need to make sure to take Foreign key relationships between tables into account. In this example, the `address` table has a reference to the `city` table via the `city_id` column, while `city` in turn has a relationship with `country`. If you were to exclude either one of the latter and your storage engine on the slave was InnoDB, replication would break because of Foreign key violations when trying to insert an address, since its dependencies were not fulfilled.

MySQL does not help you in this respect; you must make sure to identify all tables and their relationships manually before setting up the replication.

## There's more...

In this example, we clearly specified three tables by their full names. There are more options available, not only to include but also to exclude tables. See the MySQL online manual's chapter 16.1.3.3 on *Replication Slave Options and Variables* for more information on these at `http://dev.mysql.com/doc/refman/5.1/en/replication-options-slave.html`.

# Setting up automatically updated slaves using data file copy

Even though replication is designed to keep your data in sync, circumstances might require you to set up slaves afresh. One such scenario might be severely changing the master data, making replication too expensive. Using a SQL dump to re-initialize the slaves might be too time-consuming, depending on the size of the data set and the power of the slave machines.

In cases where master and slave databases are the same size anyway (meaning, you do not have filters in place to sync data only partially) and if you can afford a downtime on the master database, there is another way of providing slaves with a fresh starting point: copying the master's data files to the slave.

 Beware that this approach will lose all data that was changed on the slave alone. So make sure that this is what you want!

## Getting ready

To follow along with this recipe you will need privileges to shut down both master and slave MySQL instances and access the data and log directories on both machines. Depending on the size of your database you will have to judge which method of copying will be the best between the machines. If both are part of a local area network, copying via a shared drive or something like FTP will probably be the fastest way. You might, however, need to resort to other means of data transfer like external hard disks or the like, when only limited bandwidth is available.

Moreover, you will need administrative MySQL user accounts on both sides to execute the necessary statements to control replication.

## How to do it...

1.  Open the master's configuration file with a text editor. Locate the line controlling the name of the binlog files. It is located in the `[mysqld]` section and will look similar to this:

    ```
    [mysql]

    . . .

    log-bin=master-bin

    . . .
    ```

2.  Change the value of that setting to a different name. In this example, we will use `log-bin=new-master-bin`. This will cause the master MySQL server to start with a new sequence of binlogs upon its next launch, making a convenient starting point for the replication.

3.  Shut down the master database.

4.  Navigate to the MySQL data directory. The exact location can be found in the MySQL configuration file. Make sure to find both InnoDB data and log locations.

5.  Optionally, copy data and log files to another location locally on the master. This might be faster than copying via network or USB drives, and allows for a quick restart of the master. If you do this, use this temporary location to copy the data in the next step.

6.  Copy the data to the slave machine. We recommend a temporary target location on the slave because this allows the slave to continue running for the time the copying takes. Unless you want to bring along all the user accounts and privilege information from the master to the slaves, you should exclude the `mysql` folder from the data directory. You also need not copy the binary logs (in this example called `master-bin.*`).

7.  Stop the slave server.

8.  You can restart the master once the original data and transaction log files have been copied. Make sure it starts with a new sequence of binlogs called `new-master-bin.000001`.

9. Write down the names and sizes of InnoDB data and log files you copied to the slave. These will have to be entered into the slave's configuration because, otherwise, InnoDB will not start up. Also, pay attention to an `autoextend` option, which the last of the data files might have attached. Make sure you carry over this option, should it be there on the master. You can also take these values from the master's configuration file, of course.

10. Replace the original slave data and log files with those of the master. Make sure you keep the `mysql` database directory if you decided not to copy it from the master.

11. Make sure you delete the `master.info` file and any relay-logs from the slave—those do not match the current state anymore and would cause trouble when the slave is restarted.

12. Edit the slave's configuration file to match the names and sizes of the data files you wrote down a minute ago.

13. Start the slave server again. It should come up without any problems using the new data files. If not, make sure you got everything right in the config file regarding names and sizes of the data files.

14. Re-initialize the replication on the slave. This is rather easy because we altered the master's configuration to log any changes that occurred after the snapshot copy was taken to a new series of binlog files. Fill in the appropriate host name, user, and password values for your master:

```
slave> CHANGE MASTER TO MASTER_HOST='master', MASTER_USER='repl',
MASTER_PASSWORD='slavepass', MASTER_LOG_FILE='new-master-
bin.000001';
slave> START SLAVE;
```

As we want the slave to start reading the `new-master-bin.000001` file from the beginning, no `MASTER_LOG_POS` has to be specified.

15. Verify whether the slave is running with:

```
slave> SHOW SLAVE STATUS\G
*********************** 1. row ***************************
                        . . .
        Slave_IO_Running: Yes
       Slave_SQL_Running: Yes
                        . . .
```

## How it works...

The principle of this recipe is very simple: replication needs a common starting point on master and slave. What could be better than a 1:1 copy of the original master's data? As the master is shut down during the process, no more writes can happen. Configuring it to start with a new binlog file on its next start makes it trivial to point the slave to the right position because it is right at the new file's beginning.

If you cannot change the master binlogs' file names, the process is slightly more complicated. First you need to make sure nobody can modify any data for a short period of time. You do so with a FLUSH TABLES WITH READ LOCK; statement. Then issue a SHOW MASTER STATUS; and note the values. Now, without closing the client connection or releasing the lock, shut down the master server. Only if the lock is kept while shutting down the master can you be sure no write operations take place and invalidate the binlog position you just gathered.

Copy the data and transaction log files as described above. The remaining steps are the same, except of course, when you issue the CHANGE MASTER TO on the slave. Here you need to insert the MASTER_LOG_FILE and MASTER_LOG_POS you got from SHOW MASTER STATUS.

## There's more...

The steps described above require you to take down both master and slave databases, albeit not necessarily at the same time. Nevertheless, this might not be an option if you are dealing with a production system that cannot be shut down easily.

In these cases, you have some other options that are, however, not explained in detail here.

### Conserving data file by using LVM snapshots

If your data and log files are stored on a logical volume managed by LVM, you can use its snapshot feature to conserve the data files' state once you have got the SHOW MASTER STATUS information. As soon as the snapshot has been taken, you can release the lock again and proceed as described above, copying not the most current version but the snapshot files. Be advised, however, that this approach might take a significant hit on the I/O performance of you master!

### Backing up data using Percona xtrabackup

At the time of writing, an open-source alternative to the commercially available *innobackup* tool (available from http://www.innodb.com/products/hot-backup/) is under active development. While being primarily a backup tool that allows backing up InnoDB databases while the server is up and running, the documentation contains a (currently empty) section on setting up a slave from a backup in replication. Experience tells that Percona—the company behind xtrabackup—is very engaged in the MySQL ecosystem and might very well have completed its set of instructions by the time you read this. To check on the current status of the project go to `https://launchpad.net/percona-xtrabackup`.

# Sharing read load across multiple machines

Often you have a very unequal distribution of read and write operations on a database. Websites usually get many more visitors just browsing and reading contents than actually contributing contents. This results in the database server being mainly busy reading information instead of adding or modifying existing material.

Replication can be used to alleviate scalability issues when your site reaches a certain size and a single machine might reach the limits of its performance reserves.

Unfortunately, MySQL does not offer this load-balancing functionality itself, so you will need to take appropriate actions on the application level.

In this recipe, we will show you the general procedure to follow when sharing read accesses between two slave machines while still aiming writes at the master. Beware that due to the asynchronous nature of MySQL replication, your application must be able to handle slightly out-of-date results because issuing an INSERT, UPDATE, or DELETE against the master will not mean that you can read the modified data back immediately as the slave might take some time to catch up. Usually, on a local network this should be a couple of seconds at most, but nevertheless the application code must be ready for that.

To simplify the scheme, you should design your application to exclusively read from the slaves and only use the master for modifications. This brings the additional benefit of being able to keep the overall system up and running while switching to a read-only mode temporarily, backing up the master server. This is not part of this recipe, however.

The example used in this recipe uses three database servers. The sample application is written in Java, using the *MySQL Connector/J* JDBC database driver. Depending on what application platform you are using, syntax and function names will differ, but the general principle is language independent.

 The source code shown later has been abbreviated to show only the most relevant portions. You can find the complete file on the book's website.

## Getting ready

Depending on your application infrastructure, you will need privileges to change its database connectivity configuration and the source code. This is usually a task that requires cooperation with application developers.

To follow along with this example you should be familiar with the Java language and its basic constructs.

Moreover, you will need three MySQL servers—one configured as the master and two others as slaves. They will be referred to as *master, slave1,* and *slave2* in this example. Substitute your concrete host names appropriately.

You will also need the Java Standard Edition development tools available from `http://java.sun.com`, and the MySQL Connector/JDBC driver available from `http://dev.mysql.com`. Download and install both if you do not already have them.

## How to do it...

1.  Download the file called `MySQLBalancingDemo.java` from the book's website. It contains the following code:

    ```
    ...

    Connection conn = driver.connect("jdbc:mysql://master:3306,slave1:
    3307,slave2:3308/sakila?user=testuser&password=testpass&roundRobin
    LoadBalance=true", null);

    conn.setReadOnly(false); // target the MASTER

    rs = conn.createStatement().executeQuery(
      "SELECT @@server_id;");
    rs.next();
    System.out.println("Master: " + rs.getString(1));

    conn.setReadOnly(true); // switch to one of the slaves

    rs = conn.createStatement().executeQuery(
      "SELECT @@server_id;");
    rs.next();
    System.out.println("Slave: " + rs.getString(1));
    conn.close();

    ...
    ```

2. Compile the file using the `javac` compiler. Alternatively, an integrated development environment like Eclipse or Netbeans can take care of this for you:

```
$ javac -cp mysql-connector-java-5.1.7-bin.jar MySQLBalancingDemo.
java
```

3. Run the sample application and see how it automatically distributes the read requests between the two slaves:

```
$ java -cp .:mysql-connector-java-5.1.7-bin.jar MySQLBalancingDemo
Master: 1000
Slave: 13308
```

## How it works...

You just compiled and ran a small program that demonstrates round-robin load balancing.

The first line of output is the master's `server-ID` setting, because the first connection was *not* set to read only. The connection is then declared to be targeted at the slaves via `setReadOnly(true)`. The next query will then return the `server ID` of the particular slave it was balanced to. You might need to run the demo a few times to see a different slave being used because the algorithm that balances the load does not strictly toggle each time, but might direct a few connections against the same slave.

## There's more...

While the JDBC driver makes it relatively easy to use read load balancing across several slaves, it only helps you take the first step on the way. You must take care that the application knows which connection to use for write operations and which for read. It must also cope with slaves and master possibly being slightly out of sync all the time. Concentrating that this special logic in a class of its own, is advisable to limit the effect on the rest of the application.

### Working with connection pools

When working with connection pooling, be sure to initialize any connection you get to the correct mode using the `setReadOnly()` method, to be sure you know what state it is in. You might be handed a connection that was set to the wrong mode when it was put back into the pool.

### Working on other programming environments

In development environments not using Java, you might have to take care of managing the cycling between slaves yourself. Independent of the actual language or environment you are using, a good practice is to channel all database operations through a set of functions or methods that centrally manage the balancing. You could provide functions that handle

INSERT, UPDATE, and DELETE operations, always connecting to the master and a SELECT function going to the slaves for data reads.

In case you need to select something back that you just wrote and cannot allow for the replication lag, you might also provide a read function querying the master machine. You should use this sparingly, however, because it definitely counteracts the intention of relieving the master from the read load.

### Considering efficiency while adding slaves

Of course, the slaves have to perform write operations as well to keep up with the master. This means their performance is not fully available for reads, limiting scalability.

So adding more slaves does not proportionally improve performance of the overall system.

# Using replication to provide full-text indexing for InnoDB tables

The InnoDB storage engine is the one most commonly used nowadays because it provides more enterprise-level features than MyISAM and most other engines. However, InnoDB tables do have a major drawback: they do not support full-text indexing. This can be a significant obstacle when you have to design any sort of application that relies on atomic operations and must store text data in a searchable manner.

While there are third-party products available to redress this shortcoming, there are times you may need to refrain from using these and stick to the out-of-the-box functionality. If you are willing to provide an additional server and make slight adjustments to your application code, replication can help you provide a full-text index for InnoDB tables indirectly.

This recipe is similar to the one about *Sharing read load across multiple machines* in this chapter. In contrast, only queries that are targeted at the full-text index need to be sent to a slave machine. This will require slight changes to the application code.

## Getting ready

To follow along with this recipe, you will need two MySQL servers available—a master and a slave. For testing, these might reside on the same physical machine. In a production environment we do, however, recommend two separate pieces of equipment.

They will be referred to as *master* and *slave* in this example. Substitute your concrete host names appropriately.

You will need privileges to change the application source code. This is usually a task that requires cooperation with the application developers.

## How to do it...

1. On the master, identify the table that contains the column(s) that you want to equip with a full-text index. In this example, we use the following table definition from a fictional forum application of some sort:

```
CREATE TABLE `posts` (
  `id` int(11) NOT NULL auto_increment,
  `title` varchar(100) NOT NULL,
  `posttext` text NOT NULL,
  PRIMARY KEY  (`id`)
) ENGINE=InnoDB;
```

The `posttext` column contains the text of forum posts. As the table is created with `ENGINE=InnoDB`, we cannot add a full-text index to it.

2. On the slave, create the same table, but with a slightly modified definition:

```
CREATE TABLE `posts` (
  `id` int(11) NOT NULL auto_increment,
  `title` varchar(100) NOT NULL,
  `posttext` text NOT NULL,
  PRIMARY KEY  (`id`),
  FULLTEXT KEY `FT_text` (`posttext`)
) ENGINE=MyISAM;
```

The storage engine is set to `MyISAM`, allowing the `FULLTEXT KEY` `FT_text` (`posttext`) definition. Trying to add this on the master would result in an error message.

3. Make sure the replication rules between master and slave include the `posts` table.

4. Modify your application to access the slave when doing full-text queries. It is generally considered a good practice to concentrate all database access to a dedicated module or class, so that you can easily modify your application's interaction with the underlying data store.

## How it works...

In this replication setup, whenever you make changes to the master's *posts* table, those will be replicated to the slave, but the target table uses a different storage engine than the master. As SBR simply sends over SQL statements without any information about the origin, the slave will execute the instructions blindly. While this can be a problem in other circumstances because it makes the whole process somewhat fragile, it plays to our advantage in this case.

Upon UPDATE or INSERT to the posttext column the MyISAM engine will update the full-text index appropriately. This enables the application to issue queries using the full-text query syntax against the slave.

 An important drawback you must take into account is that you cannot JOIN tables between different MySQL servers!

A workaround is required when you have to, for example, join the posts with a user accounts table via the posts.id column. To implement this you will need to issue two separate queries. The first one using the full-text search on the slave will bring up all posts containing the search terms. From the resulting rows you can then take the id column values and run a second query against the master database, substituting the text search with an id lookup.

## There's more...

MyISAM's full-text index has existed for several years, but has not been improved a great deal over time. If you have many concurrent requests you will notice significant resource usage, limiting scalability.

Over the past few years, several third-party vendors have stepped up with alternative solutions to the problem of full-text search, offering more features and better performance.

One of those products, offering tight integration with MySQL and PHP, is *Sphinx*—an open-source product available for free from http://www.sphinxsearch.com. If you find that MySQL's built-in capabilities are either too slow or too limited in other respects to meet your application's requirements, you should definitely have a look at it.

### Setting up new slaves in this scenario

You should not simply use a regular SQL dump to initialize the slave, as it will contain a create table statement that specifies InnoDB and does not include the full-text index. Of course, you could change the table type after the import is complete. However, this can be time consuming. Instead, we recommend you first create the target schema on the slave, making sure the tables in question are created with ENGINE=MyISAM.

Then go ahead and import the data into the table. Only after that, add the full-text index. This is typically much faster than having the index in place beforehand because MySQL must then update it all the way through the bulk insert of rows. This is a very expensive operation compared to the delayed index creation.

## See also

▶ *Adding a full-text index* in Chapter 2

# Estimating network and slave I/O load

Especially when using replication over a wide-area network connection with limited bandwidth, it is interesting to be able to predict the amount of data that needs to be transported between master and slaves.

While MySQL does not use the most efficient strategy to deliver data, it is at least relatively easy to calculate the requirements in advance.

This is less of a step-by-step recipe than an annotated walkthrough of the basic formula that can be used to estimate the traffic you will have to be prepared for.

## Getting ready

In order to follow along, you must have some key data points available because otherwise there is not much to calculate. You will need:

▶ The number of slaves (to be) connected to the master.

▶ An idea about the average amount of binlogs written when using the master under regular load. Knowing about peak times can be interesting as well.

▶ The bandwidth of the connection between master and slaves. This includes the speed of the network interfaces on the master and, in general, the whole route between them (possibly including Internet connections).

We assume that there are no other network-intensive applications running on the master or slaves, so that practically all the speed your network card can provide is usable for MySQL.

In this example, we will keep matters simple, assuming the following:

| Data point | Value |
| --- | --- |
| Master's Connectivity | Gigabit LAN interface (approx. 100MB/s) |
| Slaves' Connectivity | 2MBit/s DSL line, of which 1MBit/s can be assumed available for MySQL. 1MBit/s comes down to approximately 100kb/s. |
| Average amount of binlogs created on master | 175MB per hour, approx. 50kb/s. |
| Number of Slaves | 5 |
| Speed of the slowest link in the connection between Master and Slaves. | Master is connected to the Internet via a 10MBit/s connection, approx. 1MB/s. |

## How to do it...

1. **Check the master's network speed**: Multiply the number of slaves with the average amount of binlogs: 5x175MB/hour = 875MB/hour or about 250kb/second. The gigabit connection can handle this easily.

2. **Check individual slaves' network speed**: The 1MBit portion of the DSL line is sufficient for an average amount of data of 50kb/second. Often binlog production is not linear over time—there might be peaks, but there is still a reserve.

3. **Check if the slowest part of the route between master and slaves can handle the load**: 250kb/second should be no problem for the 10MBit/second Internet connection.

4. Disk I/O load on each slave, caused by the replication, is the amount of relay logs being written. This is equivalent to the amount of binlogs the master produces. Provided the slave's I/O is not already saturated by other things, an additional 175MB per hour should not pose a problem either.

## How it works...

Basically, replication simply needs sufficient resources to copy the master's binlogs to the slaves. This really all there is to it. Depending on the network route between them this can be easily done (say most LANs), or can be tricky (as in cases with slow Internet connections).

In this example, we see there should be no problem on any part of the system, as there is still room for a higher load on each resource. The most limiting factor in this scenario seems to be the master's outgoing Internet connection. If you add more slaves to the scenario, each new one will add another 50KB per second of outgoing bandwidth. Assuming replication can use the full 1MB/s outgoing speed, which is not very realistic, that part of the route could theoretically service 20 slaves at most. In reality, it will be more like 10 to 15.

## There's more...

There are two more general considerations you might want to think about when planning a replication setup.

### Handling intermittent connectivity between master and slave

If the connection between master and slaves is only available for a limited period of time, the slaves will start to lag behind while disconnected. The slaves will download new data as quickly as possible when the connection is resumed and store it locally in the relay logs, asynchronously executing the statements. So expect higher network load during these times.

You will also want to take that into account when there are multiple slaves trying to catch up at the same time. Under such circumstances, the route between master and slaves might become saturated more quickly.

## Enabling compression with the slave_compressed_protocol option

Particularly useful for low bandwidth connections between master and slaves is the compression feature for replication traffic. Provided it is switched on on both master and slave machines, it can significantly reduce the amount of data that is actually transferred over the network at the cost of increased CPU loads. The master will then send out the binlog information in a compressed format.

In a simple comparison, measuring the network traffic while creating and loading the `sakila` sample database, 3180kb of binlogs were created. However, with the compressed protocol switched on, only about 700KB of data per slave were sent over the network.

To enable compression, add the following line to the `[mysqld]` section in the configuration files on both master and slave:

```
slave_compressed_protocol=1
```

Then restart the servers to enable the feature. Verify whether it was switched on successfully by issuing a `SHOW VARIABLES LIKE 'slave_compressed%';` command on both master and slaves.

You can achieve a similar effect with SSH compression. As we generally do not recommend replicating over the Internet without encryption, that option might even be more appealing in such scenarios as it does not require any configuration changes to MySQL.

 Naturally, the level of compression heavily depends on the data you are handling. If you store JPEG images in BLOB fields, for example, those cannot be compressed much more than they already are!

## See also

▶  *Encrypting a MySQL server connection with SSH in Chapter 3*

▶  *Creating an encrypted MySQL console via SSH in Chapter 3*

▶  *Using a PuTTY template connection for SSH secured connections in Chapter 3*

# Limiting network and slave I/O load in heavy write scenarios using the blackhole storage engine

If you have a large number of slaves and a rather busy master machine, the network load can become significant, even when using compression. This is because all statements that are written to the binlog are transferred to all the slaves. They put them in their relay logs and asynchronously process them.

The main reason for the heavy network load is the *filter on the slave paradigm* that MySQL employs. Everything is sent to every one of the slaves and each one decides which statements to throw away and which to apply based on its particular configuration. In the worst case, you have to transmit every single change to a database to replicate only a single table.

## Getting ready

The following procedure is based on Linux. So in order to repeat it on Windows, you need to adapt the path names and a little shell syntax accordingly.

To follow along, you will need a MySQL daemon with the *blackhole* storage engine enabled. Verify this with the following command:

```
mysql> show variables like '%blackhole%';
```

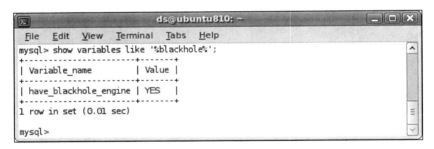

Even though you only strictly need a blackhole-enabled MySQL server on the actual filter instance, for this example we will be using only a single machine and just a single server version, but with different configuration files and data directories.

In the following steps, we assume you have installed a copy of MySQL in a folder called `blacktest` in your home directory. Modify accordingly if your setup differs.

## How to do it...

1. Create three distinct data directories—one for the master, one for the blackhole filter engine, and one for a slave.

```
~/blacktest$ mkdir data.master
~/blacktest$ mkdir data.slave
~/blacktest$ mkdir data.black
```

2. Into each of those, copy the MySQL accounts database. Ideally, you should take an empty one from a freshly downloaded distribution to make sure you do not accidentally copy users you do not want.

```
~/blacktest$ cp -R data/mysql data.master
~/blacktest$ cp -R data/mysql data.slave
~/blacktest$ cp -R data/mysql data.black
```

3. Configure the master instance. To do so, create a configuration file called `my.master` and make sure that it contains the following settings:

```
[client]
port            = 3307
socket          = /home/ds/blacktest/master.sock

[mysqld_safe]
socket          = /home/ds/blacktest/master.sock

[mysqld]
user            = mysql
pid-file        = /home/ds/blacktest/master.pid
socket          = /home/ds/blacktest/master.sock
port            = 3307
basedir         = /home/ds/blacktest
datadir         = /home/ds/blacktest/data.master
tmpdir          = /tmp
language        = /home/ds/blacktest/share/mysql/english

bind-address    = 127.0.0.1

server-id       = 1
log-bin         = /home/ds/blacktest/master-bin.log
```

Everything that is specific to the master instance has been highlighted—those values are going to be different for filter and slave instances.

4. Start the master daemon for the first time to make sure everything works so far. We recommend a dedicated window for this daemon. For example:

```
~/blacktest$ xterm -T MASTER -e bin/mysqld \
>          --defaults-file=my.master \
>          --console &
```

This will start the daemon in the background and show its output in a new window:

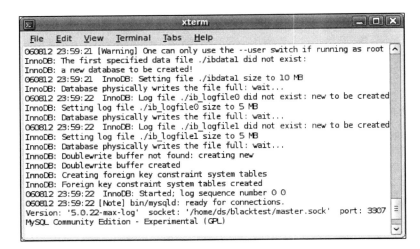

The warning about the `--user` switch can be ignored for now. Should you not get a message very similar to the one above (especially concerning the **ready for connections** part) go back and find the error in your setup before going on. Usually, the error messages issued by MySQL are rather verbose and bring you back on track pretty soon.

5. Insert some test data to be able to verify the correct function of the filter later. To do so, connect to the master instance just started and create some tables and data:

```
~/blacktest$ bin/mysql -uroot -S master.sock --prompt='master>'

master> CREATE DATABASE repdb;
master> USE repdb;
master> CREATE TABLE tblA (
    ->        id INT(10) PRIMARY KEY NOT NULL,
    ->        label VARCHAR(30)
    ->  ) ENGINE=InnoDB;
master> CREATE TABLE tblB (
    ->        name VARCHAR(20) PRIMARY KEY NOT NULL,
    ->        age INT(3)
    ->  ) ENGINE=InnoDB;
```

```
master> INSERT INTO tblA VALUES
    ->        (1, 'label 1'),
    ->        (2, 'label 2'),
    ->        (3, 'label 3');
master> INSERT INTO tblB VALUES
    ->        ('Peter', 55),
    ->        ('Paul', 43),
    ->        ('Mary', 25);
```

Inserting this data already creates binlog information. You can easily verify this by looking at the file system. The `master-bin.000001` file should have grown to around 850 bytes now. This might vary slightly if you did not enter the commands above with the exact same number of spaces—the binlog will store commands in the exact way you typed them. For example, we will only replicate changes to table `tblB` but ignore anything that happens to table `tblA`. We will assume that `tblB` needs to be written by an application on the slave. So the table should be present, but empty on the slaves to avoid key collisions.

6. Create a user account on the master for the filter to connect with:

```
master> GRANT REPLICATION SLAVE
    -> ON *.*
    -> TO 'repblack'@'localhost'
    -> IDENTIFIED BY 'blackpass';
```

7. Configure the filter (blackhole) instance with a configuration file named `my.black` that contains at least the following :

```
[client]
port            = 3308
socket          = /home/ds/blacktest/black.sock

[mysqld_safe]
socket          = /home/ds/blacktest/black.sock

[mysqld]
log-slave-updates
skip-innodb
default-storage-engine=blackhole

user            = mysql
pid-file        = /home/ds/blacktest/black.pid
socket          = /home/ds/blacktest/black.sock
port            = 3308
basedir         = /home/ds/blacktest
```

```
datadir          = /home/ds/blacktest/data.black
   tmpdir          = /tmp
   language        = /home/ds/blacktest/share/mysql/english


   bind-address    = 127.0.0.1

server-id        = 2
log-bin          = /home/ds/blacktest/black-bin.log
relay-log        = /home/ds/blacktest/black-relay.log
```

Notice that all occurrences of *master* have been replaced with *black*!

Moreover, the `server-id` setting has been changed and the `log-slave-updates`, `skip-innodb`, and `default-storage-engine` options have been added. The second one prevents this instance from creating `ibdata` table space files, which would not be used later anyway. The last one specifies which storage engine to use when a CREATE TABLE statement does not explicitly specify one or if the specified engine is not available. We will come back to this soon.

8. Make sure this instance basically works by starting it the same way as the master before (you will not see the InnoDB messages here, of course).

```
~/blacktest$ xterm -T BLACK -e bin/mysqld \
>          --defaults-file=my.black \
>          --console &
```

9. Create a set of dump files from the master to set up both the blackhole filter and an example slave. The details on why we need two and in which ways they are different will be explained later. Use these commands to create the files needed:

```
~/blacktest$ bin/mysqldump -S master.sock -uroot \
>                --master-data \
>                --single-transaction \
>                --no-create-info \
>                --ignore-table=repdb.tblA \
>                repdb > master_data.sql

~/blacktest$ bin/mysqldump -S master.sock -uroot \
>                --no-data \
>                repdb > master_struct.sql
```

10. Connect to the filter server, create the database, make it the default database, and finally, import the structure information created before:

```
~/blacktest$ bin/mysql -uroot -S black.sock --prompt='black> '

black> CREATE DATABASE repdb;
black> USE repdb;
black> source master_black.sql;
```

At this point we now have the structure of the master transferred to the filter engine adapted to use the blackhole engine for all the tables.

11. Set up the replication between master and filter engine. To do so, we need to know the exact position from where the filter will start replicating. Extract this information from the previously taken data dump like this:

```
~/blacktest$ head -n 30 master_data.sql | grep 'CHANGE MASTER TO'
```

Write down that information; we will need it in a moment.

12. Modify the `my.black` configuration file to contain the following in the `[mysqld]` section:

```
replicate-ignore-table=repdb.tblA
replicate-do-table=repdb.tblB
```

This is a very simple filter setup; in a real application scenario these rules will probably be more complex.

13. Restart the filter engine to activate the new configuration:

```
~/blacktest$ bin/mysqladmin -uroot -S black.sock shutdown

~/blacktest$ xterm -T BLACK -e bin/mysqld \
>          --defaults-file=my.black \
>          --console &
```

14. Reconnect the client connected to the blackhole engine. To do this, just issue a `SELECT 1;` command.

15. Execute the following command to hook up the filter to the master. Be sure to fill in the values you wrote down a moment ago in the statement:

```
black> CHANGE MASTER TO
    -> master_host='localhost',
    -> master_port=3307,
    -> master_user='repblack',
    -> master_password='blackpass',
    -> master_log_file='master-bin.000001',
    -> master_log_pos=1074;
```

16. Retrieve information required to set up the filter/slave portion. Write down the results of the SHOW MASTER STATUS command, they will be needed later:

```
black> FLUSH LOGS;
black> SHOW MASTER STATUS;
+------------------+----------+---+---+
| File             | Position | … | … |
+------------------+----------+---+---+
| black-bin.000003 |       98 |   |   |
+------------------+----------+---+---+
```

17. Start the slave thread on the filter engine and verify that everything is going well:

```
black> START SLAVE;
black> SHOW SLAVE STATUS \G
*************************** 1. row ***************************
               Slave_IO_State: Waiting for master to send event
                  Master_Host: localhost
                  Master_User: repblack
                  Master_Port: 3307
                Connect_Retry: 60
              Master_Log_File: master-bin.000001
          Read_Master_Log_Pos: 1074
               Relay_Log_File: black-relay.000003
                Relay_Log_Pos: 236
        Relay_Master_Log_File: master-bin.000001
             Slave_IO_Running: Yes
            Slave_SQL_Running: Yes
                          . . .
           Replicate_Do_Table: repdb.tblB
       Replicate_Ignore_Table: repdb.tblA
                          . . .
                   Last_Errno: 0
                   Last_Error:
                 Skip_Counter: 0
          Exec_Master_Log_Pos: 1074
              Relay_Log_Space: 236
                          . . .
        Seconds_Behind_Master: 0
```

At this point we have successfully established a replication connection between the master database and the blackhole-based filter instance.

18. Check that nothing has yet been written to the filter's binlogs. Because we issued a `FLUSH LOGS` command on the filter instance, there should be nothing in the most recent binlog file. Verify this as follows:

```
~/blacktest$ bin/mysqlbinlog black-bin.000003
```

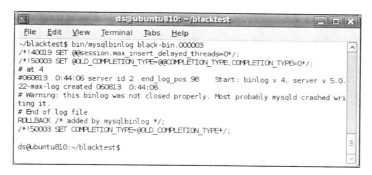

19. Test the filter setup with some statements issued on the master:

```
master> UPDATE repdb.tblA
    -> SET label='modified label 3'
    -> WHERE id=3;
master> INSERT INTO repdb.tblB
    -> VALUES ('John', 39);
```

We would expect to see the `INSERT` in the binlog file of the filter instance, but not the `UPDATE` statement, because it modifies `tblA`, which is to be ignored.

20. Verify that the rules work as expected by having another look at the filter's binlogs:

```
~/blacktest$ bin/mysqlbinlog black-bin.000003
```

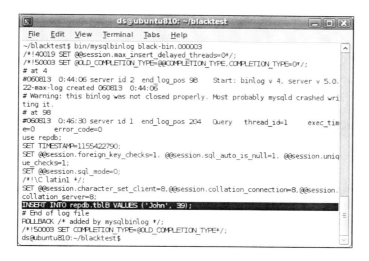

This looks precisely as expected—the INSERT is present, the UPDATE is nowhere to be seen.

21. Set up the configuration of a slave using these settings:

```
[client]
port            = 3309
socket          = /home/ds/blacktest/slave.sock

[mysqld_safe]
socket          = /home/ds/blacktest/slave.sock

[mysqld]
user            = mysql
pid-file        = /home/ds/blacktest/slave.pid
socket          = /home/ds/blacktest/slave.sock
port            = 3309
basedir         = /home/ds/blacktest
datadir         = /home/ds/blacktest/data.slave
tmpdir          = /tmp
language        = /home/ds/blacktest/share/mysql/english

bind-address    = 127.0.0.1

server-id       = 3
relay-log       = /home/ds/blacktest/slave-relay.log
```

 Notice that all occurrences of *master* have been replaced with *slave*!

Again the server-id setting has been changed and the log-slave-updates, skip-innodb, and default-storage-engine options that were part of the filter instance's configuration are *not* included. Also, the log-bin parameter has been removed because changes on the slave need not be recorded separately.

22. Start up the slave engine. You will see the familiar messages about InnoDB filling up the data files and finally, the **Ready for connections** line:

```
~/blacktest$ xterm -T SLAVE -e bin/mysqld \
>          --defaults-file=my.slave \
>          --console &
```

23. Then connect a client to the slave and create the database:

```
~/blacktest$ bin/mysql -uroot -S slave.sock --prompt='slave> '

slave> CREATE DATABASE repdb;
slave> USE repdb;
```

   At this point, the slave is set up and has an empty `repdb` database.

24. Fill up the slave database with the initial snapshot of the master. We need to load two files here. The details of why are explained further down in the *How it works...* section.

```
slave> source master_struct.sql;
...

slave> source master_data.sql;
...
```

25. Verify that you can find the data from the master on the slave now by doing a `SELECT * FROM` first table `repdb.tblA` and then `repdb.tblB`.

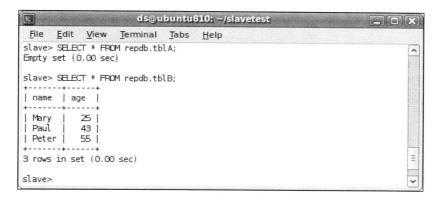

   The first `SELECT` shows no records because `tblA` was excluded from the dump. Table `tblB` contains the three records we inserted on the master.

26. Create a replication user account on the filter instance for the slaves to use:

```
black> GRANT REPLICATION SLAVE
    -> ON *.*
    -> TO 'repslave'@'localhost'
    -> IDENTIFIED BY 'slavepass';
```

27. Connect the slave to the filter engine. Be sure to insert the correct values for `MASTER_LOG_FILE` and `MASTER_LOG_POS` in the statement. Those are the values you wrote down when you issued the `SHOW MASTER STATUS` command on the filter server before starting the replication there:

```
slave> CHANGE MASTER TO
    -> master_host='localhost',
    -> master_port=3308,
    -> master_user='repslave',
    -> master_password='slavepass',
    -> master_log_file='black-bin.000003',
    -> master_log_pos=98;
Query OK, 0 rows affected (0.01 sec)
```

28. Start the slave and verify that it starts up correctly:

```
slave> START SLAVE
slave> SHOW SLAVE STATUS \G
*************************** 1. row ***************************
            Slave_IO_State: Waiting for master to send event
                         . . .
      Relay_Master_Log_File: black-bin.000003
            Slave_IO_Running: Yes
           Slave_SQL_Running: Yes
                         . . .
      Seconds_Behind_Master: 0
```

29. As soon as the previous step is complete, the replication should already have updated tblB on the slave and inserted the new **("John", 39)** record. Verify it like this:

```
slave> SELECT * FROM repdb.tblB;
```

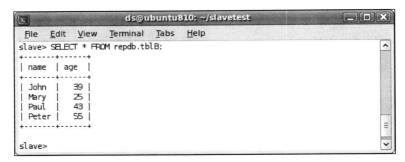

Apparently, the replication works. You can now try to modify some data on the master and check if the results match on the slave. Anything you do to modify tblB should be reflected on the slave. Remember to use fully qualified statements; otherwise changes will not match the replication rules.

## How it works...

Though MySQL did not implement a *filter on the master* feature literally, another way of doing similar things was provided. While MyISAM and InnoDB implement ways of storing data on disk, another engine was created that is basically an empty shell. It just answers **OK** to all `INSERT`, `UPDATE`, or `DELETE` requests coming from the SQL layer above. `SELECT` statements always return an empty result set. This engine is suitably called the blackhole storage engine, as everything you put into it just vanishes.

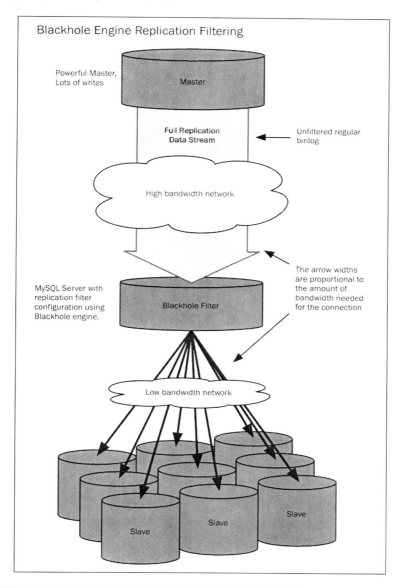

In the upper part you see the main master server. All modifying statements are written on the master's binlog files and sent over the network to subscribed slaves. In this case, there is only a single slave: the filter server in the middle. The thick arrow in between them represents the large amount of data that is sent to it.

In the lower part of the picture, there are a number of slaves. In a regular setup, a thick arrow would be drawn from the master to each of those—meaning that the same massive amount of replication data would be sent over the network multiple times. In this picture, the filter server is configured to ignore statements for certain tables. It is also configured to write the statements received from a replication master to its own binlogs. This is different from regular slaves because usually those do not write replicated statements to their binlogs again. The filter server's binlogs are much smaller than those of the main master because lots of statements have been left out. This would normally have taken place on each and every regular slave.

The regular slaves are configured against the filter server. That means they only receive the pre-filtered stream of statements that have made it into the filter's binlogs through the `replicate-ignore-*` and `replicate-do-*` directives. This is represented by thin arrows in the picture.

Because slaves can go offline for extended amounts of time, binlogs could easily mount up to dozens of gigabytes in a few days. With the much smaller filtered binlogs you can more often purge the large main master's binlogs as soon as you have made a full backup, in the end freeing more space than is needed by the additional filter instance.

## Other storage engines than InnoDB

Be advised that if you are using a different storage engine than InnoDB for your tables (especially MyISAM), you will need to do a little more tweaking. This is because the InnoDB example relies on MySQL's being very lenient concerning errors in many cases. We put the `skip-innodb` option into the `my.black` config file. This means that InnoDB will not be available at runtime. Because the `master_struct.sql` dump file contains `CREATE TABLE ... ENGINE=InnoDB` statements, MySQL falls back to the default storage engine that we configured to be the blackhole engine.

If you are using MyISAM tables, there is no need for the server to automatically change the table type because MyISAM is always available (MySQL stores its user information apart from other things in MyISAM tables). So you would need to adapt the `master_struct.sql` dump file before sourcing it into the filter server. I recommend using `sed`, like this:

```
~/blacktest$ sed -e 's/ENGINE=InnoDB/ENGINE=BLACKHOLE/g' \
>        master_struct.sql > master_black.sql
```

This will replace all occurrences of the InnoDB engine with the blackhole engine and put the result into a new file. Please keep the original file, too, as it will be needed for the slave machines.

# Setting up slaves via network streaming

If you need to reset one or more slaves regularly, say every morning before business hours begin, importing a SQL dump might take too much time, especially if the slaves are relatively low-end machines without a sophisticated I/O subsystem.

In this recipe, we will present a way to set up a MySQL slave with minimal I/O load on the hard drive and the network adapter of the slave. The example assumes a Linux-based slave machine; however, you should be able to apply this to Windows as well. but you will need to download some free tools most Linux distributions come with out of the box.

The general idea is to have a more powerful machine, which can be the master if resources allow, to prepare a complete set of data files for the slaves and later stream them directly to the slave's disk from a web server.

## Getting ready

To try this out, you will need a master server with at least one slave. Additionally, a machine with a web server installed is required. Depending on your setup, the master server might be suitable for this task. In the example that follows, we will assume that the master server has a web server running.

## How to do it...

1. Set up a fresh temporary MySQL daemon with a configuration similar to the clients.
2. Dump the data from the master with the `--master-data` option and feed it into the temporary server.
3. Shut down the temporary server and compress its data.
4. Transfer the archive to the slaves and unpack.
5. Adapt the slaves' config files.
6. Run the slaves and let them connect and catch up with the master.

## How it works...

This recipe is based on the fact that you can quite easily copy MySQL's data files (including InnoDB table space files) from one machine to another, as long as you copy them all. So, we first create a ready-to-go set of slave data files on a relatively powerful machine and transfer them to multiple slaves with weaker hardware. Usually, those files will be bigger than a simple SQL dump file that is usually used for slave setups. But no parsing and processing is required on the target system. This makes the whole thing mostly network and linear disk I/O bound.

The idea behind this concept is to relieve the individual slaves from importing SQL files themselves. As their hardware is rather slow and MySQL only supports single threaded slave SQL execution, this can be very time consuming. Instead, we use the master's better resources temporarily as a single *power-slave* and let it handle the process of importing. We then provide any number of identical slaves with its data files. This will reduce the burden of the other slaves to simply unpacking some files.

While this does not really save anything in terms of bytes that need to be written to each slave's disk, the access pattern is much more sensible. The following table compares the disk transfers for a regular SQL import from local disk and the proposed alternative for a 60MB gzipped SQL file, which will lead to approximately 2GB of InnoDB table space files:

| Regular SQL Import | Prepared Data File Deployment |
|---|---|
| Linear write 60MB download to local disk | Download 60MB, directly streamed to 2GB data files, written linearly |
| Linear write 2GB initial creation of InnoDB data files | n/a |
| Linear read 60MB SQL.gz, interleaved with random write 2GB to data files | n/a |
| **4GB total read/written randomly** | **2GB linear write** |

Importing a SQL file from the local hard disk means there are continual seeks between the current position in the SQL text file and the server's data files. Moreover, as the database schema may define lots of indexes, there is even more random disk write activity when executing simple INSERT statements.

In contrast unpacking ready-made InnoDB table spaces (or MyISAM table files for that matter) is basically just linear writing.

## Temporary daemon

The SQL dump needs to be executed at least once. So, we set up a temporary MySQL daemon with a stripped down configuration that is close to the actual slaves—meaning all the parameters that affect the storage files must match the slaves to create compatible data files.

Every time you want to prepare such a new slave installation image, the temporary daemon should be started with an empty data directory. While not strictly necessary, we prefer to delete the table space and transaction log files every time because it allows for better compression rates later.

The data files should be created close to the size that will be needed, maybe a little more to prevent the need for them to grow. Nevertheless, specify the last data file to be auto-extending. Otherwise the process of importing the SQL data may lead to filling the table space prematurely, especially when used in an automated process that can be difficult to handle.

Also, you should allow InnoDB to add larger chunks to the last data file if needed (default: 8MB). Extending the files is associated with some overhead, but using bigger chunks reduces the impact on the I/O subsystem. You should be fine with 50MB or 100MB. The bigger this is, the less often InnoDB will have to extend the file. See the manual section on InnoDB configuration for more info.

## Dumping master data

Once you have the temporary daemon running, use the `mysqldump` tool with the `--master-data` and `--single-transaction` options to create a dump of the database(s) you need to replicate. In order to save time and disk space, you may find it useful to pipe the output directly through the `mysql` command-line client and feed it into the target temporary server.

## Shutting down and compressing

You can now shut down the temporary server. Compress the data directory. Depending on how you want to configure permissions, you may include or exclude the *mysql* schema. We usually have the temporary server set up with as low permissions as possible and do not move the *mysql* schema along.

For compression, you should not use the ZIP format. It contains a catalog of all files included at its very end; so piping it through a decompression program on the fly will not work. Instead, we use a gzipped tarball. This allows us to download and to pipe the data stream through `gunzip` before directing it to disk.

## Transferring to the slave and uncompressing

On the slave we suggest `curl` as a download tool. It is important that the tool you choose be able to output the downloaded file directly to standard out. With `curl` that is quite simple—it is its default behavior. It also handles files larger than 2GB, which some versions of `wget` have problems with. The command line should look similar to this:

```
curl http://the.server/mysql_data.tgz | tar -C /the/target/datadir -xzf -
```

`curl` will download the file and pipe it to `tar` to decompress into the target data directory.

 Do not miss the final - at the end of the command!

You will find that on a local area network, downloading and unpacking will be considerably faster than having MySQL to first create the empty data file and then import the SQL, for the reasons stated above.

## Adjusting slave configuration

When the data files have reached their destination on the slave, you may need to adjust the slave settings. This especially depends on whether you copied fixed size data files (in which case you can prepare the config file in advance) or used the `autoextend` option on the last table space file. In that case, you could write a little script that takes a template `my.cnf` file with your basic settings and replaces some placeholders for the data file-related settings via `sed`. One of those is the size of the last InnoDB data file from the archive. It will become a fixed size file on the slave. Another file will then be added at the first slave start.

## Connecting to the master

One last thing that needs to be done is to read the master's current binlog file name and position from the `master.info` file. This is required because once the slave server has been started you will need to provide correct credentials for the replication user. You must also explicitly tell the slave which master host to connect to. Unfortunately, when issuing a CHANGE MASTER TO command on the slave, which includes a master host name, all information about previous master binlogs—the corresponding offset—is discarded (see MySQL online manual, chapter 12.6.2.1 *CHANGE MASTER TO Syntax* at `http://dev.mysql.com/doc/refman/5.1/en/change-master-to.html`).

Therefore, you will need to tell the slave again where to begin replication.

One possible solution is to read the contents of the `master.info` file that was brought along with the data files into a bash script array and inject the values into the statement:

```
arr = ( $(cat master.info) )
mysql -e "CHANGE MASTER TO master_host='the.master.server', master_
user='replication_user', master_password='the_password',
master_log_file='${arr[2]}', master_log_pos=${arr[3]}"
```

The format of the `master.info` file is described in the MySQL manual.

## Starting the slave

As soon as you issue a START SLAVE statement, the slave will connect to the master and begin to catch up with whatever has happened since the time when the dump was taken.

# Skipping problematic queries

There are occasions where something goes wrong and a problem prevents one or more slave servers from updating. The reasons for this can be several, but most often some sort of discrepancy between the master's and the slave's data set will cause a statement to fail on the slave that was executed properly on the master (otherwise it would not have made it to the binlog).

This is where the basic principle of assuming master and slave being equal becomes a little too simple. It can lead to a potentially long series of statements executing on the slave, but on a different set of data than the master has. Depending on how long this goes unnoticed, the master and slave can drift out of sync unnoticed, until a statement cannot be executed successfully on the slave—for example because a foreign key constraint fails on the slave.

Fortunately, not every problem stems from such a serious error, which can often only be repaired by resetting the affected slaves to a known good state.

Often a slave stops the replication because a record to be inserted is already present, resulting in key uniqueness violation error. This is especially likely when (accidentally or on purpose) you are working on the master and the slaves, modifying data on both sides maybe even to fix a replication problem.

In this recipe, we will show you how to skip one or more problematic queries—meaning instructions replicated from the master that will not execute correctly on the slave machine.

## Getting ready

We will demonstrate the skipping of problematic queries in a contrived error scenario. To try this for yourself, you will need two MySQL servers set up as master and slave, being currently in sync. As an example, we will use the `sakila` sample database to demonstrate a record `INSERT` that fails on the slave because it was previously inserted manually by accident.

## How to do it...

1. Connect to the master using a MySQL client. Make `sakila` the default database.
2. With a second client, connect to the slave. Make `sakila` the default schema here as well.
3. On the slave, enter the following command to insert a new category:

   ```
   slave> INSERT INTO category (name) VALUES ('Inserted On Slave');
   ```

```
slave> INSERT INTO category (name) VALUES ('Inserted On Slave');

slave> SELECT * FROM category WHERE name='Inserted On Slave';
+-------------+-------------------+---------------------+
| category_id | name              | last_update         |
+-------------+-------------------+---------------------+
|          17 | Inserted On Slave | 2009-07-22 19:22:21 |
+-------------+-------------------+---------------------+
1 row in set (0.00 sec)

slave>
```

In this case, the **category_id** column was automatically set because it is defined as auto-incrementing. At this point, the master and the slave are already out of sync because this record does not exist on the master.

4. On the master, insert a new record as well:

```
master> INSERT INTO category (name) VALUES ('Inserted On Master');
```

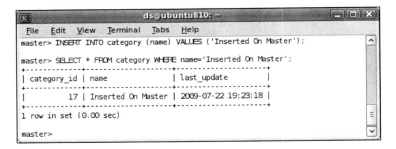

You can see that the master also picked **17** as the **category_id**. It has been written to the binlog and has by now probably been replicated to the slave.

5. Have a look at the replication status on the slave:

```
slave> SHOW SLAVE STATUS \G
************************** 1. row **************************
            . . .
        Slave_IO_Running: Yes
      Slave_SQL_Running: No
            . . .
    Seconds_Behind_Master: NULL
```

You can see that the replicated insert has failed. No more statements replicated from the master will be executed (Slave_SQL_Running: No).

6. Repair the damage by making sure the slave records are identical:

```
slave> UPDATE category SET name='Inserted On Master' WHERE
category_id=17;
```

Now the data on master and slave are identical again.

7. Tell the slave that you want to skip the (one) INSERT statement that came from the master and that cannot be executed:

```
slave> SET GLOBAL SQL_SLAVE_SKIP_COUNTER=1;
```

8. Start the slave SQL thread again and check the replication status:

```
slave> START SLAVE;
```

```
slave> SHOW SLAVE STATUS \G
*********************** 1. row ***************************
                . . .
        Slave_IO_Running: Yes
       Slave_SQL_Running: Yes
                . . .
    Seconds_Behind_Master: 0
```

You can see that the replication is up and running again.

## How it works...

When the slave data was out of sync in such a way that a statement from the master would fail (in this case because of a duplicate identity column value), the slave server stopped executing any more SQL statements, even though in the background they were still read from the master and stored in the relay logs. This is what the `Slave_IO_State` and `Slave_IO_Running` columns from the output of SHOW SLAVE STATUS say.

MySQL does this to give you a chance to look at the problem and determine if you can repair the situation somehow. In this very simple example, the solution is simple because we can easily bring the slave's data back in sync with the master by modifying the record in question to match the contents that were sent from the master and then skip the INSERT replicated from the master using the `SQL_SLAVE_SKIP_COUNTER` global variable. This will skip exactly one statement from the relay logs, when the slave is next told to start. In our case, this is the problematic INSERT.

After that the replication is back in sync, as master and slave are now based on identical data sets again, allowing the following statements to be replicated normally.

## There's more...

Another solution in this particular case could have been to delete the record on the slave and then restart the replication with START SLAVE. As the INSERT from the master has not been executed yet, replication would continue as if nothing had happened.

However, under more realistic circumstances, when confronted with a situation like this, you might not have a chance to delete the row on the slave due to foreign key constraints. Only because we immediately took care of the problem and we were sure that in the meantime no programs could have written to the slave, possibly creating new references to that record, were we able to remove it.

Depending on your application architecture and how fast you noticed the problem, some process might have been writing data to the slaves to tables that are designed for this purpose, linking to the now present `category_id` 17 and effectively preventing you from deleting it.

While in this simple case, we would be sure that the replication setup is now back to normal again, you often will not be able to tell for certain at which point in time a replication problem originated. INSERT statements of duplicate keys will immediately cause an error to become apparent. UPDATE or DELETE statements will often succeed in executing, but would have different effects on the slave than on the master, when they were previously out of sync.

Problems like this can corrupt the data on your slaves silently for extended periods of time. When you find out in the end, it is often too late to recover without resorting to setting up the slave afresh.

When in doubt, we recommend to first use mk-table-checksum as described in the *Checking if servers are in sync* recipe in this chapter, or more generally to set up the slave from a well-known good state to be completely sure!

# Checking if servers are in sync

As MySQL cannot detect if two servers are in sync (that is they contain the same records and tables), one would often like to verify that master and slave are still working on identical data sets to be sure no corruption has occurred yet.

For this purpose, the excellent Maatkit suite of programs (see http://www.maatkit.org) contains a handy tool called mk-table-checksum. It automatically calculates checksums of tables on one or more servers, which can then be compared. Should the checksums differ, then the table in question is not identical on the machines involved in the check.

The servers involved need not necessarily be a replication master and slaves, but can be any set of servers you wish to compare. mk-table-checksum has an additional alternative means of checking the special case in replication environments to see if a master and its slaves are in sync. See the *There's more...* section at the end of this recipe for more details on this feature.

## Getting ready

Maatkit is written in Perl. While on most Unix-like systems this scripting language is already installed by default or can be easily downloaded and set up, Windows users will not be so lucky in general. If you are stuck with Windows, you might want to take a look at ActivePerl, a mature Perl implementation for Windows.

Moreover, you are definitely going to need the Maatkit mk-table-checksum tool. You can get it directly from http://www.maatkit.org. Also, download the mk-checksum-filter companion tool and put it in the same directory as mk-table-checksum.

In this example, we will compare two MySQL servers that differ in the `sakila` database's `country` table located on machines called *serverA* and *serverB*.

You will need to have user accounts for both machines that have permission to connect and execute statements remotely.

The command lines in this recipe might change with newer versions of Maatkit, as it is under active development. Double-check with the online manual that the instructions printed here are still current before trying them out.

## How to do it...

1. On a command shell prompt, enter the following line, assuming `mk-table-checksum` is in the current directory and executable:

   ```
   $ ./mk-table-checksum h=serverA,u=userA,p=passwordA
   h=serverB,u=userB,p=passwordB  | ./mk-checksum-filter
   ```

2. Check the output of this command (formatted and abbreviated for printing):

| Database | Table | Chunk | Host | Engine | Count | Checksum |
|----------|-------|-------|------|--------|-------|----------|
| sakila | country | 0 | serverA | InnoDB | NULL | 2771817858 |
| sakila | country | 0 | serverB | InnoDB | NULL | 3823671353 |

Notice the last column: The checksums do not match—the tables are not identical.

## How it works...

`mk-table-checksum` connects to all servers listed on the command line and calculates checksums for all tables. Identical table contents result in identical checksums. So if the checksums from two servers do not match for any given table, there must be a difference in their contents. The `mk-checksum-filter` tool removes all lines from the output that do *not* indicate a checksum mismatch.

 It is important to know that the checksums are different if you employ different versions of MySQL across servers. In this case, a different checksum might just be the result of the different versions!

`mk-table-checksum` offers several algorithms for checksumming, each with different speeds and different levels of resilience against certain kinds of data differences that might cancel each other out, leading to identical checksums, but for different data. The Maatkit online manual contains detailed and current information on this topic.

## There's more...

Due to the asynchronous nature of MySQL replication, executing the checksum statements remotely from a single machine may not yield reliable results. This is because the master database might already contain modifications that have not been executed by each slave yet.

To compensate, `mk-table-checksum` offers a special mode to check slaves and masters. Instead of executing the calculations remotely, the statements to do so are written to the master's binlog and then sent off to the slaves via the regular replication mechanism. This ensures that each slave will calculate the checksum at the correct time with respect to the transaction order. The results are then stored in a table on the slave that can be retrieved with a second command remotely later on. To use this feature, you need a user with sufficient privileges to create a table for this purpose on the slaves.

For more details, see the `--replicate` and `--create-replicate-table` options in the Maatkit online manual.

# Avoiding duplicate server IDs

A key configuration item in any replication setup is server IDs. They must be unique across all participating master and slave machines. Unfortunately, there is no official way to verify this reliably. Instead, when you introduce duplicates by mistake, strange behavior may surface. Generally, this happens when cloning the machines from an image.

Most importantly, on the master server you will not see any indication of the problem. The problem arises only on the slaves without clearly stating the root cause of the problem. See the *There's more...* section of this recipe for more details.

## Getting ready

The `server-id` setting does not carry any meaning in and of itself, but is only used to internally distinguish servers from each other. Generally, administrators setting up new MySQL servers enter sequential or random values for this field. This requires a list of server IDs already issued, preferably including the host name. As with most things in life that need to be done manually, maintaining this list is likely to become a burden and will be forgotten.

Instead, you can assign server IDs based on features of the individual machines that are usually unique already, for example, the network interface's MAC address or the IP address, which should remain reasonably fixed for any server machine as well.

IP addresses are usually shown in a dotted notation of four numbers between 0 and 255. Because MySQL requires `server-id` to be specified as single decimal value, you need to convert it first.

## How to do it...

1. Determine your server's IP address. Make sure not to use the loop-back adapter or a similar pseudo-interface. In this example we assume an IP address of `10.0.159.22`.

2. Convert the 4 bytes of the address to hexadecimal. Mostly any calculator application can do this for you. You enter each of the four numbers in decimal mode and then switch to hexadecimal mode. Just replace each individual decimal value with its hexadecimal counterpart. For the address above you will come up with: `0a.00.9f.16`

3. Append the bytes (that is just remove the dots between them) and convert them back to decimal by switching modes: $0a009f16_{HEX}=167812886_{DEC}$

4. Insert that final value as the server ID in the [mysqld] section of that server's configuration file:

   ```
   [mysqld]
   server-id=167812886
   ```

## How it works...

The IP address serves to uniquely identify a network interface (and therefore a machine) on a network. We leverage this uniqueness by recycling the IP address as the server ID. Most operating systems will issue a warning when an IP address conflict is detected, so this indirectly points to a replication problem as well.

 Of course, traditional IPv4 addresses (those usually noted in the above notation) are only unique in their respective subnet. That means you should not rely on this recipe alone for your server IDs if master and slave machines are located in different locations from a network topology point of view!

## There's more...

The IP address is only one possible unique value you can use. Anything that you can fit in the valid numeric range of the `server-id` setting can be used. Ideally that value should never change over the lifetime of a server, much like a good Primary key, just not for a single database record, but the server as a whole.

You could use any sort of serial number your hardware vendor already assigns to the machine, if it is purely numeric and fits the valid range of 4 bytes. However, this ties you to the vendor's idea of uniqueness, which you cannot verify reliably. Alternatively, the last 4 bytes of the server's MAC address (those are 6 bytes long, starting with a vendor specific prefix) could be used as well. However, beware that unless you exclusively use network adapter chip sets from a single vendor, there remains a certain danger of duplicates.

### Recognizing symptoms of duplicate server IDs

Despite all care, errors can happen and duplicate `server-ids` can be issued. Unfortunately, MySQL will not tell you explicitly when you have non-unique `server-ids` in your replication setup. While on the master, you will not see any evidence in the log files that something is wrong, slaves will show strange behavior and issue seemingly unrelated error messages to their log files in short succession:

Of course, the names of machines, log files, and positions will vary, but the message of an assumed shutdown of the master, followed by immediate retries and failing again is a clear indication of a problem with replication `server-ids`.

# Setting up slaves to report custom information about themselves to the master

When you issue a SHOW SLAVE HOSTS command on a replication master server, you will get a list of slaves connected, provided that they are set up correctly.

Unfortunately, by default they are not, so unless you specifically configure them to do so, slaves will not register themselves with the master. In a default setup you might not see any slave in the output of the above command or in the Replication Status pane in MySQL Administrator at all, even though there might be several configured against this master.

In this recipe, we will show you how to configure a slave to tell its master some details that might come in handy when troubleshooting

Please note that due to a bug in MySQL the output of the SHOW SLAVE HOSTS command is not always reliable! Sometimes it will report hosts being available when in fact they are currently not. The only way that seems to fix an erroneous display is to stop and start the master server.

This effectively makes this feature unsuitable for the purpose of the actual current health of the slaves. It, nevertheless, provides a way to gather some inventory information on their location and some other details described below.

The bug report is tracked at
`http://bugs.mysql.com/bug.php?id=13963`.

## Getting ready

To follow along, you will need sufficient operating system privileges to modify the slave's configuration file (`my.cnf` or `my.ini` depending on your operation system). To actually see that status on the master you will need a MySQL user there as well.

## How to do it...

1. Shut down the slave.

2. Open its configuration file in a text editor.

3. Make sure the following line is present in the `[mysqld]` section:

   ```
   report-host=slave_1701.example.com
   ```

4. Save the configuration.

5. Restart the slave.

6. On the master, issue this command to verify your change was successful:

   ```
   mysql> show slave hosts \G
   ```

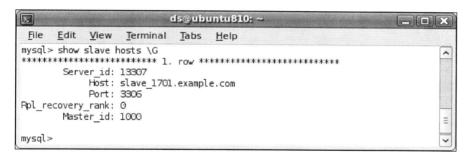

You might of course see many more slaves here, depending on how they are configured.

Should you ask yourself what the `Rpl_recovery_rank` line in the output means, you may simply ignore it. It seems it was introduced some years ago but never put to active use.

## How it works...

Usually, slaves do not report any details about themselves when they connect to the master. By adding some options in their configuration you can, however, make them announce details about themselves.

We strongly recommend setting up all your slaves to register with the master, especially when you are dealing with many masters and slaves. This can be very helpful to keep on top of things.

MySQL Administrator allows you to remember all slaves it has seen once and display a warning on its **Replication Status** pane when a machine previously known does not register later. This particular piece of information is not reliable. however; see the warning in this recipe's introduction for more information.

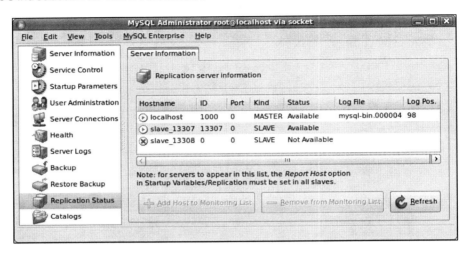

## There's more...

The general idea behind the `report-host` setting is to give an idea about how to reach the slave machine via the network. As the slave might be located behind some sort of firewall or NAT router, its IP address might not be very helpful. So, in general, it can be helpful to have the slave report a fully qualified domain name that can be used to reach it, if applicable.

However, it is by no means mandatory to do so. If you do not intend to access the slave remotely, you might just enter any other piece of information you like to see in the output of the command mentioned in this recipe or the MySQL Administrator pane. As you can see in the previous screenshot, I set up the slaves to report back a name suffixed with the server-ID value. Doing so works around a bug in MySQL Administrator that knows how to remember slaves it has seen before, but sometimes forgets their `server-id`.

Showing slaves currently unavailable is a feature of MySQL Administrator; the SHOW SLAVE HOSTS command will not mention them at all. To leverage this you must click the **Add Host to Monitoring List** button for each slave once it is connected. Otherwise, they will not appear at all when they are not connected.

Apart from the `report-host` configuration setting there are three more options you should know about:

| Setting | Description |
|---|---|
| report-port | Informs about the port that must be used to reach the slave on the domain name reported by report-host. This can be sensible if port forwarding has been set up. |
| report-user | Report a username that can be used to connect to the slave. Not recommended to use! |
| report-password | Report a password that can be used to connect to the slave. Not recommended to use! |

For completeness, this is what the output of SHOW SLAVE HOSTS will look like if you go against our advice and configure the slave to report a set of login credentials and the master has been started with the `show-slave-auth-info` option:

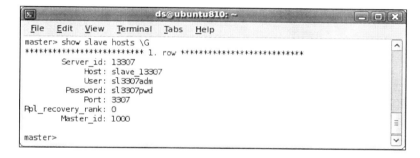

While the `report-port` setting might be useful, we strongly suggest to refrain from using the `report-user` and `report-password` options for security reasons.

Even though the master server will only display these values when it is started with the `show-slave-auth-info` option, it is still very risky to send login credentials over the network in this manner. You should always use more secure ways to exchange login information!

# 2
# Indexing

In this chapter, we will cover:

- ► Adding indexes to tables
- ► Adding a fulltext index
- ► Creating a normalized text search column
- ► Removing indexes from tables
- ► Estimating InnoDB index space requirements
- ► Using prefix primary keys
- ► Choosing InnoDB primary key columns
- ► Speeding up searches for (sub)domains
- ► Finding duplicate indexes

## Introduction

One of the most important features of relational database management systems—MySQL being no exception—is the use of indexes to allow rapid and efficient access to the enormous amounts of data they keep safe for us. In this chapter, we will provide some useful recipes for you to get the most out of your databases.

## Infinite storage, infinite expectations

We have got accustomed to nearly infinite storage space at our disposal—storing everything from music to movies to high resolution medical imagery, detailed geographical information, or just plain old business data. While we take it for granted that we hardly ever run out of space, we also expect to be able to locate and retrieve every bit of information we save in an instant. There are examples everywhere in our lives—business and personal:

- Your pocket music player's library can easily contain tens of thousands of songs and yet can be browsed effortlessly by artist name or album title, or show you last week's top 10 rock songs.

- Search engines provide thousands of results in milliseconds for any arbitrary search term or combination.

- A line of business application can render your sales numbers charted and displayed on a map, grouped by sales district in real-time.

These are a few simple examples, yet for each of them huge amounts of data must be combed to quickly provide just the right subset to satisfy each request. Even with the immense speed of modern hardware, this is not a trivial task to do and requires some clever techniques.

## Speed by redundancy

Indexes are based on the principle that searching in sorted data sets is way faster than searching in unsorted collections of records. So when MySQL is told to create an index on one or more columns, it copies these columns' contents and stores them in a sorted manner. The remaining columns are replaced by a reference to the original table with the unsorted data.

This combines two benefits—providing fast retrieval while maintaining reasonably efficient storage requirements. So, without wasting too much space this approach enables you to create several of those indexes (or *indices*, both are correct) at a relatively low cost.

However, there is a drawback to this as well: while reading data, indexes allow for immense speeds, especially in large databases; however, they do slow down writing operations. In the course of **INSERT**s, **UPDATE**s, and **DELETE**s, all indexes need to be updated in addition to the data table itself. This can place significant additional load on the server, slowing down all operations.

For this reason, keeping the number of indexes as low as possible is paramount, especially for the largest tables where they are most important. In this chapter, you'll find some recipes that will help you to decide how to define indexes and show you some pitfalls to avoid.

## Storage engine differences

We will not go into much detail here about the differences between the MyISAM and the InnoDB storage engines offered by MySQL. However, regarding indexes there are some important differences to know between MySQL's two most important storage engines. They influence some decisions you will have to make.

# MyISAM

In the figure below you can see a simplified schema of how indexes work with the MyISAM storage engine. Their most important property can be summed up as "all indexes are created equal". This means that there is no technical difference between the primary and secondary keys.

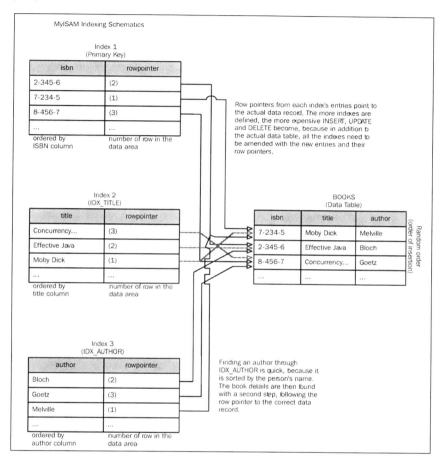

The diagram shows a single (theoretical) data table called **books**. It has three columns named **isbn**, **title**, and **author**. This is a very simple schema, but it is sufficient for explanation purposes. The exact definition can be found in the *Adding indexes to tables* recipe in this chapter. For now, it is not important.

MyISAM tables store information in the order it is inserted. In the example, there are three records representing a single book each. The ISBN number is declared as the *primary key* for this table. As you can see, the records are not ordered in the table itself—the ISBN numbers are out of what would be their lexical order. Let's assume they have been inserted by someone in this order.

Now, have a look at the first index—the **PRIMARY KEY**. The index is sorted by the **isbn** column. Associated with each index entry is a row pointer that leads to the actual data record in the **books** table. When looking up a specific ISBN number in the primary key index, the database server follows the row pointer to retrieve the remaining data fields. The same holds true for the other two indexes *IDX_TITLE* and *IDX_AUTHOR*, which are sorted by the respective fields and also contain a row pointer each.

Looking up a book's details by any one of the three possible search criteria is a two-part operation: first, find the index record, and then follow the row pointer to get the rest of the data.

With this technique you can insert data very quickly because the actual data records are simply appended to the table. Only the relatively small index records need to be kept in order, meaning much less data has to be shuffled around on the disk.

There are drawbacks to this approach as well. Even in cases where you only ever want to look up data by a single search column, there will be two accesses to the storage subsystem—one for the index, another for the data.

## InnoDB

However, InnoDB is different. Its index system is a little more complicated, but it has some advantages:

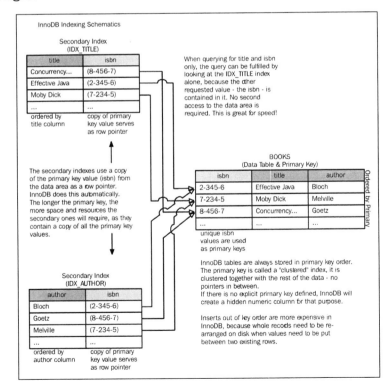

## Primary (clustered) indexes

Whereas in MyISAM all indexes are structured identically, InnoDB makes a distinction between the primary key and additional secondary ones.

The primary index in InnoDB is a *clustered index*. This means that one or more columns of each record make up a unique key that identifies this exact record. In contrast to other indexes, a clustered index's main property is that it itself is part of the data instead of being stored in a different location. Both data and index are *clustered* together.

An index is only serving its purpose if it is stored in a sorted fashion. As a result, whenever you insert data or modify the key column(s), it needs to be put in the correct location according to the sort order. For a clustered index, the whole record with all its data has to be relocated.

That is why bulk data insertion into InnoDB tables is best performed in correct primary key order to minimize the amount of disk I/O needed to keep the records in index order. Moreover, the clustered index should be defined so that it is hardly ever changed for existing rows, as that too would mean relocating full records to different sectors on the disk.

Of course, there are significant advantages to this approach. One of the most important aspects of a clustered key is that it actually *is a part* of the data. This means that when accessing data through a primary key lookup, there is no need for a two-part operation as with MyISAM indexes. The location of the index is at the same time the location of the data itself—there is no need for following a row pointer to get the rest of the column data, saving an expensive disk access.

Looking up a book by ISBN in our example table simply means locating it quickly, as it is stored in order, and then reading the complete record in one go.

## Secondary indexes

Consider if you were to search for a book by title to find out the ISBN number. An index on the name column is required to prevent the database from scanning through the whole (ISBN-sorted) table. In contrast to MyISAM, the InnoDB storage engine creates secondary indexes differently.

Instead of record pointers, it uses a copy of the whole primary key for each record to establish the connection to the actual data contents.

In the previous figure, have a look at the *IDX_TITLE* index. Instead of a simple pointer to the corresponding record in the data table, you can see the ISBN number duplicated as well. This is because the **isbn** column is the primary key of the **books** table. The same goes for the other indexes in the figure—they all contain the book ISBN number as well. You do not need to (and should not) specify this yourself when creating and indexing on InnoDB tables, it all happens automatically under the covers.

Lookups by secondary index are similar to MyISAM index lookups. In the first step, the index record that matches your search term is located. Then secondly, the remaining data is retrieved from the data table by means of another access—this time by primary key.

As you might have figured, the second access is optional, depending on what information you request in your query. Consider a query looking for the ISBN numbers of all known issues of Moby Dick:

```
SELECT isbn FROM books WHERE title LIKE 'Moby Dick%';
```

Issued against a presumably large library database, it will most certainly result in an index lookup on the *IDX_TITLE* key. Once the index records are found, there is no need for another lookup to the actual data pages on disk because the ISBN number is already present in the index. Even though you cannot see the column in the index definition, MySQL will skip the second seek saving valuable I/O operations.

But there is a drawback to this as well. MyISAM's row pointers are comparatively small. The primary key of an InnoDB table can be much bigger—the longer the key, the more the data that is stored redundantly.

In the end, it can often be quite difficult to decide on the optimal balance between increased space requirements and maintenance costs on index updates. But do not worry; we are going to provide help on that in this chapter as well.

## General requirements for the recipes in this chapter

All the recipes in this chapter revolve around changing the database schema. In order to add indexes or remove them, you will need access to a user account that has an effective **INDEX** privilege or the **ALTER** privilege on the tables you are going to modify.

While the **INDEX** privilege allows for use of the **CREATE INDEX** command, **ALTER** is required for the **ALTER TABLE ADD INDEX** syntax. The MySQL manual states that the former is mapped to the latter automatically. However, an important difference exists: **CREATE INDEX** can only be used to add a single index at a time, while **ALTER TABLE ADD INDEX** can be used to add more than one index to a table in a single go.

This is especially relevant for InnoDB tables because up to MySQL version 5.1 every change to the definition of a table internally performs a copy of the whole table. While for small databases this might not be of any concern, it quickly becomes infeasible for large tables due to the high load copying may put on the server. With more recent versions this might have changed, but make sure to consult your version's manual.

In the recipes throughout this chapter, we will consistently use the **ALTER TABLE ADD INDEX** syntax to modify tables, assuming you have the appropriate privileges. If you do not, you will have to rewrite the statements to use the **CREATE INDEX** syntax.

# Adding indexes to tables

Over time requirements for a software product usually change and affect the underlying database as well. Often the need for new types of queries arises, which makes it necessary to add one or more new indexes to perform these new queries fast enough.

In this recipe, we will add two new indexes to an existing table called `books` in the `library` schema. One will cover the `author` column, the other the `title` column. The schema and table can be created like this:

```
mysql> CREATE DATABASE library;
mysql> USE library;
mysql> CREATE TABLE books (
    isbn char(13) NOT NULL,
    author varchar(64) default NULL,
    title varchar(64) NOT NULL,
    PRIMARY KEY  (isbn)
) ENGINE=InnoDB;
```

## Getting ready

Connect to the database server with your administrative account.

## How to do it...

1. Change the default database to library:
   ```
   USE library;
   ```

2. Create both indexes in one go using the following command:
   ```
   ALTER TABLE books ADD INDEX IDX_author(author), ADD INDEX IDX_title(title);
   ```

## How it works...

The `ALTER` table statement shown above is almost self-explanatory. The `books` table is altered to be indexed with individual indexes on the `author` and the `title` columns. Each index is given an easily recognizable name: `IDX_author` and `IDX_title` for the `author` and `title` columns respectively.

Index names are helpful when you later decide to remove an index from a table. Instead of listing all the columns again, you can just refer to the index name.

**Index names**

It is very common to name indexes with some sort of prefix like `IDX_` and then append the column name(s) the index spans.

This is not strictly necessary and you might want to establish a different naming scheme. Whatever you choose, make sure you follow your scheme and assign names consistent with it for all your indexes.

## There's more...

There are some more details worth knowing about when creating indexes on any given table.

### Using MySQL Query Browser to generate the SQL statements

Setting up indexes can be done either through a command line as shown earlier or using an arguably more comfortable graphical tool like MySQL Query Browser. Especially when dealing with more complex table setups, the graphical presentation can provide additional clarity. Before applying any changes to your database, the product will display and allow you to copy or save the full SQL statement(s) that are equivalent to the changes you made in the graphical editor.

This is very convenient because this way you can be sure not to make any mistakes concerning statement syntax, table, or column names. We usually make changes using MySQL Query Browser on a development or testing machine just to grab the SQL statements and put them into SQL update script files for later execution, for example, as a part of our software update routine. The following figure shows what the changes made in this example look like. Note that the generated statements contain all table and column names in backtick quotes. This is generally not required as long as those identifiers do not collide with MySQL keywords—something you should avoid anyway. Also, the statements will be *fully qualified*, which means the database name is put before the table name. This is also not strictly required if you set the default database to the right schema beforehand.

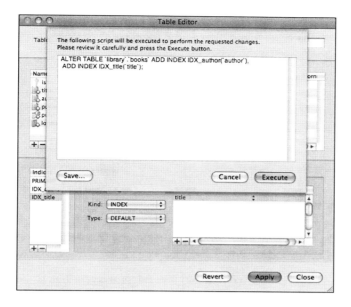

## Prefix indexes

In the example above, we created an index with default settings. This will create an index that is usually "just right". You may, however, have special requirements or possess knowledge about the table data that cannot be derived from the schema definition alone, making a custom index a better choice than the default one.

The detail most often changed in an index definition is the length of the index fields. MySQL provides support for so-called *prefix indexes*. As the database does not know about the nature of the contents that are going to be stored in any particular column apart from the data type, it has no choice but to take the safe route and consider the full length of the column in its sorted index copy.

For long columns in large tables, it can be a waste of space to copy the complete column values to the index, which in turn can have negative impact on performance just because there's more data involved.

You can aid the database to work more efficiently with your domain knowledge. In the *books* example table the title can be up to 64 characters long. However, it is very unlikely that there will be a lot of books whose titles start alike and only differ in the last few characters. So, having the index cover the maximum length is probably not necessary for quick lookups. By changing the index creation statement to include a prefix length (say 20 characters) for the column to be indexed, you can tell MySQL to only copy the first 20 characters of the title to the index:

```
ALTER TABLE books ADD INDEX IDX_title(title(20));
```

As a result, the index will use less space—in terms of both disk usage and memory when used for queries. As long as the book title differs within the first 20 characters, this index will be more efficient than one covering the full column.

Even when there is a certain number of titles that are identical within this 20 character prefix, the index will still be useful. This is because as long as MySQL can rule out all but a few records, having to look at the actual table data for the final decision as to which rows fulfill the query conditions is still significantly faster than having to scan the whole table with all books.

Unfortunately, there is no easy-to-use formula to determine the ideal prefix length because it heavily depends on the actual data content. This is why by default the whole column is indexed.

### Prefix primary keys

Most documentation on indexing in some way or another covers the topic of prefix indexes for text type columns, using only a portion at the beginning of column contents instead of the whole values for the actual index.

However, often this topic is presented in a way that might suggest this only works for secondary keys; but that is not true. You can also use a *prefix primary key*, as long as the most important requirement of a primary key is not violated: the uniqueness of each key value must be guaranteed.

## See also

- ▸ *Estimating InnoDB index space requirements*
- ▸ *Removing indexes from tables*

# Adding a fulltext index

Indexes are an important means of making sure a database performs well and responds quickly when queried. However, they can only live up to their full potential when applied to well-structured data. Unfortunately, not all information we would like to query can be made to fit into regular relational database tables and columns.

A prime example of this is free text. It does not follow any well-defined structure and does not lend itself to the principle by which regular indexes work. For example, a fulltext index allows querying for search terms no matter where in the indexed column they occur and not only at the beginning of the column as would be the case with normal indexes.

Fulltext indexes require you to use a special syntax to express your queries. Querying with the **LIKE** keyword will not be accelerated by a fulltext index. In this recipe you will learn how to create a fulltext index on an existing database column. For the purpose of this example, we assume a fictional *forum* database with a *posts* table that in turn has a *content* column storing the actual text of a forum entry.

InnoDB tables do not support fulltext indexing. This feature is only available for tables using the MyISAM storage engine.

## Getting ready

Connect to the database using your administrative account.

## How to do it...

1.  Change the default database to forum:

    ```
    USE forum;
    ```

2.  Create the fulltext index using the following command:

    ```
    ALTER TABLE posts ADD FULLTEXT INDEX IDX_content(content);
    ```

## How it works...

While regular indexes create ordered copies of the relevant columns to enable quick lookups, fulltext indexes are a more complicated matter.

**Dropping and recreating fulltext indexes for bulk data imports**

When (first) inserting bulk data into a table, it is faster to first drop an existing fulltext index and then later recreate it. This will speed up the data insertion significantly because keeping the fulltext index up to date during data insert is an expensive operation.

## There's more...

Here are some details that are important to know when including fulltext indexing in your applications.

 Please be aware that changes to any of the parameters that follow require a rebuild of any fulltext index that was created before the change!

See the MySQL online manual at `http://dev.mysql.com/doc/refman/5.1/en/fulltext-fine-tuning.html` for more details.

## Case sensitivity

Fulltext index queries are usually run in a case-insensitive way. If you need case-sensitive fulltext search, you will have to change the collation of the affected underlying columns to a binary variant.

## Word length

When a fulltext index is created, only words within a configurable range of lengths are considered. This helps to prevent acronyms and abbreviations being included in the index. You can configure the acceptable length range using the `ft_min_word_len` and `ft_max_word_len` variables. The default value for the minimum length is 4 characters.

## Stopwords

In every language, there are many words that are usually not wanted in fulltext search matching. These so called stopwords might be "is, a, be, there, because, done" among others. They appear so frequently in most texts that searching for them is hardly useful. To conserve resources, these stopwords are ignored when building a fulltext index. MySQL uses a default stopword list that defines what is to be ignored, which contains a list of about 550 English stopwords. You can change this list of stopwords with the `ft_stopword_file` variable. It takes a filename with a plain text file containing the stopwords you would like to use. Disabling stopwords can be achieved by setting this variable to an empty string.

## Ignoring frequent words

Frequent words will be ignored: if a search term is present in more than half of the rows searched, it will be considered a stopword and effectively ignored. This is useful especially in large tables; otherwise you would get half of the table as query hits, which can hardly be considered useful.

 When experimenting with fulltext search, make sure you have a reasonably large dataset to play with. Otherwise you will easily hit the 50 percent mark described above and not get any query results. This can be confusing and will make you think you did something wrong, while in fact everything is perfectly in order.

## Query modes

Apart from the default *human query* mode you can use a *boolean query* mode, which enables special search-engine-like operators to be used—for example, the plus and minus signs to include or exclude words in the search.

This would allow you to use query terms such as `'+apple -macintosh'` to find all records containing the word `apple`, but not the word `macintosh`.

For all the possible operators, have a look at the MySQL online manual at `http://dev.mysql.com/doc/refman/5.1/en/fulltext-boolean.html`

## Sphinx

MySQL's built-in fulltext search is only available for MyISAM tables. In particular, InnoDB is not supported. If you cannot or do not want to use MyISAM, have a look at Sphinx—an open source, free fulltext search engine that was designed to integrate nicely with MySQL. See `http://sphinxsearch.com/` for more information.

### See also

▸ *Removing indexes from tables*

# Creating a normalized text search column

Usually, regular and fulltext indexing as supported by MySQL are sufficient for most use cases. There are, however, situations where they are not perfectly usable:

▸ InnoDB tables cannot use fulltext indexes. At the time of writing there were no signs of this changing in the foreseeable future.

▸ There are different ways to spell the search terms

Especially in non-English speaking countries, a problem often arises that does not surface as often in American or British environments. Words in the English language consist of the letters from A to Z without diacritics. From a software development perspective this is a welcome simplification because it allows for simpler implementations.

One problem you are often faced with German, for example, is different ways to spell the same word, making it complicated to formulate suitable search terms.

Consider the German words "Dübel" (dowel) and "Mörtel" (mortar). In a merchandise management database you might find several variants of similar products, but each could be spelled in different ways:

| productID | name | stock |
|---|---|---|
| 12352323 | DÜBEL GROß 22 | 76 |
| 23982942 | "Flacher-Einser" Mörtel | 23 |
| 29885897 | DÜBEL GROSS 4 | 44 |
| 83767742 | Duebel Groß 68 | 31 |

As an end user of the corresponding application searching for those becomes cumbersome because to find exactly what you are looking for you might have to attempt several searches.

In this recipe, we will present an idea that needs some support on the application level but will allow you to use simple regular indexes to quickly search and find relevant records in situations like the above.

 To implement the ideas presented in this recipe, modifications to the software accessing the database as well as the table definition will be necessary. We advise that this is a process that usually entails a higher complexity and increased testing efforts than simply adding an index.

## Getting ready

To implement the ideas presented here, you will need to connect to the database server with your administrative account for the schema modifications. Because apart from the database modifications application program code changes will be necessary as well, you should contact an application developer.

In the example, we are going to assume a table definition as follows:

```
CREATE TABLE products (
    productID int(11) NOT NULL,
    name char(30) default NULL,
    stock int(11) default NULL,
    PRIMARY KEY  (productID)
) ENGINE=InnoDB
```

## How to do it...

1.  Connect to the database server using your administrative account and make `test` the default schema:

    ```
    use test;
    ```

2.  Add a new column `norm_name` to the `products` table:

    ```
    mysql> ALTER TABLE products ADD COLUMN norm_name CHAR(90) AFTER name;
    ```

    The column needs to be at least as long as your original column. Depending on the character mapping rules you are going to implement, the projected values might take up more space.

3.  Define an index on the new column. Make sure it is not set to `UNIQUE`:

    ```
    mysql> ALTER TABLE products ADD INDEX IDX_norm_name (norm_name);
    ```

4.  Optionally, consider dropping an existing index on the original column. Also, consider modifying other indexes currently containing the original column to include the new one instead.

Implement the replacement algorithm depending on your language. For German language substitutions, the following substitutions could be used. This is just an excerpt from the `Transformers.java` class you can find on the book's website.

```
private static String[] replacements = {
   "ä", "ae",     "null", "0",    ":", "",
   "ö", "oe",     "eins", "1",    ":", "",
   "ü", "ue",     "zwei", "2",    ".", "",
   "ß", "ss",     /* ... */       "-", "",
   " ", "",       "neun", "9",    ",", "",
   // ... further replacements...
};
```

5.  Modify your application code to use the new mapping function and issue queries against the new `norm_name` column where previously the original `name` column was used. Depending on how you decide to expose the search features to your end users, you might want to make searching the new or the old column an option.

6.  Modify your application code to update the new column parallel to the original one. Depending on the application scenario, you might decide to only update the normalized search column periodically instead.

7.  Before handing out a new version of your software containing the new code, make sure the normalized search column gets populated with the correct values.

8.  Optionally, declare the new column **NOT NULL**, after it has been initially filled.

## How it works...

By implementing the mapping algorithm, we make the application think about the different ways to spell things, not the end user. Instead of creating all possible variants, which could become a large set of permutations depending on the length and content of the original input, we project the search terms to a normalized form for both the original data and later for queries issued against it. As both use the same mapping functions, only a single—index supported—query against MySQL is needed. The application of course usually never reveals these internals. The person in front of the computer will just be pleased to find the desired records easily.

The mapping rules from input to search terms depend on the language and application-specific needs. For German words, they are rather short—only the umlaut characters need to be transformed to a normalized form. Other languages might require more complex rules.

In the example code earlier, we also transform the input to lowercase and remove several special characters like dashes and colons, and also the whitespace. For the sample data set of products we used, this is the result of the transformation:

| productID | Name | name_nrm | stock |
|-----------|------|----------|-------|
| 12352323 | DÜBEL GROß 22 | duebelgross22 | 76 |
| 23982942 | "Flacher-Einser" Mörtel | flacher1ermoertel | 23 |
| 29885897 | DÜBEL GROSS 4 | duebelgross4 | 44 |
| 83767742 | Duebel Groß 68 | duebelgross68 | 31 |

Now instead of querying the original data column, we ask the database to search for the transformed representation of the search terms in the additional norm_name (normalized) column. For this it can use regular indexes and provide results quickly and efficiently.

Note that the Transformer.java code available from the book's website is nowhere near production quality but only serves for demonstration purposes. It does not, for example, contain any error checking or exception handling and the mapping algorithm is very simple, too.

## There is more...

If you do not care about international specialties but still want to improve user experience by allowing for less strict searches, you might want to have a look at the SOUNDEX() function. It is designed to work for English language words only and allows you to query for results that sound like the search terms.

However, note that the results of using it may not be what you expect—opinions on the Internet range from extreme enthusiasm to complete disappointment. You can find its documentation at http://dev.mysql.com/doc/refman/5.1/en/string-functions.html#function_soundex.

# Removing indexes from tables

Once-useful indexes may become obsolete as requirements change with the evolving database. In this chapter, we will show you how to get rid of the *IDX_author* index created in the *Adding indexes to tables recipe*.

## Getting ready

Connect to the database server with your administrative account.

## How to do it...

1. Change the default database to `library`:

   ```
   USE library;
   ```

2. Drop the `IDX_author` index using the following command:

   ```
   ALTER TABLE books DROP INDEX IDX_author;
   ```

## How it works...

Using the `ALTER TABLE` statement, we tell the database that we want to remove (`DROP`) the index named `IDX_author` from the `books` table.

## There's more...

As with the creation of new indexes, you can drop multiple indexes at once using the `ALTER TABLE` statement by simply adding more `DROP INDEX` clauses, separated by comma. If you were to delete both indexes defined in *Adding indexes to tables,* you could use this statement:

```
ALTER TABLE books DROP INDEX IDX_author, DROP INDEX IDX_title;
```

## See also

- *Adding indexes to tables*

# Estimating InnoDB index space requirements

While indexes might very well be the single most important key in database performance tuning, they come at the price of redundancy.

There are two main disadvantages tightly connected to redundant data storage:

- The danger of inconsistencies between the redundant copies of data that should be at all times identical.
- Increased storage and memory consumption because the same data is physically duplicated.

Fortunately, the former is a non-issue with indexes. As the database server takes care of keeping data and indexes consistent without human intervention, you cannot get into a situation where two columns that should contain equal data at all times are out of sync due to programming errors or the like. This is usually a problem when violating normalization rules.

In contrast to that, there is no way to prevent the latter disadvantage. We need to store multiple copies if we want different sort orders for quick lookups. What we can do, however, is to attempt to minimize the negative effect by trying to limit the amount of duplicated information as far as possible.

The `employees` database is an open source test database available for free. It contains examples for many MySQL features including large tables, foreign key constraints, views, and more. It can be found along with some documentation at `http://dev.mysql.com/doc/employee/en/employee.html`.

In the example below, we assume the existence of the employees test database with an `employees` table defined as follows:

```
CREATE TABLE employees (
    emp_no int(11) NOT NULL,
    birth_date date NOT NULL,
    first_name varchar(14) NOT NULL,
    last_name varchar(16) NOT NULL,
    gender enum('M','F') NOT NULL,
    hire_date date NOT NULL,
    PRIMARY KEY (emp_no)
) ENGINE=InnoDB DEFAULT CHARSET=latin1;
```

We will add an index each to the `last_name` and the `first_name` columns and try to predict the necessary space.

Please note that the results will never be exact. The storage requirements—especially of text-value table columns (**VARCHAR**, **TEXT**, **CHAR**, and so on)—can be difficult to determine because there are multiple factors that influence the calculation. Apart from differences between storage engines, an important aspect is the character set used. For details refer to the online manual for your server version: `http://dev.mysql.com/doc/refman/5.1/en/storage-requirements.html`.

Moreover, it is not possible to find out the exact size even for existing indexes because MySQL's `SHOW TABLE STATUS` command only gives approximate results for InnoDB tables.

## Getting ready...

Connect to the database server with your administrative account.

## How to do it...

1. Find out the size of one primary key entry.

   To do so, look at the primary key definition in the table structure. Add the sizes of all primary key columns as documented in the MySQL Online Manual. In the example, the INT column takes 4 bytes. Write this number down.

2. Determine the size of each column to be included in the new indexes and add them up per index. In the example, both `first_name` and `last_name` are VARCHAR columns—this means their lengths are not fixed as with the INT type. For simplicity, we will assume completely filled columns, meaning 14 bytes for `first_name` and 16 bytes for the `last_name` column.

3. For each index, add the lengths of all relevant columns and the size of the primary key. In our example, this gives the following results:

| Index | Column size | Primary Key Size | Index Record Size |
|---|---|---|---|
| IDX_FIRST_NAME | 14 | 4 | 18 |
| IDX_LAST_NAME | 16 | 4 | 20 |

The rightmost column contains the pure data size of a single index record including the implicit primary key.

4. Multiply the size per index record with the number of rows in the table:

| Index | Rows | Index record size | Est. index size |
|---|---|---|---|
| IDX_FIRST_NAME | 300024 | 18 | 5400432 |
| IDX_LAST_NAME | 300024 | 20 | 6000480 |

The rightmost column contains the estimated size of the index, based on the current number of records, and the overhead taken by InnoDB to internally organize and store the data.

## How it works

In the previous steps, we simply added up the sizes of all columns that will form a secondary index entry. This includes all columns of the secondary index itself and also those of the primary key because, as explained in the chapter introduction, InnoDB implicitly adds those to every index.

Internally, the server of course needs a little more than just the raw column contents—all sorts of management overhead (such as column widths, information on which columns can be null, as well as some constant overhead) add to the required space. Calculating these in detail is complicated and error-prone because they rely on many parameters and implementation details can change between MySQL versions. This is not required, however, because our aim is a ballpark number. As table contents often change quickly, exact numbers would not be valid for long.

You can see this in our example—the values are too low. In reality, you will need to experiment with these values. You are usually going to be on the safe side when you multiply your results with a factor of 1.5 to 2.5.

You will find that depending on the lengths of the columns indexed and those that make up the primary key, the accuracy of the estimates can vary.

## There's more...

Predicting space requirements is not an exact science. The following items are intended to give some more hints on what you might want to think about.

### Considering actual data lengths in your estimate

When adding an index to an existing column, you can try to use the average length of the column values:

```
SELECT AVG(LENGTH(first_name)) AS avg_first, AVG(LENGTH(last_name)) AS avg_last FROM employees;
```

For the sample data the results are:

| avg_first | avg_last |
| --- | --- |
| 6.2157 | 7.1539 |

Round this up to the next integer (7/8). Note that especially for short columns like this, the estimates can be much less reliable because relative to internal database overhead data size is less significant. This is why in the recipe earlier we went with declared maximum length of the VARCHAR columns instead.

## Minding character sets

For columns storing text information—such as CHAR and VARCHAR, VARBINARY, and TEXT—the storage requirements depend on the character set used for the text inside. For most English-speaking countries, this is something like the Latin-1 character set, which uses a single byte per character of text. However, in international environments, this encoding is hardly sufficient. To accommodate German text, for example, you need some special characters—not to mention Chinese, Japanese, or other non-Latin languages.

MySQL supports different character sets on a per column basis. However, often you will define a default character set for a database including all its tables and their columns.

When estimating index (and data) sizes for Unicode-aware columns (MySQL supports UTF-8 and UCS2 character sets for this purpose), you need to take into account that those may require more than a single byte per character. The very popular UTF-8 encoding uses between 1 and 4 (even though 4 are only used in very special cases) bytes per character. UCS2 has a constant size of 2 bytes per character. For details on how UTF-8 works, see http://en.wikipedia.org/wiki/UTF-8.

# Using prefix primary keys

In this example we will add indexes to two tables that are almost identical. The only difference will be the definition of their primary keys. You will see the difference in space consumption for secondary indexes between a regular full column primary key and a prefix primary key. The sample table structure and data are designed to demonstrate the effect very evidently. In real-world scenarios the effect will most certainly be less severe.

## Getting ready...

Connect to the database server with your administrative account.

## How to do it...

1. Download the sample script for this chapter from the book's website and save it to your local disk. In the example below, we will assume it is stored in /tmp/idxsizeestimate_sample.sql.

2. Create a new database and make it the default database:

```
CREATE DATABASE pktests;
USE pktests;
```

3. Import the sample data from the downloaded file. When done, you will be presented with some statistics about the two tables loaded. Note that both tables have an Index Length of 0.

```
SOURCE /tmp/idxsizeestimate_sample.sql;
```

4. Now with the sample tables present, add an index to each of them:

```
ALTER TABLE LongCharKey ADD INDEX IDX_PAY_10(Payload(10));
ALTER TABLE LongCharKey10 ADD INDEX IDX_PAY_10(Payload(10));
```

5. Display the data and index sizes of the tables now:

```
SHOW TABLE STATUS LIKE 'LongCharKey%';
```

6. Add another index to each table to make the difference even more evident:

```
ALTER TABLE LongCharKey ADD INDEX IDX2_PAY_10(Payload(10));
ALTER TABLE LongCharKey10 ADD INDEX IDX2_PAY_10(Payload(10));
```

7. Display the data and index sizes of the tables again and compare with the previous values:

```
SHOW TABLE STATUS LIKE 'LongCharKey%';
```

| Name | Rows | Data Length | Index Length | Index/Data Ratio |
|---|---|---|---|---|
| LongCharKey | 50045 | 30392320 | 28868608 | 94.99% |
| LongCharKey10 | 50045 | 29949952 | 3178496 | 10.61% |

With the second index added, the difference in index length becomes even clearer.

## How it works...

Executing the downloaded script will set up two tables with the following structures:

```
CREATE TABLE `LongCharKey` (
  `LongChar` char(255) NOT NULL,
  `Payload` char(255) DEFAULT NULL,
  PRIMARY KEY (`LongChar`)
) ENGINE=InnoDB DEFAULT CHARSET=latin1;

CREATE TABLE `LongCharKey10` (
  `LongChar` char(255) NOT NULL,
  `Payload` char(255) DEFAULT NULL,
  PRIMARY KEY (`LongChar`(10))
) ENGINE=InnoDB DEFAULT CHARSET=latin1;
```

The two tables are almost identical, except for the primary key definition. They are pre-filled with 50,000 records of sample data.

The tables are populated with exactly the same 50,000 records of pseudo-random data. The `Payload` column is filled with sequences of 255 random letters each. The `LongChar` column is filled with a sequential number in the first 10 characters and then filled up to use all remaining 245 character with the same sort of random data.

```
SELECT LEFT(LongChar,20), LEFT(Payload, 20) from LongCharKey LIMIT 5;
```

| LEFT(LongChar,20) | LEFT(Payload, 20) |
|---|---|
| **0000000000**KEAFAYVEJD | RHSKMEJITOVBPOVAGOGM |
| **0000000001**WSSGKGMIJR | VARLGOYEONSLEJVTVYRP |
| **0000000002**RMNCFBJSTL | OVWGTTSHEQHJHTHMFEXV |
| **0000000003**SAQVOQSINQ | AHDYUXTAEWRSHCLJYSMW |
| **0000000004**ALHYUDSRBH | DPLPXJVERYHUOYGGUFOS |

While the *LongKeyChar* table simply marks the whole *LongChar* column as a primary key with its entire 255 characters length, the *LongCharKey10* table limits the primary key to the first 10 characters of that column. This is perfectly fine for this table, because the test data was crafted to be unique in this range.

Neither one of the two tables has any secondary indexes defined. Looking at some relevant table data shows they are equally big (some columns left out for brevity):

```
SHOW TABLE STATUS LIKE 'LongCharKey%';
```

| Name | Rows | Data Length | Index Length |
|---|---|---|---|
| LongCharKey | 50045 | 30392320 | 0 |
| LongCharKey10 | 50045 | 29949952 | 0 |

With each index added, the Index Length for the first table will increase significantly, while for the second one its growth is much slower.

In case of the *LongCharKey* table, each secondary index record will carry around with it a complete copy of the *LongChar* column because it is the primary key without limitation. Assuming a single byte character encoding, this means every secondary index record is blown up in size by 255 bytes on top of the 10 bytes needed for the actual index entry. **This means a whole kilobyte is spent just for the primary key reference for every 4 records!**

In contrast to that, the primary key definition of the *LongCharKey10* table only includes the leading 10 characters of the *LongChar* column, making the secondary index entry 245 bytes shorter and thereby explaining the much slower growth upon adding further indexes.

# Choosing InnoDB primary key columns

In the chapter introduction we promised to shed some light on how to choose your InnoDB primary key columns sensibly. Be advised that choosing good primary key columns is not an exact science—there are multiple aspects that influence this decision. Depending on your needs and preconditions you will want to prioritize them differently from one table to the next. Consider the following as general advice rather than hard rules that must be obeyed unconditionally.

## Getting ready

In order to make reasonable decisions on primary key columns, it is important to have a very clear understanding of what the data looks like in the table at hand. If you already have existing data that is to be stored in an InnoDB table—for example in MyISAM format—it can be helpful to compare it with the criteria below.

If you are planning a new schema, you might have to guess about some characteristics of the future data. As is often the case, the quality of your choices is directly proportional to how good those guesses are.

This recipe is less strict step-by-step instructions that must be followed from top to bottom and should be considered a list of properties a good primary key should have, even though you might decide some of them do not apply to your actual environment. As a rule of thumb, however, a column that fulfills all or most of the attributes described below is most probably a sensible choice for a primary key. See the *How it works...* section for details on the individual items.

## How to do it...

1. **Identify unique attributes**: This is an absolute (technical) requirement for primary keys in general. Any data attribute that is not strictly guaranteed to be free of duplicates cannot be used alone as a primary key.

2. **Identify immutable attributes**: While not absolutely necessary, a good primary key is never changed once it has been assigned. For all intents and purposes, you should avoid columns that have even a small chance of being changed for existing records.

3. **Use reasonably short keys**: This is the "softest" criterion of all. In general, longer keys have negative impacts on overall database performance—the longer the worse. Also, consider a prefix primary key. See *Using prefix primary keys* earlier in this chapter for more information.

4. **Prefer single-column keys**: Even though nothing prevents you from choosing a composite primary key (a combination of columns that together form the uniqueness), this can easily become a hassle to work with, especially when handling foreign keys.

5. **Consider the clustered index nature of the primary key**: As InnoDB's primary key is also clustered, you should take this special nature into account as well. It can speed up read access a lot, if you often have to query for key ranges, because disk seek times will be minimized.

## How it works...

In the following sections, we will try to shed some light on what each step of the recipe is concerned with in a little more detail.

## Uniqueness

An absolute requirement for primary keys is their uniqueness. Every record in your table will have to have a distinct value for primary keys. Otherwise, neither MySQL nor any other database product for that matter could be sure about whether it was operating on exactly the right rows when executing your queries.

Usually, most entities you might want to store in a relational database have some sort of unique characteristics that might be a suitable Primary key. If they do not, you can always assign a so-called surrogate key for each record. Often this is some sort of unique numeric value, either generated by an application working on top of the database or MySQL itself using an **AUTO_INCREMENT** column.

## Immutability

Primary key columns should generally be (virtually) immutable, that is, under no circumstances should you have to modify their values, once they are inserted into the database.

In our books example, the ISBN number cannot be changed once a book has been published. The same would apply for a car's chassis number.

Technically, of course, they can be changed after their creation. However, this will be very difficult to perform in practice, once the original value has been used to establish foreign key relationships between tables. In these cases, you will often have to revert to complicated and even unsafe methods (risking data inconsistencies) to perform the changes.

Moreover, as the primary key is stored as a clustered key in InnoDB, changing its value will require the whole record—including all columns—to be moved to its new location on disk, causing additional disk I/O.

Note that sometimes columns that may at first seem constant over time really are not. For example, consider a person's social security number. It is designed to be unique and can never change or be reassigned to a different human being. Consequentially, it would seem like a good choice for primary key in a table of people.

But consider that in most cases data will be entered into the database manually—be it through forms, text file imports, among others. In some form or another, someone will have typed it in through a keyboard.

Manual input is by definition an error prone process. So you might end up with a person's record that has two digits transposed in their primary key social security number without immediately knowing it. Gradually, this wrong value will spread through your database—it will be used in foreign key relationships, forming complex data structures. When you later find out about the error—for example, because another person who really owns that number needs to be inserted—then you are facing a real problem.

Unless you are absolutely and positively sure a value can never change once it has been assigned to a record, you should consider adding a new column to your table and use a surrogate key, for example, an auto-incrementing number.

## Key length

There are several reasons for keys being as short as possible. InnoDB basically only uses one single large heap of memory—the buffer pool—for its caching purposes. It is used for both row and index data, which are stored as memory cached copies of individual pages straight from the tablespace data files. The shorter each key value is, the more of them fit into a single data page (the default size is 16 KB). For an index with 16 bytes per index value, a single page will contain about a thousand index entries. For an index with only 8 bytes per entry, twice as many values can be cached in the same amount of space. So to utilize the effects of memory-based caching, smaller indexes are better.

For the data record as a whole there might not be much of a difference between 8 or 16 bytes compared with the overall record length. But remember (or refer to the chapter introduction if you don't) that the primary key length is added to each secondary index's length again. For example, a secondary index on an 8 byte field will actually be 16 bytes long if the primary key also has 8 bytes per entry. A 16 KB data page would provide space for roughly 1,000 index entries in this scenario. If the primary key is 16 bytes long, it would only be sufficient for about 680 entries, reducing the effectiveness of cache memory.

## Single column keys

Depending on the data you intend to store in an InnoDB table, you might consider using a composite primary key. This means that no single column's value alone uniquely identifies a single record but only the combination of several independent columns allows uniqueness. From a technical point of view, this is perfectly feasible and might even be a good choice from a semantic point of view.

However, you should very carefully weigh the alternatives because composite keys can quickly become a burden. The more secondary tables define foreign key relationships with a table using a composite primary key, the more complicated your queries will become because whenever you join the two, you have to define a join condition on at least four columns. For more complex queries with multiple joins, this quickly becomes very hard to maintain and therefore, carries a great risk of errors that might be hard to find.

In addition, you also have to consider the increased size of each key entry and that the sizes of all the participating columns must be added.

As general advice, you should definitely consider using a surrogate key when you cannot find any candidate that fulfills the other criteria just discussed.

## Clustered Index

As data is physically stored on disk in the order of the clustered key, similar key values end up in neighboring locations. This makes clustered indexes very efficient for queries that retrieve ranges of records by this key. If, for example, the clustered key is a timestamp of some sort, retrieving all records within a contiguous timespan is likely to require relatively little physical disk I/O because ideally all requested result rows are stored in the same data page, therefore only needing a single read operation (which might even be cached). Even if multiple pages had to be read, this will only require a sequential read operation, which leverages linear disk read performance best.

Unfortunately, InnoDB does not allow a non-primary key to be clustered—other DBMS do—so you have to weigh the alternatives and maybe live with a compromise when deciding on the primary key for your InnoDB tables.

# Speeding up searches for (sub)domains

In a column with domain e-mail addresses, searching for all addresses of a given domain is a non-trivial task performance-wise. Given the following table structure, the only way to find all addresses @gmail.com is to use a LIKE query with a wildcard:

```
SELECT * FROM clients WHERE email LIKE '%@gmail.com';
```

Of course, storing the address and domain parts in separate columns would solve this particular problem. But as soon as you were asked for a quick way to find all clients with an e-mail address from a British provider, you would be out of luck again, resorting to:

```
SELECT * FROM clients WHERE maildomain LIKE '%.co.uk';
```

Both queries would cause a full table scan because no index can support the wildcard at the beginning of the search term.

In this recipe, you will be given a simple but effective approach to enable the use of indexes for both of the problems just presented. Notice that you will need to make minor adjustments to the queries sent against the database. This might involve some code adjustments in your application.

## Getting ready

To implement the ideas presented here, you will need to connect to the database server with your administrative account for the schema modifications. Apart from the database modifications, application program code changes will be necessary as well and you should contact an application developer.

## How to do it...

1. Identify which column is currently used to store domain-related data. In the example, we will be using the `maildomain` column of the `clients` table.

2. Update this column and reverse the contents of the field like this:

   ```
   UPDATE clients SET maildomain=REVERSE(maildomain);
   ```

3. If not already set up, add an index to the column:

   ```
   ALTER TABLE clients ADD INDEX IDXR_MAILDOMAIN(maildomain);
   ```

4. Change all queries in your application as follows:

   Before:

   ```
   SELECT name, maildomain FROM clients WHERE maildomain LIKE
    '%.co.uk';
   ```

   After:

   ```
   SELECT name, REVERSE(maildomain) AS maildomain FROM clients WHERE
    maildomain LIKE REVERSE('%.co.uk');
   ```

   The point here is to reverse the search condition as well as the column in the column list. `SELECT` statements using the star placeholder instead of column names need to be rewritten to reverse the `maildomain` column.

## How it works...

Indexes are designed to speed up queries by sorting the relevant column contents, which makes finding records with a given search prefix easy.

Searching for all people whose name starts with an "S", for example, is supported by this technique. The more characters you provide the more specific the search gets, again supported ideally by an index.

Domain names are a different story, however, because those belonging together do not share a common prefix but suffix. There is no immediate way of telling MySQL to create an index supporting this kind of data.

The first idea that comes to mind to work around this would be to use a query along the lines of:

```
SELECT * FROM clients
WHERE REVERSE(maildomain) LIKE 'ku.oc.%';
```

Unfortunately, MySQL—in contrast to other DBMS—can neither use indexes in conjunction with functions like REVERSE() nor create an index based on a function in the first place. Instead, it resorts to full-table scans to find the results as soon as it encounters a function call applied to a column in a query's WHERE clause. In this case, the REVERSE() function is applied to the maildomain column.

With a minor adjustment to the way data is stored, this limitation can be alleviated, however: store the data backwards in the first place!

When inserting new data into the table, we reverse it first:

```
INSERT INTO clients (maildomain, …)
VALUES (REVERSE('example.co.uk'), …);
```

When retrieving data later, we just need to reapply the same function to get back at the original data:

```
SELECT REVERSE(maildomain) FROM clients
WHERE maildomain LIKE REVERSE('%.co.uk');
```

As now the query condition does not contain a function call *on a column* anymore, MySQL is happy to use an index on the maildomain column to speed up the search.

It might seem odd at first that now even with two calls to the REVERSE() function this query can in fact use an index.

> The key point is that MySQL does not have to apply the function on any *column data* but only on the *constant* condition (the '%.co.uk' string) and later—when the rows have already been fetched—on the already retrieved reverse column content of maildomain. Both of these are not a problem for index use.

The query is really executed in two phases. In the first phase, MySQL will have a look at the condition and check if it can replace any function call with constants. So, when we write;

```
SELECT REVERSE(maildomain) FROM clients
WHERE maildomain LIKE REVERSE('%.co.uk');
```

after the first phase, internally the query looks like this:

```
SELECT REVERSE(maildomain) FROM clients
WHERE maildomain LIKE 'ku.oc.%';
```

In this query, there is no function call left in the condition. So the index on the `maildomain` column can be used, speeding up the execution as desired.

## There's more...

If your application typically issues queries that need to retrieve contiguous ranges of domains—as in the preceding example—you might consider using the reversed domain name as primary (and therefore clustered) key.

The advantage would be that the related records would be stored closely together on disk, in the same or adjacent data pages.

 However, updating an existing table on its primary key column can be both very time consuming, as all data rows need to be physically rearranged, and sometimes complicated to do when foreign key constraints are in place.

## See also

► *Choosing InnoDB primary key columns*

# Finding duplicate indexes

Over time database schemata are subject to changes such as index additions and deletions. It is not uncommon to end up with multiple indexes that are equivalent in terms of query execution but might be defined with different names or even different columns.

This duplication of indexes has negative consequences for your database:

► **Increased size**: The more the indexes, the bigger the database.

► **Lower performance**: Each index has to be updated on modifications of the respective table, wasting precious I/O and CPU resources.

► **Increased schema complexity**: Schema maintenance and understanding of the tables and relationships gets more complicated.

For those reasons, you should be concerned about superfluous indexes.

In this recipe, we will present a way to quickly find out which indexes can be dropped from a table as they are functionally equivalent (if not necessarily formally identical) to another one.

## Getting ready

In order to run the program presented here, you will need a Java Runtime Environment (JRE or just *Java*) installed. You can download it for free from `http://www.java.com`.

Download the Index Analyzer for MySQL from the book's website.

You will also need login credentials with administrative privileges for the server and the database you want to analyze.

## How to do it...

1. Launch the downloaded application by double-clicking its icon. The connection window will appear.

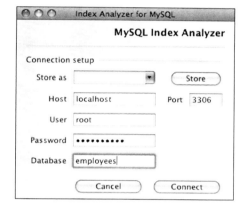

2. Enter the connection data for your MySQL server and specify the database to check. If you like, you can store these settings for later use.

3. Hit the **Connect** button. The analysis will begin. Stand by—this might take a minute or two, depending on the number of tables, columns, and indexes in that database.

4.  When the analysis is complete, review the proposed changes the tool makes. Apart from the tree-like display, you can use the Generate SQL button to copy ALTER TABLE statements to either the clipboard or a file that will apply the changes suggested to the database.

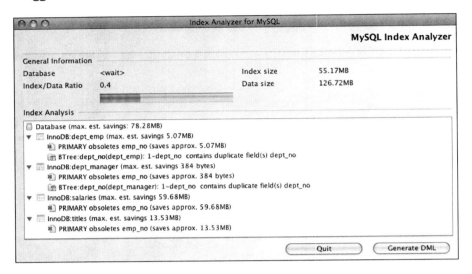

Make sure you do not just blindly execute the proposed statements against your database!

You must always carefully review anything that an automated tool suggests you do to your data. No program can replace your professional judgment about whether or not an index is obsolete or required for some specific reason beyond the computer's understanding.

## How it works

The Index Analyzer for MySQL tool connects to your database and retrieves information about the indexes defined in the database you specified. It then checks for indexes that are redundant compared with one or more of the others. It will detect the following situations:

▶   Two indexes are completely identical.

▶   One index is a prefix of a second longer one. As MySQL can use the second one for the same queries (ignoring the superfluous columns) the shorter index is redundant.

An index on an InnoDB table is defined so that it ends with the primary key column(s). As MySQL internally appends the primary key columns, they should be removed from the explicit definition. The tree display's root node is the database you selected, followed by the tables with redundant indexes. For each table, one or more detail nodes describe the analysis results in terms of which index is made obsolete by which other.

Each node also contains a rough estimate on how much space could be saved by dropping the redundant index. Note that this is just a ballpark figure to get an idea. In the example earlier, the actual savings are lower according to the statistics MySQL offers via the SHOW TABLE STATUS command:

| Table / Index | Index Size before | Estimated Savings | Actual Savings |
|---|---|---|---|
| dept_emp / emp_no | 10MB | 5.5MB | 4.5MB |
| dept_manager / emp_no | 32k | 384 bytes | 16k |
| Salaries / emp_no | 34.6MB | 59.7MB | 35MB |
| Titles / emp_no | 11MB | 13.5MB | 11MB |

All tables were defined with an extra index on the *emp_no* column, which was made obsolete by the primary key. Note that the difference between estimated and actual savings is most significant. This is because MySQL estimates are based on multiples of the data page size—16 KB—while the Index Analyzer application uses average column lengths.

## There's more...

Apart from the Index Analyzer for MySQL available from this book's website, there are other tools available for the same purpose as well. If you do not want to, or cannot, install a Java Runtime Environment, you might be more content with Maatkit's *mk-duplicate-key-checker*. It is a free command-line tool based on Perl and can be used on a variety of platforms as well. You can get it from http://www.maatkit.org including the full documentation.

# 3
# Tools

In this chapter, we will discuss about:

- ▸ Transferring connection settings between different machines using a network share
- ▸ Sorting MySQL GUI Tools' stored connections
- ▸ Automatically creating stored connections
- ▸ Adding custom graphs to MySQL Administrator
- ▸ Displaying query results page by page and with scrolling, using the `mysql` command-line client
- ▸ Extracting information from verbose output using the `mysql` command-line client
- ▸ Specifying a default pager
- ▸ Using a custom prompt to distinguish connections
- ▸ Encrypting a MySQL server connection with SSH
- ▸ Creating an encrypted MySQL console via SSH
- ▸ Using a PuTTY template connection for SSH secured connections

## Introduction

Everyone expects a DBA to keep database servers running smoothly day in and day out, handing out data to maybe thousands of clients or even more simultaneously, quickly and reliably.

Apart from a solid knowledge about the inner workings of the server(s) you manage, what's as important are the tools at your disposal. They enable you to inspect and tune the server's running parameters, configuration options, and so on.

While there is a plethora of utilities and tools, both free and commercial—each of them with its respective strengths and weaknesses—the *official* tools available directly and (mostly) for free from the MySQL website are often underestimated or even overlooked.

While they may not be the most polished and may certainly have their quirks, they should, nevertheless, not escape your attention because either on their own or sometimes amended by some other (free) software, they are capable of helping you a great deal with your everyday MySQL administration tasks.

## Tools used in this recipe

In this chapter, we will look at the MySQL command-line client `mysql`, which is available for free with the server, and the MySQL GUI Toolkit parts *MySQL Query Browser* and *MySQL Administrator*.

The command-line client lies at the heart of many scripts and other command-line tools. This is because it is quite flexible and lends itself to automation by its very nature as a purely text-based tool. It can generally be used on all platforms supported by MySQL. However, the respective underlying operating system and the shell used play an important role in what you can do with `mysql`.

Most Linux distributions and other Unix-like systems—this includes Apple's Mac OS X—by default come with rich support for scripting and automation. On Microsoft Windows, the story has become better over the years. However, some funny things that you get for free with Linux and the like will just not work. In some cases, such lack of functionality can be alleviated with the installation of some additional packages. In other cases, Windows users, unfortunately, are simply out of luck due to restrictions posed by the operating system's very core.

Nevertheless, wherever possible we will give advice on how to work around such problems should the need arise in any of the following recipes.

MySQL GUI Tools have become a respectable set of tools over the past couple of years. Although sometimes they still have issues with stability, they have reached a level of maturity where they can be recommended for everyday use without hesitation. In this chapter, you will find some recipes that revolve around MySQL Administrator and MySQL Query Browser to make using them an even more pleasant experience. You can get them from the MySQL home page at `http://dev.mysql.com/downloads/gui-tools`.

This chapter is not a manual to these tools in general. In fact, some experience with them is recommended to take full advantage of the recipes presented here. To follow along, you need to have the GUI Tools installed on your machine.

## Platform differences

MySQL GUI Tools are available for major operating system platforms. The recipes regarding them presented in this book should work equally well on Windows, Linux, and Mac OS X. However, there are some differences between these platforms, for instance, where the preferences files are stored or what the user interface looks like. Whenever necessary, aspects that need different handling depending on the underlying platform will be discussed separatwely.

## MySQL GUI Tools config file locations

One major difference between operating systems is the location of the MySQL GUI Tools' configuration files. Some recipes manipulate those directly; so instead of describing time and again where to find them on each operating system, please have a look at the following list whenever you need to locate one of them.

In Mac OS X, the preferences files are stored in the `Library/Application Support` folder of the user's home directory shown as follows:

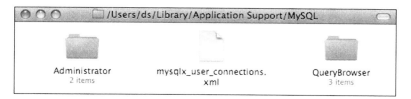

In Linux, the settings are stored in a hidden directory `.mysqlgui` inside the user's home directory.

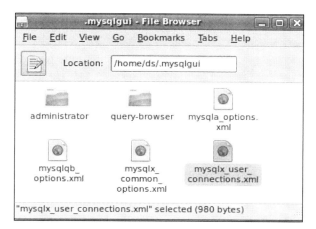

In Windows, the settings are stored in the `%APPDATA%/MySQL` folder located in the user's profile. The next screenshot shows Windows 7, but with XP it is just the same.

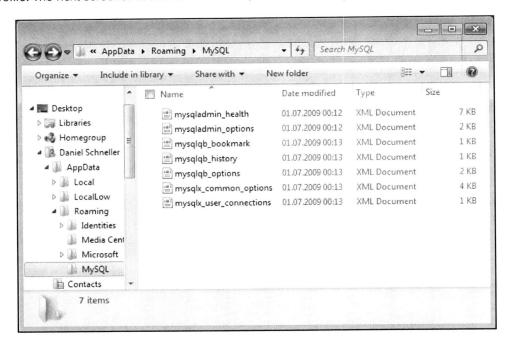

# Transferring connection settings between different machines using a network share

MySQL Administrator and MySQL Query Browser allow storing connection profiles for hosts that you regularly use. These are stored locally as part of the user profile you are logged in with. Unless you only ever work from a single machine with a single user account, you would usually have to recreate and maintain each and every machine's list of stored connections manually, which is neither a fun nor a productive task.

This recipe will show you how to store connection profile settings in a way that allows them to be used from multiple user accounts and even multiple machines.

The next steps will demonstrate how to share connection settings between Ubuntu Linux and a Windows 7 machine using a network share.

You can apply this to any combination of machines with any supported operating system.

## Getting ready

Make sure you have some sort of a shared medium ready with write permissions. This could be a directory on the local machine accessible by several user accounts, a USB pen-drive to carry around with you, a web server, or a network share accessible by anyone you want to share the connections with.

See the chapter introduction for a guide on where to find the stored connection file on each platform.

## How to do it...

1.  Set up one or more connections in MySQL Administrator on the Linux machine. The screenshots in this example were taken on a machine with two connection profiles called **Development Server A** and **QA Server**.

2.  Close MySQL Administrator and also MySQL Query Browser (if running).
3.  Navigate to `~/.mysqlgui` and copy the file called `mysqlx_user_connections.xml` to the network share.
4.  On Windows 7 open an explorer window and enter `%appdata%\MySQL` in the address bar. Click *Enter* to open the folder.
5.  Open another Explorer window and point it to the network share.
6.  Drag `mysqlx_user_connections.xml` from the network to the local directory, making a copy.

7. Start MySQL Administrator or Query Browser and find the connections defined on the Linux machine also present in Windows 7.

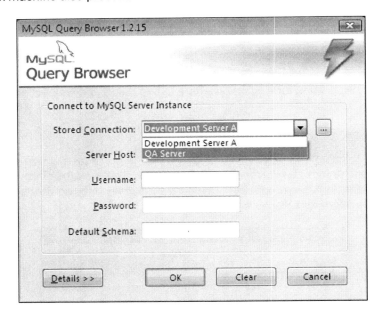

## How it works...

MySQL GUI Tools store information about the connections you enter and store using their graphical user interface in an XML file. As there are no other places to consider (such as the registry or binary files), it is rather easy to copy them around and use them in different places.

All the settings—including host names, user account names, and even the notes you can bind to a stored connection—are saved to this XML file. It is used by both MySQL Administrator and MySQL Query Browser, so you need not do anything to share a common set of connections between the two on the same machine. Passwords can optionally be stored and are put into this file too, if you choose so. However, storing passwords is generally not recommended because they are not securely encrypted.

Ideally, the tools would optionally allow you to specify which file to use so you could just point them all at the common location like the network drive employed in the previous section. While this would work great in theory, there would be all kinds of unwanted consequences. For example, what would you do if two people on different machines tried to modify and save the same stored connection?

Because of this, it is necessary to provide each machine (or user account to be precise because the `%appdata%` portion of the path named in the previous steps takes you into a subdirectory of the user's profile) with its own copy of the file to work with. This is what you just did by copying the file from one machine to the network drive and from there on to the second machine. To MySQL GUI Tools it makes no difference whether they created the file themselves or got spoonfed by a different instance, even on a different piece of hardware.

## There's more...

For simple setups and with a limited number of people sharing connection settings, this very basic approach works quite well. However, maybe you'd like some more pointers on where to go from here.

### Dealing with changes

As we already discussed, each workstation machine gets its own copy of the connections XML file. While this is a technical necessity, it brings along the problem of concurrent changes to connection profiles on different machines.

As soon as at least two people modify different local copies of the file, they will have to agree on who is to copy his or her new version to the network drive. Only one of them can do so because the second one would overwrite their colleague's edits.

For small teams, the simplest approach could be to agree on a dedicated PC on which the changes are made. All other machines only update their local copy of the file from the network, but never push them back.

Alternatively, you can name a single user who makes all of the changes and puts them on the shared medium.

For larger teams, you may consider using a version control system like Subversion or CVS. This can be especially practical for larger organizations already having a repository in place that could be put to good use here. The local XML file could be a working copy checked out from the repository. Whenever someone changes it, he or she would check it into the repository for others to fetch. In case of conflicting changes, you would be notified by the version control software and would have to merge both changes into a new combined version.

If you do this, you might consider using some kind of XML formatting tool because MySQL GUI Tools tend to write out the file with platform-specific line endings, making it a little more cumbersome compared to the files originating from Windows and Unix-like platforms.

For Windows you might want to check out a program called *firstobject XML Editor* freely available at `http://www.firstobject.com`, which has a formatting feature.

# Sorting MySQL GUI Tools' stored connections

MySQL Administrator and MySQL Query Browser both include a connection editor that allows you to manage your stored connection profiles. While this offers a comfortable way to create new or edit existing profiles including a lot of settings and even comments, this editor provides no way to sort your profiles. Especially, if you work with a lot of stored settings, you will want to maintain a certain tidiness to quickly find specific profiles from the drop-down list in the **Connections** dialog.

This recipe will show you how to sort connection profile settings by **Connection Name**, assuming Mac OS X as the platform.

For Linux and Windows, the instructions are mostly identical. However, you will have to replace the path names with the appropriate values for your system. Instead of the terminal application, Windows users use **Start | Run | cmd.exe** to launch a command interpreter. Also, note that the cp command is called copy on Windows, so make sure you change that too!

## Getting ready

To try this you will need several stored connection profiles. You can create those in either MySQL Administrator or MySQL Query Browser as they both share the same set of connections. In this example, there are five connections that appear unsorted in the connection editor:

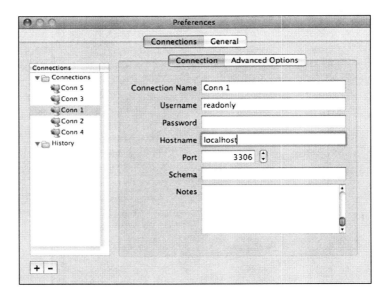

You will need an XSLT processor installed. Most Linux distributions and Mac OS X come preinstalled with a command called `xsltproc`. Windows users can download a binary version of this tool for their platform from `http://www.xmlsoft.org/XSLT`.

## How to do it...

1. Save the following code to a file called `sortconnections.xsl` and place it in your home directory. You can download this file from the book's website (`www.packtpub.com`) too.

```
<xsl:stylesheet version="1.0"
 xmlns:xsl="http://www.w3.org/1999/XSL/Transform">
<xsl:output omit-xml-declaration="yes" indent="yes"/>
<xsl:strip-space elements="*"/>
 <xsl:template match="node()|@*">
   <xsl:copy>
     <xsl:apply-templates select="node()|@*"/>
   </xsl:copy>
 </xsl:template>
 <xsl:template match="user_connections">
   <xsl:copy>
     <xsl:apply-templates select="@*"/>
     <xsl:apply-templates select="*[name()!='user_connection']"/>
     <xsl:apply-templates select="user_connection">
       <xsl:sort select="connection_name"/>
     </xsl:apply-templates>
   </xsl:copy>
 </xsl:template>
</xsl:stylesheet>
```

2. Close MySQL Administrator and also MySQL Query Browser (if running).

3. Open `Terminal.app`.

4. Enter the following commands. The first `cd` command will take you to your home directory in case you have configured a different default.

```
$ cd ~/Library/Application\ Support/MySQL/
$ cp mysqlx_user_connections.xml mysqlx_user_connections.xml.
unsorted
$ xsltproc ~/sortconnections.xsl mysqlx_user_connections.xml.
unsorted > mysqlx_user_connections.xml
```

5. Close the terminal.

6. Start MySQL Administrator or MySQL Query Browser and find the connections sorted in the connection editor.

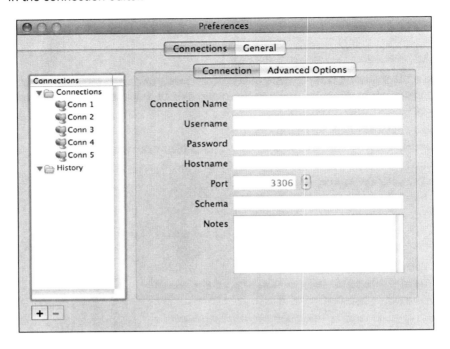

## How it works...

MySQL GUI Tools store information about the connections that you enter using their graphical user interface in an XML file. Each connection is represented by an XML element called `<user_connection>`. The order of these elements in the file determines in which order the GUI will display them.

As there is no way to rearrange the connection profiles using the user interface we sort the underlying data file.

 Because the data file is locked by the GUI Tools while they are running, it is important to quit them before beginning the procedure. Otherwise your changes might get lost, because next time you close the GUI Tools, the file gets rewritten in the order that the running instance knew!

Using a simple XSL stylesheet and a suitable processing tool (xsltproc), the unsorted XML is read and transformed into a new version with the <user_connection> elements sorted by their <connection_name> sub-element. To make sure nothing goes wrong, we first make a backup copy of the original file and save it as mysqlx_user_connections.xml. unsorted.

Finally, the xsltproc command applies the sortconnections.xsl stylesheet, and the resulting output is stored back into mysqlx_user_connections.xml where it will be found the next time a MySQL GUI Tool starts.

## There's more...

Sorting by name is just one way of organizing your connection templates and probably, the one most often used. However, XSL stylesheets are a very versatile and powerful means to manipulate XML files such as the connection profiles store. There are lots of resources on the Web and in printed form that can teach you how to filter, group, and rearrange XML data. For a good tutorial on XSL transformations, for example, go to http://www.w3schools.com/xsl/.

Here are some more pointers as to what you might do to make stored connections more useful:

- Instead of sorting by connection name, you might sort by hostname. This can be useful if you manage a large number of machines following a naming convention that allows for sensible sorting.
- A combination of sort criteria might prove useful if you store several profiles for a single server. You might sort by host first and then by database or username.

Even in cases where the predefined fields are insufficient, there is a way to define almost arbitrary sort criteria by leveraging the otherwise seldom-used **Notes** field in the query editor. For example, in a scenario where you have to manage hosts in different locations (cities, countries, subsidiaries, and so on) you could store the city name in the **Notes** field and use this as a sorting criterion.

## Automatically creating stored connections

Although managing a handful of connections is no problem with the built-in connection managers in MySQL GUI Tools, creating a larger series of them tends to become tedious. For example, when managing a shared database server there might be several hundred databases—one or even more for each customer. In a different scenario you may have numerous servers, for each of which you might want a separate stored connection entry to allow easy access.

This recipe presents a way to automatically generate new connection entries based on a simple CSV (comma-separated-value) file using a short shell script. This very simple format allows for a wide range of data sources. For example, you might already have a spreadsheet with all of the important information or extract it from some sort of database.

Refer to the *MySQL GUI Tools config file locations* section in the chapter introduction to check where you can find the connection storage XML file for each operating system.

## Getting ready

To try this you should know your way around with a command line. There is no need for you to be experienced with advanced shell scripting, but you should be familiar with navigation around the file system and some basic commands. Moreover, you will need a file containing the basic information about each connection profile you would like to include in your MySQL GUI Tools stored connections. The steps outlined in this recipe require a `bash` shell. This is default in many Linux distributions and Mac OS X 10.3 and later.

In Windows, you can either install the Cygwin toolkit from `http://www.cygwin.com` that provides a `bash` shell and `sed` tool, or modify the script to match the batch file syntax. The `sed` command can be downloaded as a.native Windows executable as part of the Unix utilities from `http://unxutils.sourceforge.net/`. We definitely recommend you have a look at Cygwin, unless you are really experienced with Windows batch scripting.

Connections will be generated from a CSV file, which should contain one line per new connection. Each line will contain the connection information in a fixed order separated by commas like this:

```
Title,Username,Hostname,Port,Schema,Notes,Password
```

All fields are optional. However, the number of commas per line must be obeyed, even when nothing more follows in the same line!

Everything that you don't include in this file must either be entered manually each time you choose this connection profile, or be a fixed value that all connections have in common. The following file contains several valid sample lines to demonstrate the idea. The example below assumes that you start with an empty list of connection profiles and add these sample entries directly from this file called `connections.csv`:

```
LocalDev,root,localhost,3310,dev_db,Version 1.5,rootpw
Web01,smith,web01.example.com,3306,cmsweb,,
Austria,guest,10.22.109.12,3306,mz011,Staging DB,
```

In order to create connections with a password taken from the CSV file, you must make sure that the template connection you are going to create in the following section is configured to use **Plain Text** password storage setting. If you do not want to store passwords in the connection profiles for security reasons, you can set this option to any of the other available settings, but make sure that you do not provide any passwords in the CSV file because they would not work.

The example in the next section assumes plain text password storage for demonstration purposes.

## How to do it...

1. Open MySQL Administrator or MySQL Query Browser, and go to the **Connection Editor**.

2. Create a new connection with this data:

| Field | Content |
|---|---|
| Connection Name | p_0 |
| Username | p_1 |
| Password | p_6 |
| Hostname | p_2 |
| Schema | p_4 |
| Notes | p_5 |

3. Close MySQL Administrator and MySQL Query Browser (if running).

4. Open the connection profiles XML file with a text editor and search for **p_0**. You will most likely find it close to the end of the file.

5. Replace the port number **3306** with **p_3**. This is necessary because you cannot enter non-numeric characters in the GUI.

6. Save the `<user_connection>` element surrounding your template profile including the `</user_connection>` line at the end to a new file called `oneconnection.template`. This file should look like this:

```
<user_connection>
  <connection_name>p_0</connection_name>
  <username>p_1</username>
  <hostname>p_2/hostname>
  <port>p_3</port>
  <schema>p_4</schema>
  <advanced_options>
  </advanced_options>
  <storage_path></storage_path>
```

```
    <notes>p_5</notes>
    <connection_type>0</connection_type>
    <storage_type>1</storage_type>
    <password_storage_type>6</password_storage_type>
    <password>p_6</password>
</user_connection>
```

7. Create a script file named `mkuserconn.sh` with the following contents:

```
#!/bin/bash
IFS=,
TMPFILE=$(mktemp ~/mkuserconn.XXXXXXXXXX) || exit 1
while read p[0] p[1] p[2] p[3] p[4] p[5] p[6] ; do
    s=""
    for ((i=0; i<${#p[*]}; i++)); do
        s=$s"s/p_${i}/${p[${i}]}/g;"
    done
    newentry=$(sed -e "${s}" oneconnection.template)
    echo "${newentry}" >> ${TMPFILE}
done < ${2}
echo "</user_connections>" >> ${TMPFILE}
sed -e "/<\/user_connections>/ {
  r ${TMPFILE}
  d
}" ${1}
```

8. Make the file executable with:

**`$ chmod u+x mkuserconn.sh`**

9. Invoke the script like this:

**`$ ./mkuserconn.sh mysqlx_user_connections.xml connections.csv`**

10. The output will be sent to `stdout` to give you a chance to verify that everything goes as planned. Once you are content, redirect it to a new file with the redirect operator > like this:

**`$ ./mkuserconn.sh mysqlx_user_connections.xml connections.csv > mysqlx_user_connections_new.xml`**

11. Replace the original `mysqlx_user_connections.xml` file with the newly created `mysqlx_user_connections_new.xml` once you are content, saving a backup of the previous version:

**`$ cp mysqlx_user_connections.xml mysqlx_user_connections.xml.bak`**
**`$ cp mysqlx_user_connections_new.xml mysqlx_user_connections.xml`**

12. Open MySQL Administrator or MySQL Query Browser and find the newly created connections ready to go:

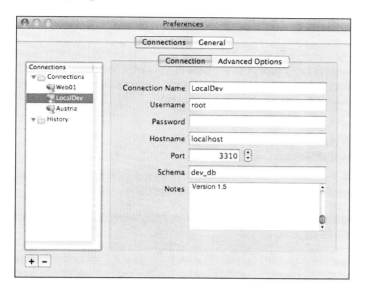

## How it works...

MySQL GUI Tools store information about the connections you enter and store using their graphical user interface in an XML file. Each connection is represented by an XML element called `<user_connection>`.

The script presented takes one such entry as a template to create new ones, replacing the `p_0`, `p_1`, `p_2`, and other similar placeholders with values from the `connections.csv` file.

First the script creates a file in your home directory (~) where the new connection data is stored temporarily. It then reads the fields from a file passed in as the second parameter and stores them in an array called `p`. The order of the fields in the file corresponds to the index in the array. In the loop body (the loop reads the CSV file one line at a time), the `sed` command-line is assembled, consisting of replace commands that fill in the information from the CSV file at the appropriate places in `oneconnection.template`.

When the command has been built, it is executed, and the output is stored in the temporary file created earlier.

This is repeated until all lines of the CSV file have been read, effectively creating a new `<user_connection>...</user_connection>` element for each line in your input file.

Finally, when the temporary file contains all new connection profiles, it is merged into the first file specified as a command-line parameter, which is your `mysqlx_user_connections.xml` file or a copy thereof, right before the end of the file.

When you open one of the GUI tools again, you will find the newly created connections based on the template you set up before. You can, of course, remove the p_0 connection at any time, once you copied it to the `oneconnection.template` file.

>  Be sure to try this on a copy of your connections XML file first to make sure everything is correct! A single typo in the script file might corrupt the file beyond repair. This is why we designed the script to output to the console by default to prevent accidental overwrites.

## There's more...

The script presented in this recipe is very basic to make it easier to understand, and you can use basic tools that are easy to get and install almost anywhere.

Of course, you could rewrite it in Perl or any other programming language, adding more features, some help texts, and so on.

Some ideas you may want to pursue could be inserting new connections in some specific order, modifying existing connections with the same name instead of creating duplicate entries, or editing the connection storage XML file in place.

# Adding custom graphs to MySQL Administrator

MySQL Administrator is one of the graphical tools that MySQL provides to manage its database servers. Apart from other things like server daemon control and a log file viewer, this tool includes visual controls to display the current load and other "vital signs" of the database server.

Even though the out-of-the-box configuration already contains some useful diagrams, it becomes even more useful with some custom-designed graphs. It might not be suitable to replace a fully featured monitoring solution, but it is definitely helpful to gain a quick impression about what stress a server is currently under, how many users are connected, and so on.

MySQL Administrator provides a graphical editor to introduce new *pages, groups,* and *graphs.* Even though I would rather use the term tab (which is what it comes down to in the GUI), we will stick to *page* here because that's what MySQL calls it.

When you open up MySQL Administrator and head to the **Health** section, you will see some default pages: **Status Variables**, **Connection Health**, **Memory Health**, and **Server Variables**. Depending on the version of your tools, there may be one more **Monitoring & Advisory Service**; however, it just contains an advertisement for a commercial monitoring solution.

In this recipe, we are going to add a new page called *Stats* and set it up to display information about the number of requests the server has to handle currently, split up by SELECT, INSERT, UPDATE, and DELETE statements as well as a bar diagram that shows the ratio of InnoDB read/write operations.

MySQL GUI Tools are not always available for all platforms in the latest version. Usually, Windows is updated more frequently. This sometimes results in minor differences like slight changes in menu item names and the like, depending on which operating system you use. For example, at the time of writing the most current Windows version was 5.0r17 while for Mac and Linux it was 5.0r12. While on Windows, the context menu mentioned in this recipe is labeled **Add Page...**, the Mac version calls the same command **New Page**. However, you should not have any problems moving along.

## Getting ready

To try this you need MySQL Administrator installed. Furthermore, you will need login credentials to a MySQL server instance, preferably a busy one to watch some real data. Of course, a locally installed instance will do just as well. Please note that you need sufficient privileges to issue SHOW STATUS commands.

One word of advice before we begin: even though it has gotten much better at this, when modifying the graphs MySQL Administrator will sometimes just crash and take everything you did so far with it. It only saves your modifications to disk when you leave the program.

 It is highly recommended to quit the application and restart every once in a while when you have got something working—the way you would like to keep it, to prevent losing your freshly made customizations!

In case you experience repeated crashes, you might want to consider editing the graph definition manually. Refer to the *How it works...* section for further information.

## How to do it...

1. Start MySQL Administrator and connect to the server.
2. Activate the **Health** section and go to the **Connection Health** page.
3. Right-click on the page and choose **New Page** from the context menu.
4. Enter **Stats** in the newly opened dialog. If asked for it, specify a descriptive text like **Statistical breakdown of different query types**.
5. Make sure the new **Stats** page is displayed and then right-click on it. Choose **New Group**.

6. Enter **DML Statements** in the naming box that will appear.

7. Right-click the (empty) **DML Statements** group. Choose **New Graph** from the menu.

8. Fill up the settings as shown in the following table. Fields not listed should be left empty:

| Field | Content |
| --- | --- |
| Display Title | Not Checked |
| Graph Type | Line Graph |
| Value Formula | ^[com_select] |
| Value Unit | Count |
| Value Caption | SELECT |
| Min Value | 0 |
| Max Value | 100 |
| Auto Extend | Checked |

9. Click **OK (Mac) / Apply (Windows)**.

10. Repeat this step for the value formulas ^[com_insert], ^[com_update], ^[com_delete], and their appropriate value captions.

11. Right-click on the page and create another group called **InnoDB**.

12. Inside this group add a new graph with these settings:

| Field | Content |
| --- | --- |
| Title | InnoDB R/W Ratio |
| Display Title | Checked |
| Graph Type | Bar Graph |
| Value Formula | ([innodb_pages_read]/([innodb_pages_read]+[innodb_pages_written]))*100 |
| Value Unit | Percentage |
| Value Caption | Reads |
| Min Value | 0 |
| Max Value | 100 |
| Max Caption | Total |

Do not forget to restart MySQL Administrator to make your changes permanent.

After filling up each field appropriately, as discussed, the final output should look like the following screenshot:

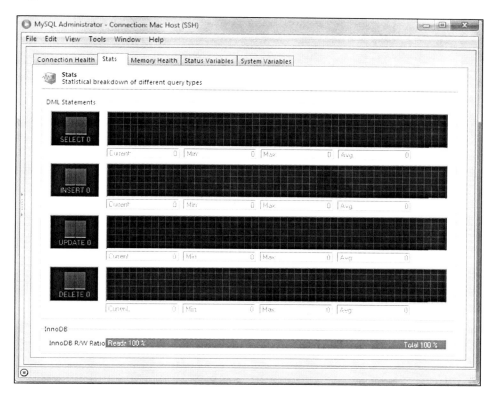

## How it works...

All graphs are based on status variables provided by the MySQL server. The MySQL online manual contains an extensive list of these at `http://dev.mysql.com/doc/refman/5.1/en/server-status-variables.html`, documenting the meaning of each variable. The value formulas allow mathematical operations using these values that will then be displayed in bar graphs or line graphs. Which type of diagram you choose depends on the type of information you would like to visualize.

Bear in mind that depending on which version of MySQL you use, the exact set of variables you can use does vary. Refer to the online manual to make sure your graph definitions match your server version.

The examples in this recipe provide a quick overview of what the server is currently working on based on the command counters for the individual data manipulation statements. More sophisticated stats can be built using some of the lower-level status variables like those starting with `Handler_`. They provide information that may allow you to identify performance problems or bad indexing.

MySQL Administrator stores your custom diagrams in an XML file. The name and location of that file are operating system dependent. In Windows and Linux, it is called `mysqladmin_health.xml`. In Windows, it is located in the same folder as `mysqlx_user_connections.xml`. In Linux and Mac OS X, there is a subfolder named `administrator`. Moreover, the Mac version uses a different filename: `mysqladmin_custom_health.xml`.

Fortunately, the contents are identical, so copying a file from one system to the other just requires you to adapt its name and place appropriately.

In certain cases you might want to edit the graph definitions manually. For example, there is no way to change the graph type from **Line** to **Bar** or vice versa once you have created it in the GUI. By directly editing the XML definition you gain a lot more flexibility.

**Caution:**
Make sure to keep a backup copy of your edits before you start MySQL Administrator and try your changes. If you make a mistake that prevents MySQL Administrator from reading and applying the file, it will overwrite it with defaults on exit!

## There's more...

While generally most recipes are agnostic to the exact version of MySQL you are running, this one has a caveat: MySQL has a known issue that leads to different behavior in different versions.

From version 5.0 on, the effect is that you cannot query the counters, for example, the number of temporary tables, without modifying it as you go. In versions prior to 5.0, the `SHOW STATUS` commands (the foundation for many of the values MySQL Administrator can display) could be executed without modifying them. Their results were sent to the client immediately. Starting with 5.0, a temporary table with the results is created automatically and its contents are sent to the client. Unfortunately, this temporary table itself is counted in the statistics.

Even though this new technique allows accessing this statistical data in stored procedures, it increases noise in measuring. As a simple workaround, some formulas can be modified to compensate, for example by subtracting the value that an idle server would display. This of course is not viable for all types of calculations. Also, consider that there might be multiple simultaneous connections that execute the same queries. You cannot reliably compensate for this.

In the end you will have to keep this in mind when interpreting the stats you see.

For more details, we suggest you read the discussion that is part of the bug report available at `http://bugs.mysql.com/bug.php?id=10210`.

# Displaying query results page by page and with scrolling using the MySQL command-line client

The `mysql` program is part of every MySQL installation. It is a powerful tool, even though some of its functionality is only available on non-Windows platforms. It may not be graphically pleasing, but can be used as a versatile client to the database server both interactively and in scripted scenarios.

When using the MySQL command-line client `mysql`, you are certainly familiar with outputs like the following screenshot:

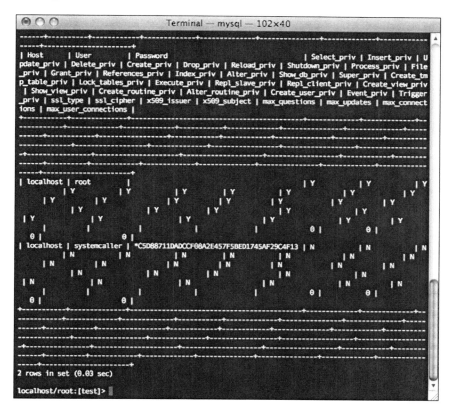

It only shows two rows of data, but you have almost no chance of getting the information you wanted. When you have larger result sets, it gets even worse because then vertical scrolling might even prevent you from reading the column titles (depending on how large your console's buffer is). Fortunately, there is a way to process the output of any MySQL command before sending it to the screen.

This recipe will show you how to view a result that is too large to fit on one screen in a way that allows both vertical and horizontal navigation as well as some other operations.

The next example assumes that you have an instance of the MySQL server running on your local machine. Of course, you can connect to any other host as well.

## Getting ready

To try this you will need the `mysql` command-line client on Mac OS X, Linux, or any other Unix-like platform.

 Unfortunately, for Windows users there is no way to apply this recipe because the client cannot provide the necessary functionality in Windows as it is based on some underlying functions that are not available in Microsoft's operating system!

You will also need the `less` pager utility. This is available on Mac OS X and virtually every Linux distribution, so you should not have any problems here. For simplicity, the example assumes that you have privileges to `SELECT` from the *mysql* system database. This is not required, however, as any `SELECT` will do.

## How to do it...

1. Run the `mysql` command-line client:

   ```
   $ mysql
   ```

2. Enter the following commands at the `mysql` prompt:

   ```
   mysql> pager less -SFX
   mysql> SELECT * FROM mysql.user;
   ```

3. You will get an output similar to this:

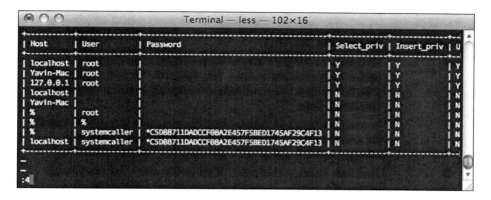

In this view you can scroll horizontally and vertically using your cursor keys. Hitting the *q* key will bring you back to the command prompt.

4. Optionally, to unset the pager type this:

```
mysql> nopager
```

## How it works...

The `pager` command allows you to specify an arbitrary program, which is executed whenever you would normally see the result of a subsequent command. This includes results from SELECT statements as well as any other output, for example, from SHOW ENGINE INNODB STATUS.

The program receives exactly the same output that would otherwise be printed to the console.

In this example, the query result is handed over to the `less` utility, a common tool to display information that would usually be too large to fit on a single screen. `less` allows free navigation using the cursor keys, which is what you just tried. It also knows a command called `q` that we used earlier and that exits the program, effectively taking you back to the MySQL command prompt.

The -SFX parameters passed to less in this example specify some options that are recommended for use with mysql.

| Parameter | Description |
|-----------|-------------|
| -S | Causes lines longer than the screen width to be chopped rather than wrapped around. This keeps the table format of the SELECT output intact and allows to navigate horizontally using the cursor keys. |
| -F | In case the result of a command fits on screen without the need for any scrolling, less automatically terminates, effectively saving you from typing "q" to get ready for the next command. |
| -X | Instructs less to skip some initialization that would otherwise potentially lead to undesirable screen layout problems. |

less offers a large number of other parameters you may pass to further customize its behavior. For a complete list, refer to the manual page available from a command shell:

```
$ man less
```

# Extracting information from verbose output using the MySQL command-line client

Output from MySQL commands can be rather verbose. For example, the SHOW ENGINE INNODB STATUS command usually produces enough text to cause your typical terminal window to scroll.

Often you are not interested in everything the output contains, but only want to know about a particular detail that easily gets lost in the overall amount of text.

This recipe will show you how to easily extract information from such output using a search term. In particular, we will extract the **BUFFER POOL AND MEMORY** section from the InnoDB status output.

## Getting ready

To try this, you will need the mysql command-line client on Mac OS X, Linux, or any other Unix-like platform.

Unfortunately, for Windows users there is no way to apply this recipe because the client cannot provide the necessary functionality in Windows as it is based on some underlying functions that are not available in Microsoft's operating system!

Furthermore, you will need the `grep` text search utility. This is available on Mac OS X and virtually every Linux distribution by default, so you should not have any problems here.

## How to do it...

1. Open a connection to the MySQL server using the `mysql` command-line client.

2. Set the pager to the following command:

   ```
   mysql> pager grep -A 12 -e "BUFFER POOL AND MEMORY"
   ```

3. Request the InnoDB status using the following command:

   ```
   mysql> SHOW ENGINE INNODB STATUS\G
   ```

4. Instead of the complete InnoDB status output, you will only see the 12 lines following the **BUFFER POOL AND MEMORY** heading:

```
Terminal — mysql — 70×20

localhost/root:[test]> pager grep -A 12 -e "BUFFER POOL AND MEMORY"
PAGER set to 'grep -A 12 -e "BUFFER POOL AND MEMORY"'
localhost/root:[test]> SHOW ENGINE INNODB STATUS \G
BUFFER POOL AND MEMORY
-----------------------
Total memory allocated 17334612; in additional pool allocated 871296
Dictionary memory allocated 26616
Buffer pool size   512
Free buffers       476
Database pages     36
Modified db pages  0
Pending reads 0
Pending writes: LRU 0, flush list 0, single page 0
Pages read 36, created 0, written 0
0.00 reads/s, 0.00 creates/s, 0.00 writes/s
No buffer pool page gets since the last printout
1 row in set (0.00 sec)

localhost/root:[test]>
```

## How it works...

The `pager` command allows you to specify an arbitrary program, which is executed whenever you would normally see the result of a subsequent command. This includes results from `SELECT` statements as well as any other output, for example from the `SHOW ENGINE INNODB STATUS` command.

The program is handed the exact same output that would otherwise be printed to the console. In this example, the query result is handed to the `grep` utility—a common tool to search for keywords or phrases in text content. It offers a wide range of parameters and configuration options. In this example, the `-A` (number of lines to be displayed after the one that contained the search term) and `-e` (specifies the search term) options are used to first look for a line that contains the text **BUFFER POOL AND MEMORY** and outputs this and the 12 lines following it.

The exact number of lines to be used depends on the output you are filtering. In this example, the length of the relevant section is 12 (you will have to adapt this to a value suitable for your particular use case). Keeping a note at hand with the correct number of lines for your most commonly used commands is recommended.

## There's more...

`grep` is not limited to searching for fixed text fragments. It supports case-sensitive and case-insensitive modes, matching lines that do or specifically *don't* contain the search term, and much more. Apart from simple search terms, you can also specify to search using regular expressions, which makes it extremely flexible and powerful. You should have a look at the `grep` manual pages for more detailed information.

Over time you will find yourself using the same filters repeatedly. Consider putting these into small individual shell scripts that can also be used as a `pager`, saving you the trouble of typing potentially long and complex commands over and over again.

# Specifying a default pager

In the *Displaying query results page by page and with scrolling using the mysql command-line client* and *Extracting information from verbose output using the mysql command-line client* recipes, we presented a way to have the `mysql` command-line client send its output through an external program to have it formatted before displaying.

Depending on what kind of processing you need, the client's `pager` command provides a useful way of specifying the external command to use. However, this choice is lost once you exit the client. Next time you want to use it, you are back with the standard output handling (which is to simply write the data to your console).

This recipe will show you how to configure `mysql` to use an external command of your choice as the default on startup and whenever you issue the `pager` command without parameters to revert to the default setting.

The next example assumes you have an instance of the MySQL server running on your local machine. You can also connect to any other host.

## Getting ready

To try this you will need the `mysql` command-line client on Mac OS X, Linux, or any other Unix-like platform.

 Unfortunately, for Windows users there is no way to apply this recipe because the client cannot provide the necessary functionality in Windows as it is based on some underlying functions that are not available in Microsoft's operating system!

In this example, we are going to use the well-known `less` pager utility that comes pre-installed in Mac OS X and virtually every Linux distribution, and set it up as the default pager, effectively making all `mysql` output navigable if it is larger than your terminal.

## How to do it...

1. From your home directory, open the `.my.cnf` file in a text editor. Note that this is a hidden file (because of the leading dot (.) in the filename). If it does not yet exist, create an empty file with that name. Make sure you include the leading dot in the filename.

2. Look for a section called `[mysql]`. If it is not there, add it by inserting the following line at the end of the file:

   `[mysql]`

3. Below that line (and before any other section) insert this:

   `pager=less -SFX`

4. Save the file.

Each new instance of the command-line client you start from now on will default to the `less -SFX` pager. You can still use the `pager` command to specify a different command to process output inside `mysql`.

## How it works...

When the mysql client starts, it looks for options in a file called `.my.cnf` in your home directory. Inside this file it reads the `[client]` and `[mysql]` sections. By placing a `pager` setting in there we configured a pager different from the default.

> Make sure you put the `pager` setting in the `[mysql]` section, and not in the `[client]` section!
>
> While the `mysql` command-line client would work with the new setting, other client tools (such as `mysqladmin`) would also try to read it and might abort because they do not know what to do with it. `[mysql]`, however, is solely read by the command-line client.

## There's more...

The example uses the `.my.cnf` option file in your home directory to specify the default pager. In a multi-user environment this makes perfect sense, since everyone can configure their client with individual settings.

But there are several locations `mysql` looks in for its configuration that might come in handy if you want to share parts of your configuration among several user accounts. They are explained in detail in section 4.2.3.3. *Using Option Files* in the MySQL online manual at `http://dev.mysql.com/doc/refman/5.1/en/option-files.html`.

# Using a custom prompt to distinguish connections

In many situations, the `mysql` command-line client program is the first choice when connecting to MySQL servers. With its default `mysql>` prompt, it sets itself apart from the local command shell's prompt so you know where you are at a glance.

But when you need to connect to more than one server at a time (or maybe just keep multiple connections to the same one open), this simple prompt is not enough to quickly tell the sessions apart.

In this recipe, we will change the default prompt to include useful session-related information. It will be configured to show the host you are connected to, the username used to log in, and the current default database.

## Getting ready

To try this you will need the `mysql` command-line client and login credentials to at least one MySQL server. Ideally, you can access more than one machine to see the effect of all settings presented.

> In Windows, there is no `.my.cnf` but a `my.ini` file. Moreover, it is not usually located in your user profile—or home—directory, but in the Windows folder or the folder your MySQL installation resides in. If you are unsure, use the `my.ini` in the Windows directory or create one there if it does not exist yet!

## How to do it...

1. Open the `.my.cnf` file in a text editor. It is located in your home directory. If it does not yet exist, create an empty file with that name. Make sure you include the leading dot in the filename.

2. Look for a section called `[mysql]`. If it is not yet there, add it by inserting the following line:

   ```
   [mysql]
   ```

3. Below that line (and before any other section) insert this:

   ```
   prompt=\\h/\\u:[\\d]>\\_
   ```

4. Save the file.

5. Open at least two connections with different credentials and/or to different hosts. In each connection you can now see the host you are connected to, followed by your username and the name of the current default database

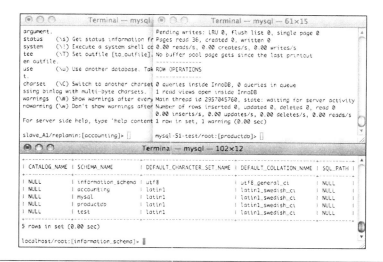

## How it works...

Basically the way this recipe works is the same as described in the *Specifying a default pager* recipe. The difference is just the parameter you set (`prompt`). Please read the description there to get a deeper insight into the preference file mechanism.

The value we set for `prompt` consists of several tokens, each of which gets replaced with a value specific to the current connection:

| Token | Replacement |
|-------|-------------|
| \\h | The name of the host you are connected to |
| \\u | Your username |
| \\d | The name of the current default database |
| \\_ | A space character |

For the machine used to write this book, the prompt in this example is expanded as follows:

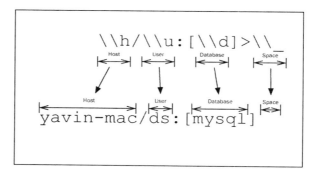

## There's more...

See the *There's more...* section of the *Specifying a default pager* recipe for more information on the parameters file.

Apart from the tokens used in this example, there are several more that allow you to further tailor the `prompt` to your needs. You can find a comprehensive list for your MySQL version in the server's online manual section 4.5.1.2. *mysql Commands* at http://dev.mysql.com/doc/refman/5.1/en/mysql-commands.html.

Configuring a `prompt` that really suits all your needs is often a matter of trial and error and can take some time before you are really satisfied. To speed up this process use the `prompt` command inside `mysql` to change the prompt for only the current session interactively. Once you are done you can put it into the option file to automatically use it the next time the client starts.

## See also

▸   *Specifying a default pager*

# Encrypting a MySQL server connection with SSH

When connecting to MySQL server over the Internet, you should be aware that any communications between your client and the host machine are transferred without any encryption. This applies to both the login credentials and the actual database contents you send to or receive from the server. While the MySQL authentication schema provides some measure of protection for your password (it is not sent in the clear, but using a challenge/response type mechanism), it is not as secure as if you were using a real cryptographic encryption.

Though in a controlled environment like a corporate local area network this may not be much of an issue, sending database contents through a public network is a different thing.

Theoretically, MySQL allows SSL secured connections between the server and its clients, if both are built to support it. Unfortunately, the default MySQL packages available for download from the mysql.com website are not encryption enabled. To get that, you would have to compile the server from the source code and include the necessary encryption options. This is tedious and requires a rather substantial amount of knowledge and the appropriate tool chain.

This recipe will show you how to establish an encrypted connection to a standard MySQL server with any client program such as the command-line client or MySQL GUI Tools, and so on. In the next example, we will encrypt a connection from MySQL Administrator to a default MySQL server.

## Getting ready

For this recipe to work, the MySQL server's operating system has to support a secure shell (SSH) connection. Most Linux distributions include out-of-the-box support for this. Mac OS X 10.5 "Leopard" also supports encrypted SSH connections without third-party products. Earlier versions must be amended with appropriate software packages.

Windows users also need to install the SSH server themselves. There are several commercial offerings, but for the purpose of this recipe, the SSH server available with the Cygwin package is completely sufficient.

Make sure you have set up SSH correctly before you proceed. In Mac OS X, go to the **System Preferences** and open the **Sharing** pane (as seen in the following screenshot). Enable **Remote Login** and make sure you select the appropriate user accounts:

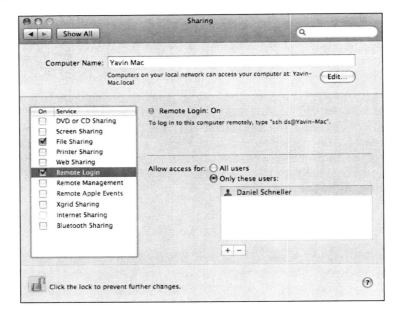

In Linux, you usually do not have to do anything.

In Windows, follow the setup instructions for the SSH server of your choice (for example, from `http://www.cygwin.com` or `http://www.freesshd.com/)`.

Please note that you will need a set of username and password for the MySQL server as well as for the operating system it runs on. This is because the SSH will check before allowing you to try to connect to the database server!

While in Linux and Mac OS X all necessary client tools are again bundled with the operating system, Windows users need to acquire an SSH client program and install it on the machine where they want to run their MySQL client. The Cygwin package includes an `SSH` client, but there is a better alternative: The excellent free *PuTTY* SSH client. It is available on the Web at `http://www.chiark.greenend.org.uk/~sgtatham/putty` (alternatively just enter `putty` into a search engine of your choice). We will use it in this and the following recipes.

In the next example, we are going to log in to a MySQL server on Mac OS X through a secure channel established via SSH from a Windows machine.

## How to do it...

1. In Linux and Mac OS X, open a command-line shell. In Windows, launch PuTTY.

2. In Linux and Mac OS X, enter the following command. Replace *OSUSER* with the operating system account name. Replace *HOST* with the SSH server hostname:

```
$ ssh -L3316:127.0.0.1:3306 OSUSER@HOST
```

 Notice that there is no mention of a MySQL username or password yet! This is purely to log on to the SSH server.

In Windows, set up a connection with PuTTY making sure you have the following settings on the **Connection/SSH/Tunnels** page:

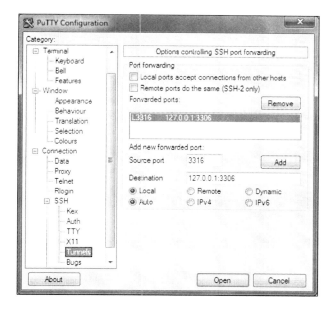

 Make sure you hit the **Add** button once you have entered the **Source port** and **Destination;** otherwise the tunnel settings will not be activated!

3. For Linux and Mac OS X, hit the *Enter* key; for Windows click the **Open** button.

4. Log in to the server using your operating system password.

5. When asked to confirm the remote host's identity, accept the key presented to you. This will only happen upon the first connection.

6.   Once the connection has been established, launch MySQL Administrator.

7.   Set up a connection like this:

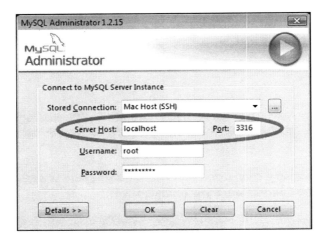

 Please note that the server host is `localhost`, even though you are about to connect remotely. Also, make sure that the port number is set to `3316`. The username and password are those for the MySQL server this time.

8.   Click on **OK** to connect.

9.   To disconnect later, first close MySQL Administrator then the SSH client program.

## How it works...

The SSH server (or daemon as it is often called) and client toolset provide a versatile and powerful way of *tunneling* network connections through the secure link they establish with one another. This feature enables encrypted data transfers for applications that are not able to do so themselves, like in our case the default MySQL server and client builds.

To make the encryption process transparent to the tunneled application (MySQL), the SSH client accepts incoming connections on a configurable TCP port on its behalf. Any connection that is established with this port gets its data encrypted and sent to the SSH daemon. The daemon then decrypts the data and relays the original information to the original target (the MySQL server).

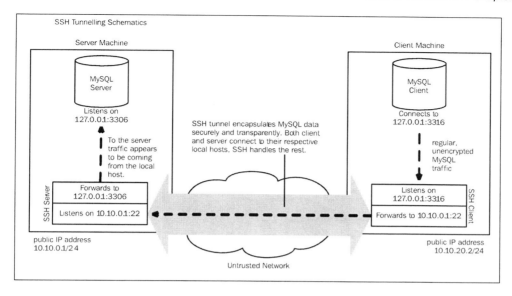

Let's have a look at the command line we used on the client machine (this is on the right side in the preceding image). The parameters in PuTTY are identical:

```
$ ssh -L3316:127.0.0.1:3306 OSUSER@HOST
```

`ssh` is the name of the client program. The `-L3316` parameter tells it to open port 3316 on the local machine (hence the `-L`).

Following that, the address and port of the target MySQL server are set. This is a little difficult to understand at first because `127.0.0.1` is the standard address of the localhost. The key to understand this is that the part after the colon is an address from the perspective of the SSH remote server machine. In the example, the MySQL server is running on the Mac. The SSH server is also running there, so from its point of view the database is reachable via `127.0.0.1` on the default port `3306` (on the left side in the earlier image).

Finally, `OSUSER@HOST` tells the client which host to connect to and which user account to log in with.

Once the secure channel is established MySQL Administrator can connect to port `3316` on its local (Windows) machine. `ssh` transparently forwards the connection to the `HOST` machine which in turn connects to the database on port `3306`. In the illustration (refer to the previous figure), this is the dashed line inside the tunnel depicted in gray.

You can also tell `ssh` to listen to connections on the regular port 3306, as long as there is no other process, such as a local MySQL server, using it already.

In the next screenshot, notice the information in the uppermost box **Connected to MySQL Server Instance**. As far as MySQL Administrator is concerned, it does not know about the HOST machine; from its point of view it is connected to localhost, port 3316. This is normal behavior in this scenario.

Server status:
**MySQL Server is running.**

Connected to MySQL Server Instance

| | |
|---|---|
| Username: | root |
| Hostname: | localhost |
| Port: | 3316 |

Server Information

| | |
|---|---|
| MySQL Version: | MySQL 5.1.30 via TCP/IP |
| Network Name: | VistaVirtual |
| IP: | 127.0.0.1 |

Client Information

| | |
|---|---|
| Version: | MySQL Client Version 5.1.11 |
| Network Name: | VistaVirtual |
| IP: | 192.168.154.129 |
| Operating System: | unknown |
| Hardware: | Intel(R) Core(TM)2 Duo CPU |

## There's more...

By now you must have already understood from the description earlier that you need not necessarily have the SSH daemon installed on the same machine as the target MySQL server. In fact in many production scenarios, you will have a single SSH gateway server from which you can reach your MySQL servers. You can then connect to this gateway server with one or more SSH clients and have it relay MySQL communications to the respective database servers.

Often hosting providers will not allow you to log in to your MySQL server directly for security reasons. They do, however, usually equip you with a set of SSH user credentials for managing the server. Usually, you get to a command shell when you log in using PuTTY or a similar client program. With this recipe you will no longer be confined to using the mysql command-line client for your database management needs, but simply run your tool of choice (for example, MySQL Query Browser) locally and just tunnel it through SSH.

If you want to attach to different MySQL hosts from the same client, be sure to specify an individual local port number (for example: 3316, 3317, 3318) for each connection, as the host name will be localhost for all of them.

# Creating an encrypted MySQL console via SSH

Often you connect to a remote machine using SSH just to launch the `mysql` command-line client as soon as you are logged in. Especially, on dedicated database machines it would be easier to get the `mysql` prompt right after you established the SSH connection.

In this recipe, we will set up a dedicated user account on the server machine that automatically launches the `mysql` command-line client and connects you to the MySQL server once you log in using SSH. When you leave the `mysql` client, you will automatically be disconnected from SSH as well.

**Important**: The procedure presented in this recipe may pose a security risk! *Effectively, users have got shell access with this!* *Therefore, apply this recipe only in tightly controlled environments with trustworthy and well-known users!* **Never use it to allow arbitrary access to your servers!**

`mysql` provides the `system` command on Unix-like operating systems. This command allows you to run operating system level commands in the context of the currently logged in user. Even though in the example we utilized a restricted user account that does not have any special rights, it can still access world-readable files (like `/etc/passwd`) and execute programs as if it were logged onto the server machine locally!

## Getting ready

For this recipe to work, the MySQL server's operating system has to support an SSH connection. Most Linux distributions include out-of-the-box support for this. Mac OS X Leopard also supports encrypted SSH connections without third-party products.

While in Mac OS X and Linux, the `ssh` client is provided out of the box, Windows users will need the free PuTTY SSH client from the Web or the Cygwin bundled `ssh` client.

You will need the necessary privileges to create a new operating system user on the SSH server machine. This need not necessarily be the same machine as the database server. Moreover, you will need a valid user account on the MySQL server.

In the next example, we will use an Ubuntu Linux machine, which is both the SSH and the database server. We assume root access on that machine. To connect to the server we will use PuTTY on Windows.

Setting up this scenario using a Windows SSH server depends on the SSH server you choose to install. While it would be technically possible to achieve this with the Cygwin SSH server, it would be rather cumbersome to do so, due to the way Cygwin integrates with the Windows user account system. Because of this, we will concentrate on Unix-like servers in this recipe and only use Windows as a client.

## How to do it...

1. Open a command shell. Create a new user group on the Linux machine using the following command:

   ```
   sudo addgroup mysqlshellusers
   ```

2. Create a new directory and set the permissions using these commands:

   ```
   sudo mkdir /usr/local/bin/mysqlshells
   sudo chmod u=rwx,g=rx,o= /usr/local/bin/mysqlshells
   sudo chgrp mysqlshellusers /usr/local/bin/mysqlshells
   ```

3. Create a new file on the SSH server with the following content. Save it as `/usr/local/bin/mysqlshells/mysqladmin.sh`:

   ```
   #!/bin/bash
   echo ----------------------------
   echo Connecting to MySQL...
   echo ----------------------------
   /usr/bin/mysql -uroot -p
   ```

4. Set the permissions on the new file as follows:

   ```
   sudo chmod u=rx,g=rx,o= /usr/local/bin/mysqlshells/mysqladmin.sh
   sudo chgrp mysqlshellusers /usr/local/bin/mysqlshells/mysqladmin.sh
   ```

5. Create a new user account using this command:

   ```
   sudo useradd -d /tmp -g mysqlshellusers -s /usr/local/bin/mysqlshells/mysqladmin.sh mysqladmin
   ```

6. Set a password for the new user using this command:

   ```
   sudo passwd myadmin
   ```

7. On the client machine launch PuTTY. Connect to the SSH server. Use `mysqladmin` as the username and supply the password that you set in step 5.

8. Once you have logged into the host machine, enter the MySQL password for the database root account:

```
192.168.154.134 - PuTTY
login as: mysqladmin
mysqladmin@192.168.154.134's password:
Linux ubuntu810 2.6.27-11-generic #1 SMP Thu Jan 29 19:24:39 UTC 2009 i686

The programs included with the Ubuntu system are free software;
the exact distribution terms for each program are described in the
individual files in /usr/share/doc/*/copyright.

Ubuntu comes with ABSOLUTELY NO WARRANTY, to the extent permitted by
applicable law.

To access official Ubuntu documentation, please visit:
http://help.ubuntu.com/
Last login: Mon Mar 30 23:10:00 2009 from 192.168.154.129
-----------------------------
Connecting to MySQL...
-----------------------------
Enter password:
Welcome to the MySQL monitor.  Commands end with ; or \g.
Your MySQL connection id is 45
Server version: 5.0.67-0ubuntu6 (Ubuntu)

Type 'help;' or '\h' for help. Type '\c' to clear the buffer.

mysql>
```

## How it works...

When you log in to an SSH server, the program that it will look up is set as the user's *login shell*. Usually, this is a command-line shell like `bash` or `zsh` that lets you to interact with the server's operating system, launch programs, and so on. It need not be a general purpose command-line interpreter, however, it is perfectly fine to specify any executable command or script. On some Linux systems, for example Mandriva, you need to add the path of this special shell in `/etc/shells`.

When we created the new `mysqladmin` user account, we used the `useradd` command's `-s` parameter to tell it that we wanted `/usr/local/bin/mysqlshells/mysqladmin.sh` as our login shell, which we had just created and placed there.

Upon login, the SSH server opened and ran this script, effectively starting our `mysql` command-line client with the `-u root` and `-p` parameters. This is why you were asked for the second password. For security reasons we did not put the password into the script file, even though that would have been possible and only required us to enter one instead of two passwords to log in. In a tightly controlled environment this might be a viable solution, but it is definitely not recommended.

The rest of the commands discussed earlier create a new user group called `mysqlshellusers` and restrict access to the `/usr/local/bin/mysqlshells` directory to the members of this group to prevent unauthorized users from even viewing the scripts.

## There's more...

Of course, you are not limited to a single user account or just one script. You can create as many specialized scripts as you like and assign them to different user accounts. In the previous example, the script logged on to the MySQL server as root, which is necessary for some administrative tasks. You should, however, generally use an account with more restricted privileges.

To prevent you from having to enter two passwords each time you log in, you might want to look into SSH public/private key pairs that can be used to log in to SSH instead of a password without compromising security.

# Using a PuTTY template connection for SSH secured connections

In the previous recipe, we used SSH to tunnel MySQL connections through insecure networks like the Internet and prevented the data and login information from traveling in clear text. While for a single server such connections can quite easily be set up manually, it quickly gets tedious and inflexible once you have more than just a few servers to regularly connect to. In Mac OS X and Linux, it is very easy to create a little shell script that uses variables for all of the relevant options you need to pass to the ssh client tool.

PuTTY users in Windows might find themselves in a situation where they would like to do the same, but unfortunately PuTTY does not provide command-line options for everything that can be configured through the GUI. For example, you might want to specify your favorite terminal font or have production systems use a different terminal background color than internal test machines.

You might be tempted to create individual connection profiles in PuTTY (if you prefer Windows) for every MySQL server you have to manage or multiply the corresponding registry entries where PuTTY stores its connection profiles.

Both these approaches work fine up to the point where you need to change a setting that is common to all of your profiles. In that case, you would need to load, modify, and save each and every connection the change is applied to.

This recipe will show you how to establish encrypted connections to MySQL servers through SSH tunnels that are set up using a connection template. As an example, this template will include a red signal color background for the terminal window to easily visually distinguish production systems from test machines.

**Important:** The procedure presented in this recipe may pose a security risk! Please make sure you understand the implications by reading the information box in the *Creating an encrypted MySQL console via SSH* recipe!

## Getting ready

For this recipe to work, the MySQL server's operating system has to support an SSH connection. Most Linux distributions include out-of-the-box support for this. Mac OS X Leopard also supports encrypted SSH connections without third-party products.

Windows users need to install the SSH server themselves. There are several commercial offerings, but for the purpose of this recipe the SSH server available with the Cygwin package is completely sufficient.

While in Mac OS X and Linux, the `ssh` client is provided out of the box, Windows users will need the free PuTTY SSH client from the Web.

## How to do it...

1. Open Notepad and save the following code as `MySQLTunnel_PROD.cmd`:
   ```
   @echo off
   echo Production System Hostname:
   set /p hst=
   echo Connecting to %hst%
   putty.exe -L 3316:127.0.0.1:3306 -ssh -load "TMPL_PROD" %hst%
   ```
2. Launch PuTTY.
3. Choose the **Window/Appearance** panel from the left-hand tree.
4. Select **Default Background** from the list and set the RGB value to `120,0,0`.
5. Choose the **Connection/Data** panel from the left-hand tree.
6. Enter the remote operating system username in the **Auto-login username** field. In the example this is `ds`.
7. Save the connection from the **Session** panel under the name `TMPL_PROD`.
8. Close PuTTY.

9. Double-click on the `MySQLTunnel_PROD.cmd` file. You will be prompted with a window where you can enter the SSH server's hostname. In this example we've entered `yavin-mac`:

10 PuTTY will be automatically launched and will connect to the host you entered, applying both settings from the batch file (the tunnel setup) as well as from the `TMPL_PROD` session (background color, username):

11. Launch your MySQL client program (for example: MySQL Administrator) and point it to `localhost` port `3316` to connect through the tunnel.

## How it works...

Instead of creating a single connection for every server you need to connect to, we created a template that contains all settings common to a group of connections (for example, one for production systems and a different one for internal test machines).

Using only one set of placeholder settings allows for easy changes later on. If you copied the initial settings for every new host, you would have to edit each copy separately.

A batch file prompts to enter the hostname to connect to, and stores it in a variable called `hst`. The batch then launches the PuTTY executable passing both the name of the prepared template session and some additional command-line parameters (the tunnel setup and the content of the `hst` variable), effectively merging both template and manually specified settings.

If you now need to change a configuration setting (for example, you'd like to enable session logging to a text file), you just need to edit the corresponding template session in PuTTY once and have the new settings applied to every subsequent connection that is established via the batch file.

## There's more...

In the example, only a limited number of settings are stored in the template session. You can customize this further, for example, by using a key pair for authentication without the need to enter a password upon each connection.

You can also introduce more variables in the batch file and hand them to one or more of PuTTY's other command-line options. Refer to the online documentation to find out which options can be set directly from the command line.

If your servers are set up using a naming scheme, you might reduce the amount of typing even further. Just have the user enter only the variable portion of the hostname and build the complete hostname in the batch file like so:

```
@echo off
echo Subsidiary no:
set /p subsno=
set hst=SUBS_%subsno%.example.com
echo Connecting to %hst%
putty.exe -ssh -load "TMPL_PROD" %hst%
```

Here the hostname is built from a prefix SUBS_ which is then appended by a fictional subsidiary number and complete with a domain suffix .example.com. Adapt this to your environment appropriately.

By either duplicating the batch file or adding some sort of menu to it, you can also use different template sessions depending on which set of preferences you would like for any given connection.

# Backing Up and Restoring MySQL Data

This chapter will cover the basic tasks necessary to back up your MySQL data efficiently, and the steps to restore this data if necessary. We will discuss the following recipes:

- Using MySQL Administrator GUI Tool as a frontend for backups
- Copying all data files to a backup location
- Creating a SQL dump of all databases
- Creating a SQL dump of specific databases
- Creating a SQL dump of specific tables
- Compressing SQL dumps on-the-fly
- Rotating and purging binary logs
- Using replication to perform backups without hurting a production system's performance
- Restoring data from a dump to a previously backed-up state
- Performing a point-in-time recovery using the binary logs

# Introduction

Although MySQL has a reputation for robustness and data loss is a problem you will not likely encounter, it is best to be prepared for when your data gets corrupted or lost. Experience shows that it will eventually happen and probably when you least expect it.

The first thing you should make sure of is that you have a backup at hand. In this chapter, we will show you different ways of saving your data elsewhere. But having a backup alone is not enough, as even the most complete backup is basically useless if you are not able to restore your data from it. This chapter also covers different ways of restoring the data in the database using an existing backup.

You should, however, be aware that a backup strategy does not only consist of the technical details on how to back up and how to restore your data. You should also consider backup aspects like backup frequency, how many generations have to be kept available, suitable backup media, and constructional conditions. Is one backup per week sufficient? Or is once a day a better choice? Will you need a tape drive, or will a USB hard disk do? Is it required to store backup media in a separate fire compartment? All these questions will be answered differently depending on your application's criticality, so there are no best practice proposals.

The only thing that we strongly encourage you to do in all cases is to repeatedly and continuously test your restore process! A restore process that was tested some years ago might not work today for different reasons. One common problem with restore processes is that the documentation is outdated or not available to the people that are responsible for restoring the database ("not available" also includes "they do not know where to find it"). Another standard issue is that there are no precise responsibility definitions—the people you think are responsible for restoring the database may neither know of the responsibility nor how to do it. And the fact that the restore process worked perfectly within the given parameters last year is no guarantee that this is the case today as well (data growth often being the reason for such a difference). Restoring an almost empty database took a matter of minutes back then, but restoring the current multi-terabyte database takes more than 24 hours, which is not acceptable if the backup-restore concept states a maximum recovery time of six hours.

So, as with a fire alarm, you should try and test it on a regular basis to make sure the whole process still works as expected, and hope that you will never need it.

While definition of a full backup-recovery strategy is beyond the scope of this chapter, we will provide you with the basic technical means of saving and restoring your database.

# Using MySQL Administrator GUI Tool as a frontend for backups

## Getting ready

To follow the steps in this recipe, you will need an account that has sufficient permissions to perform a backup (you will need `SELECT` and `LOCK TABLES` privileges). We will assume a user named `backup_usr` (refer to Chapter 8, *Defining a specific user for backup*).

You should also make sure that there is no write access to your database. This is to prevent locking issues. For further explanation please refer to the *There's more...* section.

And finally, you will need sufficient space on one of your drives to store the backup file.

## How to do it...

1.  Start MySQL Administrator. Connect to your database server using the `backup_usr` account.
2.  Select the entry **Backup** either from the list on the left or from the **View** menu.
3.  Click on the **New Project** button.
4.  Enter the project name **MySQL Backup 1** in the **Project Name** field.
5.  Successively select each schema from the **Schemata** list and click on the **>** button. Exclude the **information_schema** (you will be warned if you accidentally try to add this to the list).

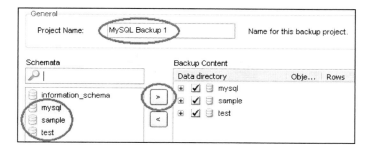

6.  Select the **Advanced Options** tab.
7.  Choose **Online with binlog pos** as the backup execution method.

8. Enable the **Complete backup** option and click on the **Save Project** button.

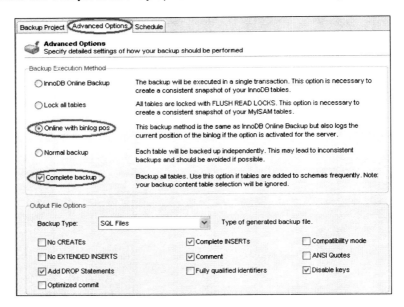

9. Click on the **Execute Backup Now** button,and select a location for the backup file in the next dialogue.

10. The backup will begin and a progress indicator will be displayed, as seen in the next screenshot:

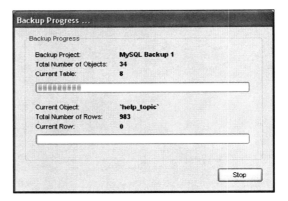

## How it works...

This recipe is a pretty straightforward way of creating a backup. With steps 1 and 2 we open the backup interface of MySQL Administrator. Steps 3 and 4 are used to create a new backup project named **MySQL Backup 1**; this name can be changed freely to your liking.

In step 5, you select all databases that will be included in your backup. If you wish not to back up all databases, but only a selected schema, you can also restrict your selection to certain databases. But please be aware that in case of cross-database dependencies you have to select all relevant databases as well, otherwise this might lead to problems later when trying to restore the data. Also, note that all MySQL accounts and their respective privileges are stored in the **mysql** schema. If you choose not to include this in your backup, you will have to restore the accounts and privileges by other means.

Steps 6 through 8 define the exact method for backing up your data. With step 7, you change the default method from **InnoDB Online Backup** to **Online with binlog pos**. We advise to use this method because its performance is identical to the default method, but includes an additional information about the current binlog position that is extremely useful in case of a restore. The **Complete backup** option selected in step 8 makes sure you can use the same backup project later without any changes even if new tables were added since the project's creation. If you do not plan on using the backup project again, you can simply skip step 8.

Step 9 is again pretty straightforward: after selecting the target for the backup file, the backup is started.

## There's more...

In addition to the steps described in this recipe, MySQL Administrator features several options regarding the backup. The following sections will discuss some of these options as well as the limitations of this backup approach.

### Scheduling backups

As backups are something you typically need on a regular basis, MySQL Administrator also provides you with a scheduling option. Under the **Schedule** tab, you can enable scheduled backups. After entering the target directory and the base name of the backup files, you can choose between daily, weekly, and monthly backup. Saving your project using the **Save Project** button will install a scheduling entry task in your operating system (either a `cron` job on Unix-based systems or a Scheduled Task on Windows—you will need to provide the respective operating system credentials for this).

### Understanding and handling limitations of using MySQL Administrator for backups

The approach of using MySQL Administrator as a graphical tool makes it very easy to perform backups, either manually or scheduled. For many purposes, this is completely sufficient. But for larger installations, you will probably need some more flexibility, for example with respect to the scheduling options or the targeted MySQL instances. If you have multiple MySQL server processes running on one server, MySQL Administrator provides no out-of-the-box solutions to create backups for all of them, as it mainly targets single instance installations. Also, an option to perform backups at sub-daily intervals (for example every 6 hours) is not covered by MySQL Administrator.

Due to these limitations, we recommend to write and schedule your own scripts for installations that deal with mission-critical data, and to simultaneously establish a monitor for these scripts, so the responsible administrators are informed if the backup is not created properly.

Regardless of whether MySQL Administrator is used or not, use of a desktop computer to backup your data is generally not recommended. Desktop machines are typically not set up to run continuously, so you can't rely on uninterrupted backups. Separate machines are also more prone to security issues, as they are often easily physically accessible by different people, which makes data theft easier. In many installations, desktop computers and database servers are also located on different networks. This possibly facilitates attacks on the networking layer, and might even be a legal problem when dealing with personal data.

## Exploring additional backup options

We will discuss a few additional options in the **Advanced Options** tab of MySQL Administrator that might be useful for some situations.

First of all, the **Add DROP Statements** option is enabled by default. This causes MySQL Administrator to include `DROP TABLE IF EXISTS` statements in the dump. This typically makes sense because it helps removing all existing data from a table before restoring it. So after restoring the data, the table contains exactly the same data as it did at the time the dump was created. It also makes sure that the restore process will not run into problems if the table's structure has changed between dump creation and restoration. So you will mostly want to leave this option enabled. But if you plan to use the dump to import additional data into an existing database, you should disable this option.

The **No CREATEs** option prevents MySQL Administrator from producing `CREATE DATABASE` statements in the dump. According to the documentation, this is intended for situations in which you want to import a dump into a different database. Unfortunately, this will not work, as the dump still contains a `USE` statement that will target the restore to the original database name and cause an error if this database does not exist. Hence, this option is basically useless and can be left disabled.

The other options provided in the **Advanced Options** tab of the **Backup** section of MySQL Administrator are not relevant for typical use. For more details, refer to the `mysqldump` manual available at: `http://dev.mysql.com/doc/refman/5.1/en/mysqldump.html`.

## See also

▶   *Defining a specific user for backup*

# Copying all data files to a backup location

The most straightforward way to back up the data of your database is to simply copy the files in which the data is stored to another location. In many cases, this is one of the most effective ways to perform a backup. This recipe will describe the steps required to successfully use this approach.

## Getting ready

For the copy-all backup, you have to shut down your database. For this you have to make sure that all connections to your database are closed. Furthermore, you have to identify the directories in which MySQL stores its data files, the InnoDB table space, and the configuration file. In the following steps, we will assume the following directories and files: `C:\Program Files\MySQL\MySQL Server 5.1\my.ini` for MySQL configuration, `C:\MySQL\Data\` as the MySQL data directory (where MyISAM data and the transaction logs are stored), and `C:\MySQL\InnoDB\` for the InnoDB table space.

And finally, you need sufficient space on a drive to copy the data files to. In this example, we will assume a directory `D:\MySQLBackup` as the target directory for the backup.

## How to do it...

1. Shut down your database instance (for example using MySQL Administrator).
2. Create the target directories.
3. Copy the full content of the data directory `C:\MySQL\Data\` to the destination directory `D:\MySQLBackup\Data`.
4. Copy the full content of the InnoDB data directory `C:\MySQL\InnoDB\` to the destination directory `D:\MySQLBackup\InnoDB\`.
5. Copy the MySQL configuration file `C:\Program Files\MySQL\MySQL Server 5.1\my.ini` to the destination directory `D:\MySQLBackup\`.
6. Start the MySQL Server instance again.

## How it works...

This recipe basically consists of copying the important MySQL files from one location to the other. It is important to understand why step 1 (shutting down the database) is necessary, without this step you risk an inconsistent or (even worse) unusable backup. If any changes are made to the tables while you copy them, you will have an undefined state in some of the files at the moment they are ready to be copied to the backup location. While MySQL is able to recover even from such inconsistent backups more often than not, it is best not to rely on this because your primary goal is to have a reliable backup.

When MySQL is stopped, it leaves a defined state in all of the files, which will not change during the backup process. This is why a file-based backup will be consistent and sufficient to restore the saved state if necessary.

You may have noticed that the binary logs are not saved in this particular recipe. This is because of the fact that the binary logs are not necessary to restore a MySQL instance from scratch. If they are missing when the database is restarted after a restore, a new binary log (together with an index file) is created automatically.

It should be noted that if you chose to write your transaction logs to a different location outside of the data directory (using the `innodb_log_group_home_dir` option), you will have to save this directory to the backup location as well, as the log position marked therein is linked to the InnoDB data files. While InnoDB usually has no problems to recover from this situation after a restore, it is advised to save the transaction logs as well.

The configuration file saved in step 5 is not vital, but it is very helpful when trying to restore data from a backup to have the original configuration at hand. Especially for InnoDB databases, the configuration of the InnoDB table space has to be reproduced identically to prevent non-recoverable errors after restore.

## There's more...

In the following sections, we will discuss restrictions of the recipe, an advanced variation of the backup method using LVM snapshots, and a few hints on how to restore data from a backup.

### Understanding the restrictions of the file-based backup method

The backup method described in the above recipe typically delivers very good performance and excellent duration predictability (especially on a restore). On the downside, the approach of backing up binary files makes it more vulnerable to data corruption problems (beside the fact that the database server needs to be restarted). If a binary file gets corrupted (for example a table that is not accessed on a regular basis), you will not necessarily notice with this kind of backup. By the time the file gets used and the error shows up, all your backup generations might already contain a corrupted version of the file, basically leaving you without a usable backup for the data stored within the respective file.

This is why we recommend complementing the file-based backup with a dump-based backup as described in the following recipe. This forces MySQL to fully read every table so data corruption is more likely to be discovered. To make use of this fact, the backup should be monitored, as errors during backup might indicate data corruption and should be reported for further evaluation.

This dump might be produced less often, but with a frequency that performs a dump before the retained backup generations of the file-based backups get overwritten again in the next cycle. For example, if you perform a daily file-based backup and keep seven generations of these, we recommend performing an additional dump-based backup once a week.

## Backing up using LVM snapshots

The major disadvantage of the copy-all approach is that a database shutdown is required. In many situations this is not a feasible option. To avoid this restriction, it is sometimes advisable to create a snapshot of the file system (typically an LVM snapshot using the Linux Logical Volume Manager). We advise you to use this approach with caution because a snapshot does not guarantee that the state the files were in when the snapshot was created is a consistent state from which MySQL can recover. Even if we assume that in most cases MySQL can recover from such a backup state, a backup that is only *likely* to be suitable for a restore is not sufficient—you have to be absolutely positive about that!

To be sure about the state of the tables at the time the snapshot is done, you have to flush all open changes to the disk. This can be done using a `FLUSH TABLES WITH READ LOCK` command right before the snapshot. Note, however, that in case of long-running transactions this might lead to significant delays for SQL statements that try to write to the database in parallel, basically causing similar problems as with a database that was shut down.

After the backup is completed, you have to unlock the tables again by executing an `UNLOCK TABLES` command. Note that if you close the connection that was used for the `FLUSH TABLES WITH READ LOCK` command, the tables are unlocked as well. By closing the connection, you do not need the `UNLOCK TABLES` statement, but this also means the connection has to stay open during the whole backup process!

Furthermore, several tests proved that the write performance of LVM snapshots is abysmal (see for example `http://www.nikhef.nl/~dennisvd/lvmcrap.html` or `http://www.mysqlperformanceblog.com/2009/02/05/disaster-lvm-performance-in-snapshot-mode/`). If there is relevant traffic on the database while the LVM snapshot gets copied to the backup destination, your database will probably suffer from significant performance degradation. A possible remedy to this might be to perform the backup on a specific backup slave as described in one of the following recipes.

## Restoring data from a file-based backup

The restore process for a file-based backup is pretty straightforward: stop the database, and copy the directories back to their original location. After starting the database again, your data is reset to the state it was in when the backup was performed. Easy as that!

## See also

▶ *Using replication to perform backups without hurting a production system's performance.*

▶ *Defining a specific user for backup*

# Creating a SQL dump of all databases

In the previous recipe the file-based backup method was presented. As was already mentioned there, this approach requires some caveats. Thus we recommend to perform additional dump-based backups, which store the content of your database as SQL files that can easily be read and are less subject to (unrecoverable) data corruption. This recipe shows you how to create such a dump-based backup.

## Getting ready

To follow the steps in this recipe, you will need a user that has sufficient permissions to perform a backup (most importantly the SELECT and LOCK TABLES privileges). We will assume a user named *backup_usr* (see *Defining a specific user for backup* in Chapter 8).

As before, you need an additional destination directory with sufficient free space to hold the backup. We will use the directory D:\MySQLBackup\ as the target directory.

## How to do it...

Execute the following command from the command line:

```
C:\>mysqldump -u backup_usr -p"B4ckM3Up!" --all-databases > "D:\
MySQLBackup\MySQLDumpAllDatabases.sql"
```

## How it works...

While it might seem somewhat awkward to call a single command a recipe, the details involved in this command justify this decision. The command-line statement consists of two basic parts: the mysqldump command itself and the output redirection clause (> D:\...\MySQLDumpAllDatabases.sql), which writes the resulting dump file to the given file. If you take a closer look at the mysqldump command, you will notice the options -u and -p that are used to pass the user credentials to use for performing the backup. The next option is --all-databases, which tells mysqldump to write the data of all databases (including the **mysql** schema) to the dump.

Now what happens on execution of this command? First of all, the default option --opt is applied in addition to the given parameters. It is active if no other option is listed explicitly, and it enables several sensible settings, most notably the --lock-tables option that locks all tables (using the LOCK TABLE ... READ LOCAL semantics) before they are dumped. This prevents concurrent modification to the tables while data is being dumped (which could result in a dump file with inconsistent data across tables). Afterwards, one database after the other is processed. For each database, the structure and data of each of the tables (in alphabetical order) are read and written to the output file in as SQL CREATE TABLE and INSERT statements. The resulting file is a valid SQL file that can be executed on an empty MySQL installation to restore its data.

It should be noted that the performance of creating a backup using mysqldump is typically not as good as creating a file-based backup (as discussed in the previous recipe). Here is a comparison of the time needed for backing up the employees example database:

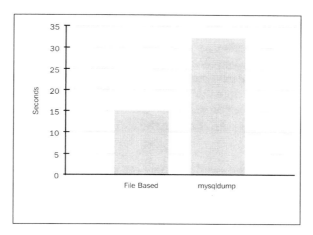

## There's more...

The default behavior of mysqldump is to lock all tables of each database before they are dumped. This has the goal of preventing inconsistencies inside the dump when concurrent modifications take place during the dump. Unfortunately, this works only within certain limits and might also have a negative impact on the database operations. The following sections discuss these caveats.

 Please note that all additional options to mysqldump mentioned next have to be placed before the --all-databases clause (you will encounter errors otherwise).

## Preventing locking issues by using InnoDB storage engine

The locking mechanism used by `mysqldump` tries to prevent concurrent data modifications during the dump. This obviously can cause significant delays due to table locks when an application tries to concurrently write to the locked tables. Depending on the size of the database and the correlated duration of the dump, this could pose a problem. If this is the case, you should consider using the InnoDB storage engine instead of MyISAM tables (which we recommend anyway for most applications), as InnoDB allows dumping a consistent snapshot of the database basically without any potentially long-lasting locks. Another alternative is to use a separate replication slave as the backup source (as described in the *Using replication to perform backups without hurting a production system's performance* recipe), which allows for backups without negative consequences for the master database server.

## Creating consistent dumps of InnoDB tables

If you deal mainly with InnoDB tables (or other tables using a different transactional storage engine), you should add the `--single-transaction` option to the previous `mysqldump` command. This option creates a consistent snapshot of all InnoDB tables, which is then written to the dump. But please note that this option ensures integrity only for transactional tables! For MyISAM tables, this option increases the risk of dumping inconsistent data across tables, as `--single-transaction` disables the `--lock-tables` and `--lock-all-tables` option.

One should also be aware that the InnoDB snapshots are not able to cope with concurrent statements that alter the table structure (such as `ALTER TABLE`, `DROP TABLE`, `TRUNCATE TABLE` or `RENAME TABLE`). You should make sure that these statements are not executed during a dump.

## Preventing dump inconsistency across databases

The default `--lock-tables` option causes `mysqldump` to lock all tables for each schema (database) separately. In case of dependencies across schemata, this might lead to inconsistent data again. Think of an entry that gets changed in schema A. The corresponding entry in schema B—which holds a reference to the first entry—is updated only after the dump of the second schema is finished. If `mysqldump` dumps schema B first, then schema A, you will have an orphan entry in schema A.

To prevent this problem, you could pass the `--lock-all-tables` option to `mysqldump`, which results in locks across all databases. As a downside, this approach produces longer lasting locks than the default method, so you should use it only if needed.

## Including binary log position in the dump

If your database has binlogging enabled, then you should use an additional option for the `mysqldump` command: `--master-data=2`. It includes the log position of your database server in your dump file. This is extremely useful when trying to perform a point-in-time recovery using the dump and additional binary log files (as described in a following recipe). This option works only if binlogging is enabled.

Please note that this option implicitly enables `--lock-all-tables` (unless used in conjunction with `--single-transaction`, which disables both table lock options).

## Performing consistent dumps for binary data

When using binary data in columns of type `BINARY`, `VARBINARY`, `BLOB` (in all sizes), or `BIT`, you should additionally include the `--hex-blob` option for `mysqldump` to ensure all data is dumped correctly. Otherwise you might encounter problems with messed up data. The reason for this problem is the conversion of special bytes sequences like line breaks that takes place when exporting and importing data. The `--hex-blob` option circumvents this conversion for binary columns.

## Reducing performance impacts by using multiple disks

When creating a dump, your computer has to perform both read and write operations in parallel—the database is read, and the dump is written. If both operations access the same disk, it results in a high load on the disk and many head movements, which in turn reduces the performance. If you have multiple physical disks available (a logical drive or partition on the same physical disk will not help), you can increase dump performance considerably by targeting the dump to a different disk than the disk that holds your database data.

## See also

▶ *Defining a specific user for backup*

▶ *Using replication to perform backups without hurting a production system's performance*

# Creating a SQL dump of specific databases

This recipe shows you how to select specific databases for backup. This might be useful for example to separate the backup processes for different databases if these have different (or even worse contradictory) backup policies.

## Getting ready

As this is only a slight adaption of the previous recipe, the preconditions are almost identical: again, you have to have a MySQL user account (here: `backup_usr`) with sufficient privileges to perform a database dump, and a target directory (here: `D:\MySQLBackup\`).

Additionally, you have to be sure that the database(s) you want to dump have no data dependencies on databases that will not be part of the dump. This could result in a dump that is not self-contained and might cause data inconsistencies in case of a restore.

Throughout this recipe, we will assume that you want to dump the content of the two databases `employees` and `suppliers`.

## How to do it...

Execute the following command from the command line:

```
C:\>mysqldump -u backup_usr -p"B4ckM3Up!" --databases employees suppliers
> "D:\MySQLBackup\MySQLDump_Employees_Suppliers.sql"
```

## How it works...

The command is basically identical to the `mysqldump` command presented in the previous recipe. The only difference is that the `--all-databases` clause is replaced by the `--databases` option. This option is followed by a database (or a list of databases, separated by blanks) that should be included in the resulting dump.

The additional options mentioned in the previous recipe are applicable for the `--databases` variant as well. You have to make sure, however, that the `--databases` option is the last option to `mysqldump`.

## There's more...

An advantage of dumping databases separately is that a database can be restored without affecting other databases. Although a full restore of all databases takes a little more work, in most situations this is outweighed by the additional flexibility of having separate dumps. Another advantage is that the dump files are typically less clumsy and are easier to handle because of their reduced size.

### Considering the side effects of automated backup

For automated backups, the idea of backing up each database to its own dump file has a side effect that should be considered: a typical simple script that basically contains one `mysqldump` command for each database has to be adapted every time a database is added or deleted. In a dynamic environment where the schema catalogue is subject to constant changes, you should consider writing a script that reads the available databases (for example using `SHOW DATABASES`) and iterates over the resulting list to dump each database.

### Increasing performance by dumping in parallel

To leverage current computers with multi-core processors, one approach to reduce the time needed for backing up a database is to parallelize the work. If you start several processes concurrently, you might be able to achieve faster backups. However, the degree of success largely depends on the available resources. If the data throughputs of your drives are the limiting factor, you will not be able to significantly speed up your backup, but in the case of fast disks (or multiple disks, as noted in the previous recipe) concurrency might help you save some time. Try concurrently backing up each database to separate disks (if applicable) for maximum performance.

If you happen to use a Linux server for your MySQL, you might also want to have a look at `mk-parallel-dump` from Maatkit that helps you to dump table sets in parallel (see `http://www.maatkit.org/doc/mk-parallel-dump.html`). Unfortunately, this is not yet available for Windows users. Also, note that the website explicitly states that `mk-parallel-dump` is not a backup program, so you might want to use a different backup strategy besides `mk-parallel-dump` (just to be sure).

## See also

> ▸ *Defining a specific user for backup*

# Creating a SQL dump of specific tables

This recipe will show you how to dump only a portion of a database by selecting specific tables to include in the dump, which comes in handy if you have specific backup requirements for special tables (for example higher backup frequency) that differ from the backup rules for the rest of the database.

## Getting ready

Again, this recipe is very similar to the previous one. We will need a suitable MySQL user account (`backup_usr`), and a target directory with sufficient space (`D:\MySQLBackup\`).

As we restrict the dump to specific tables, you should additionally check that the tables to include in this dump have no dependencies on other tables or databases that will not be included in the resulting dump.

For the following instruction we assume that the table `departments` from the schema **employees** should be written to the dump.

## How to do it...

Execute the following command from the command line:

```
C:\>mysqldump -u backup_usr -p"B4ckM3Up!" employees departments > "D:\
MySQLBackup\MySQLDump_Departments.sql"
```

## How it works...

The above command works just as explained in the previous recipe, with the only difference being that no specific option (like `--all-databases` or `--databases`) is given to pass the desired source databases to `mysqldump`. In this case, `mysqldump` reads the first "real" parameter (that is: starting without a dash) as the source database, followed by a list of tables to dump (separated by spaces). In the above example, this list consists of only one table, but others could be passed as well.

## There's more...

While this approach is sometimes very nice to produce backups that are restricted to the relevant tables only, we recommend you not to use this for automated backups. The reason for this recommendation is that data models are typically subject to a certain extent of evolution. If, for example, a new table is introduced, and this table is referenced by a table contained in the backup, you should include the new table in the backup as well. For this, the `mysqldump` command has to be changed right after the table structures were applied. Experience shows that such dependencies between data structures and scripts relying on a specific structure are typically ignored or overlooked, leaving you with a backup that contains only a part of the required data. This is why we recommend dumping the schema (or all schemata) as a whole to prevent problems arising from subsequent data model evolution.

## See also

▸ *Defining a specific user for backup*

# Compressing SQL dumps on-the-fly

When the data stored in your database grows over time, the backups get bigger as well. You often will want to reduce the space required for your backups to reduce the disk (or tape) storage requirements. If you create a backup using mysqldump, you can reduce the size of your backups considerably. The following recipe will show you how to achieve this.

## Getting ready

In addition to the prerequisites listed in the previous three recipes (a suitable MySQL account and a target directory), we also need an installed version of **gzip** (see http://www.gzip.org/#exe), which is a widely used open source compression utility.

In this recipe, we will produce a dump of all databases and compress it before it is written to the disk.

## How to do it...

Execute the following command from the command line:

```
C:\>mysqldump -u backup_usr -p"B4ckM3Up!" --all-databases | gzip --fast >
"D:\MySQLBackup\MySQLDumpAllDatabases.sql.gz"
```

## How it works...

The only difference in the above command line in comparison to the previous recipes (beside the slightly changed target file name to reflect the compressed content) lies within the | gzip --fast portion. This redirects the output of the mysqldump command to the **gzip** program, which compresses data on-the-fly. The compressed data stream is then written to the given file, resulting in a significantly reduced size.

## There's more...

While the recipe itself is not too complicated, there are some aspects to consider, which are discussed in the following sections.

## Achieving better compression ratio

As a ballpark figure for the compression ratio for typical databases, the compressed dump will probably be reduced to one-third of its uncompressed size. To achieve better compression at the expense of reduced performance and higher CPU load, you could also leave out the `--fast` option of **gzip**, resulting in a compressed file that will take less than 25% of the original size. If the size of the backup is an extremely critical issue for you, you might even try the `--best` option as a replacement for `--fast`, but be warned that this might lead to a dramatic increase in execution times with mostly minimal improvements in size; this is why we recommend not using this option.

## Considering performance factors

With the additional compression part added to the above command, you would intuitively expect that this necessarily has a negative impact on the dump performance. Surprisingly, this is not always the case, as the reduced size of the resulting file also decreases the amount of data written to your disk. This reduction in disk I/O might make up for the additional compression work or even cause a performance improvement! You should check whether the compression has any performance impact with your configuration.

A rule of thumb: the slower the target disk, and the faster your processors, the better it is for compression. And if you want to take system load into account as well: If you experience high I/O load on your target disk and low CPU load, it is well possible that the performance impact of on-the-fly compression is not too significant.

## Considering data robustness and tool availability

With the on-the-fly compression approach, the resulting dump files cannot be read without uncompressing them, which is why you need to have the **gzip** tool at hand for the restore process as well.

Moreover, due to the fact that the compressed files have a compressed binary format, they are much more susceptible to faults caused by data corruption. If data corruption occurs, it is typically more difficult to extract valid data, and the amount of data that is irrevocably lost is typically a good deal bigger.

If a partial data loss occurs for a standard dump (SQL) file, you will still be able to restore large portions of the data because you are able to read the file, extract the intact data, and maybe even correct the errors.

However, in case of a partial data loss on the compressed file the uncompress command will simply fail, basically leaving you without a usable backup since manual corrections to the compressed file are almost impossible. You should keep this in mind when deciding on the best solution to perform a backup.

## Achieving better compression with alternative tools

As an alternative to **gzip**, you could also try similar compression utilities like **bzip2** (`http://www.bzip.org/downloads.html`), **p7zip** (for Linux, `http://p7zip.sourceforge.net/`), or **7-Zip** (for Windows, `http://www.7-zip.org/`), which claim to provide a better compression than **gzip**.

### See also

> ▸ *Defining a specific user for backup*

# Rotating and purging binary logs

If you have binary logging enabled, the `binlog` files contain all changes made to your database over time. These are required for replication, but they can also be used for restoring data after a crash. This is why we strongly encourage you to enable binary logging even if you do not use replication. If you still have access to the `binlogs` produced between your last backup and the moment the disaster occurred, you can basically recover everything without losing any data at all.

To be able to do so, the binary logs should regularly be saved to a different location (best on a different drive or tape media). Moreover, you will need to remove `binlog` files that are no longer needed to prevent the disk from getting full. To be able to copy the relevant files, this recipe will show you how to make sure no concurrent access is active when backing up the data.

## Getting ready

We assume that you have a regular backup process in place, which produces a daily backup based on a MySQL dump. Your application requires that in case of a disaster you must be able to recover all data older than half an hour before the crash. To achieve this, you will have to save the binary logs at least every 30 minutes to a location that will not be affected by a possible crash on your database server.

In addition, let's assume that you will not need any `binlogs` older than 7 days for replication. This in turn means that any replication slave with a data set older than 7 days will not be able to re-enter replication again to catch up with the master (but this typically makes no sense anyway). Thus, all `binlogs` older than 7 days can be deleted.

You will again need an appropriate MySQL user account (`backup_usr`) and a place to copy the `binlogs` to. The recipe assumes a Windows system and a target directory at `D:\MySQLBackup\binlogs\`. The `log-bin` parameter of the MySQL configuration is assumed to have the value `C:/MySQL/Binlogs/bluebox`.

 The recipe is applicable to Windows systems. Please refer to the *There's more...* section for a Linux/Unix variant.

## How to do it...

Establish a scheduled task to perform the following commands at least every 30 minutes in the context of the directory `C:\MySQL\Binlogs\`:

```
copy bluebox.index idx.tmp
mysql -u backup_usr -p"B4ckM3Up!" -e "FLUSH LOGS;
    PURGE BINARY LOGS BEFORE TIMESTAMPADD(DAY, -7, NOW());"
FOR /F %i in (idx.tmp) DO xcopy /D %i D:\MySQLBackup\binlogs\
DEL idx.tmp
```

## How it works...

Let's take a look at each step of this recipe.

The line `copy bluebox.index idx.tmp` makes a (temporary) copy of the index file that contains the index list of all `binlog` files, which is needed for future reference.

The next line executes the MySQL commands `FLUSH LOGS` and `PURGE BINARY LOGS BEFORE TIMESTAMPADD(DAY, -7, NOW())` on the database. `FLUSH LOGS` causes MySQL to close and reopen all log files and to create a new `binlog` file with an incremented counter. This has the effect that write access to the previous `binlog` is finished, so we can safely back it up to another location without risking access conflicts.

The `PURGE BINARY LOGS BEFORE TIMESTAMPADD(DAY, -7, NOW())` command causes MySQL to delete all `binlog` files older than 7 days, which makes sure that the `binlog` directory does not fill up over time.

The loop command `FOR /F %i in (idx.tmp) DO` uses the old index file that we copied in the first command to iterate over all `binlog` files. The `xcopy /D %i D:\MySQLBackup\ binlogs\` command copies each `binlog` file to the backup target location. As the index file was copied before we executed the `PURGE BINARY LOGS` command, the list of files copied does not include the current `binlog` file, which is still actively accessed and possibly changed by MySQL. So we can be pretty sure no write access to the files in this list occurs. The `/D` option of the `xcopy` command is very useful to prevent the same files from being copied over and over again. This option tells `xcopy` to copy files only if the source file is newer than an existing target file, so unchanged files that are already present at the target directory will not be copied again.

The final command then simply cleans up the temporary file, which we created in the first step, so we leave the place nice and clean.

## There's more...

In this section, we will discuss some potential risks and a variant of the recipe for Linux systems.

### Rotating and purging binary logs on Linux systems

Due to syntax differences in the command-line interface, the above recipe is applicable to Windows systems only. To perform the same task for Linux systems, use the following approach (we assume `/var/mysql_backup/binlogs` as the target directory and `/var/ log/mysql` as the `log-bin` parameter):

Establish a `cron` job to perform the following commands at least every 30 minutes:

```
#!/bin/bash
cd /var/log/mysql
cp bluebox.index idx.tmp
mysql -u backup_usr -p"B4ckM3Up!" -e "FLUSH LOGS; PURGE BINARY LOGS
BEFORE TIMESTAMPADD(DAY, -7, NOW());"
cat idx.tmp | while read line; do
    cp -u $line backup/
done
rm idx.tmp
```

When comparing the script to the equivalent Windows version, you will notice some differences (we will not discuss the first two lines here, but concentrate on the actual operations). First of all, the Windows `copy` command is replaced by the Linux statement `cp`. The loop command is different as well: `cat idx.tmp | while read line; do` replaces the Windows command `FOR /F %i in (idx.tmp) DO`. It also iterates over all `binlog` files as listed in the old index file that we copied with the first `cp` command. The `/D` option of Windows' `xcopy` is reflected by the `-u` option of `cp`, which only copies files if they are new, or if the corresponding file at the target directory is older than the file to be copied.

## Considering risks of data loss

The whole mechanism of copying the `binlog` files from one place to the other makes little sense if the two directories are located on the same physical disk, because in the case of a disk failure data in both places would be lost. You should at least have two separate physical disks to store these directories on. Depending on your requirements, you could also consider copying to another host to cover the risk of fire or other disasters, which could damage all internal physical disks of your machine.

## Ensuring sufficient disk space

You will have to make sure, of course, that some kind of backup and deletion mechanism is established at the target directory as well to prevent this disk running out of space. In a typical scenario, an archiving tool might scan this directory once a day, save the files to a tape archive, and delete the archived files.

## See also

> ▸ *Defining a specific user for backup*

# Using replication to perform backups without hurting a production system's performance

A backup always produces a significant load on the server the data is read from. In addition, depending on the way the backup is performed and the storage engine used for your data, locking situations can occur, which might cause major problems for your applications. A method to circumvent both of these problems is to back up the data from a replication client instead of the server. This recipe will show you how to achieve that.

Please note that we do not consider replication itself as a backup technique! Although this is a sensible approach to deal with possible failures and to reduce downtimes, it is no proper replacement for creating regular backups.

## Getting ready

To be able to follow this recipe, you will of course need a MySQL instance that acts as a replication client. Without a working replication set up, this recipe is not helpful.

In addition, you need a MySQL account with appropriate privileges (we assume the previously used `backup_usr` here). And of course, you will need sufficient space in the target directory to save the backup to. We will assume the data directory of the slave instance is `C:\MySQLSlave\Data\`, and the backup target directory is `D:\MySQLBackup\`.

In this recipe, we will refer to the previous recipes to back up data either using the `mysqldump` tool or by copying the data files—both approaches work with this technique.

## How to do it...

1. On the replication client, execute the following statement on the command-line to stop replication processing:

   ```
   C:\>mysql -u backup_usr -p"B4ckM3Up!" -e"STOP SLAVE SQL_THREAD"
   ```

2. Perform your backup, either using `mysqldump` or by copying the data files, as presented in the previous recipes.

3. If the backup in step 2 was performed using `mysqldump`, copy the replication files to the backup target directory as well by performing the following commands (you can skip this if you copied the data files in step 2):

   ```
   C:\>copy /Y C:\MySQLSlave\Data\*.info D:\MySQLBackup\
   ```

   ```
   C:\>copy /Y C:\MySQLSlave\Data\*relay-bin.* D:\MySQLBackup\
   ```

4. Execute the following command to start replication processing again:

   ```
   C:\>mysql -u backup_usr -p"B4ckM3Up!" -e"START SLAVE SQL_THREAD"
   ```

## How it works...

The recipe basically consists of three parts: by performing the operations described in step 1, replication is disabled; in steps 2 and 3, the backup itself is performed; in step 4, replication is enabled again.

Let us have a look at the backup part first. In step 2, the backup of the data stored in the slave database is done as shown in the previous recipes. The addition of step 3 is necessary to also back up the replication state of the slave. In detail, this copies the relay log files (`[host]-relay-bin.index` and `[hostname]-relay-bin.00x`), the `relay-log.info` and the `master.info` files. These files are necessary to recover the slave from a crash because without these files, it is very hard to establish a working replication mechanism with the master. If your intention is to perform a backup only for restoring the master, these files are not absolutely necessary, but we strongly suggest including these files in the backup as well.

That's about it concerning the backup itself. Now what is the motivation for steps 1 and 4? The deactivation of the slave replication in step 1 is necessary to prevent inconsistencies during the backup. As discussed before, both the copy approach and the `mysqldump` backup have restrictions concerning data consistencies for non-transactional tables (like MyISAM) when concurrent updates occur while the data is read. You can tackle this problem for example using locking options. But for a master-slave constellation, this could (in a worst-case scenario) cause the replication to break! By stopping the SQL slave thread, the `binlog` data is still read from the master, but it is no longer processed. This prevents any concurrent data modifications and the data remains in a consistent state throughout the backup process. After the backup is done, step 4 activates replication again, and the slave will start to process the remaining changes from the master up to the point where master and slave reach a synchronous state.

In this scenario, all backup operations (together with the possible performance degradation they might provoke) are performed on the client. By this, a backup is produced, but the replication master is not affected with respect to performance issues. Note, however, that the client is out of sync with the master throughout the backup, and (depending on the way the backup is produced) locking issues might occur as well. This is the reason why this scenario is not intended for use with clients that are actively accessed by applications (for example for load balancing reasons). You are also not safe when creating the backup on a slave that is used as a hot standby for a fail-over scenario, and which is not actively accessed by any application: if the master crashes while the backup is running on the slave, the system is not ready for fail-over. The backup had to disable replication first, so your hot standby slave has a data set different from the master. Only if the replication is activated again, and the backlog is processed, can a fail-over safely take place. Whether this is acceptable has to be decided individually, but to completely separate your application from the backup, you should consider establishing a slave dedicated to backup only.

## See also

- ▶ *Defining a specific user for backup*
- ▶ *Copying all data files to a backup location*
- ▶ *Creating a SQL dump of all databases*
- ▶ *Creating a SQL dump of specific databases*
- ▶ *Creating a SQL dump of specific tables*

# Restoring data from a dump to a previously backed-up state

In the previous recipes, we dealt with creating a backup of the existing data and configuration. The sole reason for this is to be able to restore the data again if required. This recipe will show you how to restore the data created using a dump. The recipe is suitable both for full dumps and for dumps that contain only the data of specific databases.

## Getting ready

To follow the steps in this recipe, you will need a running MySQL instance and a MySQL user account that has the privileges necessary to restore all data. In a default MySQL configuration the root user can be used, but throughout this recipe we use the `admin4mysql` account with password `As,ysp4M` (see *Defining a specific user for administrative tasks* in Chapter 8). The MySQL installation should have sufficient space available to store the data from the dump, and no application connections should be active throughout the restore. And (of course) you need the dump to restore the data from. In this recipe, we assume the dump is stored in `D:\MySQLBackup\MySQLDumpAllDatabases.sql`.

## How to do it...

1.  Connect the `mysql` command-line client to your MySQL instance using the `admin4mysql` account:

    ```
    C:\>mysql -u admin4mysql -p"As,ysp4M"
    ```

2.  Restore the data from the dump by executing the following SQL command:

    ```
    mysql>source   D:\MySQLBackup\MySQLDumpAllDatabases.sql
    ```

## How it works...

Again, this is a pretty straightforward recipe: connect to the database (step 1) and restore the data from the dump (step 2).

The use of the `mysql` command-line client is not absolutely necessary, but please note that you will not be able to issue the `source` command from any other SQL client. This is because it is not a regular SQL statement, but a key word recognized by the `mysql` command-line client itself. You could of course use another SQL client to read in the whole dump file and execute its commands sequentially (for example using the **Open Script...** menu entry of MySQL Query Browser), but the `source` command is specific to `mysql`.

If the dump you want to restore contains only specific tables (as described in *Creating a SQL dump of specific tables*), use the following statement to select the target database to restore the tables into:

```
mysql>use employees;
```

You need to do so because otherwise the tables get inserted to the current default database; the dump itself contains no information about the database the dump stems from.

Please note that after performing the above steps, the content of your database is not necessarily absolutely identical to the state of the database the backup was created from. All databases that were already present before the dump are restored, but any that are not covered by the content of the dump are left unchanged. If your dump for example contains data for the `foo` database only and the database you read the dump into has a database `bar` (which was, for example, created after the dump was produced), the database `bar` will be left unchanged. To be sure you recover to an identical state, you have to:

1. Perform a full backup (using the `--all-databases` option of `mysqldump`).
2. Make sure that the target database is completely empty when restoring.

## There's more...

In the following sections, we will discuss some advanced aspects of restoring data, such as working with compressed dumps and avoiding typical performance problems.

### Restoring compressed dumps

When restoring a database from a compressed dump (for example, as created according to the *Compressing SQL dumps on-the-fly* recipe), the dump needs to be decompressed before restoring it to the database. You could either decompress the file on the disk and subsequently use the preceding recipe without any changes, or decompress on-the-fly and restore the data in one step:

```
C:\> gzip --decompress --stdout D:\MysqlBackup\DumpAllDBs.sql.gz | mysql
-u admin4mysql -p"As,ysp4M"
```

The `--decompress` option tells **gzip** to revert the compression (obviously), while `--stdout` makes sure that the compressed file itself is left unchanged, but the decompressed data is written to the `stdout` device. The pipe symbol | redirects the output from `stdout` to the `mysql` command, which then receives the decompressed content of the dump file and executes the statements contained therein.

 If you used a different compression tool like **bzip2** or **7zip** when creating the dump, you have to adapt the above command accordingly to use the respective tool here as well

## Temporarily disabling binlogs to save time and space

If binlogging is enabled on the MySQL instance you restore, all statements from the dump are not only executed against your database, but also written to the `binlogs`. This has the advantage that replication slaves perform the restore as well, but sometimes this is not necessary (or wanted). For example, if you want to keep the clients unchanged for reference in case the restore fails, or if you do not use binlogging for replication but only for better restore options, you might want to temporarily disable binlogging when processing the dump. This might save you a significant amount of disk space (depending on the size of the dump) and is also better for performance because the write access to the `binlogs` is omitted. To temporarily disable binlogging, you have to prepend the following command in step 2:

```
mysql> SET sql_log_bin=0;
mysql> source D:\...
```

This command disables binlogging for the current connection only. So as soon as the connection is terminated, the `binlogs` will again contain all changes made to your database.

Please note that for this statement your user will require `SUPER` privileges. This privilege is not usually required to perform a restore, but as restoring data is typically a task for the database administrator, it is safe to assume that an account with this privilege is available to the person in charge.

## Increasing recovery performance by using parallel restore

As parallelization is an approach to increase backup speed, it can be used for better performance for restoration as well. With multiple concurrent restore processes, your data might be reinstalled faster. However, whether this is successful or not again depends on the resources available. If the speed of your restore is limited mainly by the drive throughput, the benefit will be basically non-existent. If you have fast (or multiple) disks, however, you might see major advantages. Concurrently restoring each database separately could then be the way to maximize performance.

For Linux servers, `mk-parallel-restore` from Maatkit is available, which supports restoring data in parallel (see `http://www.maatkit.org/doc/mk-parallel-restore.html`). However, a Windows version is not available.

## Restoring tables excluding potentially very large tables

When dealing with large data sets, you sometimes encounter performance problems that require manual intervention. One real-world example of performance problems is a restore of massive tables, which might cause severe performance degradations.

Imagine a table with half a billion records (for example containing log data). While restoring such a table, you will notice a dramatic decrease of insert performance throughout the process. The first few percent of the data will be written to the table rather quickly. But as the restore continues, the write rate will gradually decrease (mostly due to internal index maintenance).

In the case of a disaster recovery, you have the choice between restoring all data (but at the price of extended downtime until the large tables are restored completely as well) and a partial restore, deliberately skipping the restore of the data from the large table, but with the advantage of a faster restore. The decision has to be made on an application level, but with the example of log data, it is often feasible to simply exclude the log data from the restore for the sake of a faster recovery.

Let us assume we have a very large dump file that contains the data you actually want to recover (`D:\MySQLBackup\MySQLDump.sql`) along with a very large table (here: `op_detail`). To be able to cope with the data contained in this potentially mammoth file, you will need access to the `grep` command (for Windows users: see `http://unxutils.sourceforge.net` for an implementation of the common GNU tools).

The following command will restore the data from the dump excluding the data from the `op_detail` table:

```
C:\>grep --invert-match "^INSERT INTO .op_detail. VALUES .*"
D:\MySQLBackup\MySQLDump.sql | mysql -u admin4mysql -p"As,ysp4M"
```

This command uses `grep` to filter all lines including an `INSERT INTO 'op_detail'` at the start of the line, leaving all other lines untouched. All other lines are piped to the `mysql` command-line client that imports the remaining dump.

Please note that if data has references to entries in the excluded table, the import of the dump will not fail. In this case, you would end up with data inconsistencies that might cause errors much later, so make sure to exclude only tables that are not referenced by foreign keys. Otherwise, you have to search for possible foreign key constraint violations manually. (Some ideas on how to achieve this are presented for example at `http://dev.mysql.com/doc/refman/5.1/en/innodb-foreign-key-constraints.html`).

## See also

- *Defining a specific user for administrative tasks*
- *Creating a SQL dump of all databases*
- *Creating a SQL dump of specific databases*

# Performing a point-in-time recovery using the binary logs

The previous recipes dealt with how to recover data from a backup. After recovery, the data should be in the same condition as it was when the backup was created. Unfortunately, the data that was changed after backup creation is not restored.

To restore the data to the point in time before the recovery, you can use the `binlog` files that were created between backup and recovery. As mentioned in the *Rotating and purge binary logs* recipe, we suggest enabling binary logging even if you do not have a replication scenario, as this gives you extended options in backup.

In this recipe, we will discuss how to use the binary logs to restore data up to the latest possible point in time before the data was lost.

## Getting ready

To be able to restore the remaining data using the binary logging information, we definitely need the binary log files. If all data from your server is lost (for example in case of a fire), the `binlogs` are hopefully available from a tape or any other media that is not affected by the data loss. If only your database data is corrupt, you often have the binary logs still present on your server's disk.

If the binary logs are still present, you should copy the binary log files to a different position *before you start recovering from a dump!* This way you have all binary log files available in exactly the state from the point in time before the recovery.

We assume the binary logs (either as a copy of the `binlog` files from your server disk, or as recovered from backup media) to be stored under `C:\tmp\binlogs\`.

To read the changes stored in the binary logs into the database, you need an appropriate MySQL user again (here: `admin4mysql` with password `As,ysp4M`).

And most importantly, you need the position at which recovery from the binary log files should start. The dump your database was restored from should have been created using the `--master-data` option (see the *There's more...* section of the *Creating an SQL dump of all databases* recipe), otherwise this information is not easily available. You could then try to manually identify the correct starting position (for example by checking the timestamps for file creation or last change or inspecting the files using the `mysqlbinlog` tool). But if you plan on using the binary logs for recovery, you should definitely use the `--master-data` option to create a dump.

Find out about the log position by using the `more` command to display the first few lines of the dump. Look for a line like the following:

```
CHANGE MASTER TO MASTER_LOG_FILE='myhost.000005', MASTER_LOG_POS=201;
```

In this line, note the values noted after `MASTER_LOG_FILE` and `MASTER_LOG_POS` for future reference. We, furthermore, assume that you have binary log files through `myhost.000008` available for recovery. Throughout the following recipe, we will use the above noted values. You have to replace them with your respective values accordingly.

## How to do it...

1.  Recover the data from the dump according to the previous recipes.

2.  Execute the following command from the command line in the context of directory `C:\tmp\binlogs\` (change directory accordingly):

    ```
    C:\>mysqlbinlog --start-position=201 myhost.000005 myhost.000006
    myhost.000007 myhost.000008 | mysql -u admin4mysql -p"As,ysp4M"
    ```

## How it works...

The command executed in step 2 reads the given binary logs, translates the changes stored therein into SQL commands and passes these to the MySQL database. The `--start-position` option tells `mysqlbinlog` to begin reading the first given file (here: `myhost.000005`) at position `201`, which starts the recovery process at exactly the point where the dump was created. After this, the next files (`000006` through `000008`) are read completely into the database.

## There's more...

The following sections address partial restores by introducing means to extend the recipe either to restore specific databases, or to restore data only up to a certain point in time.

### Restoring only a specific database

If you have to recover only the data of a specific database but want to leave all other databases unchanged, you must not import the full content of the binary log files because these might contain changes of other databases as well. In this case, add the option `--database=dbname` to `mysqlbinlog`. This restricts the SQL statements passed to the MySQL instance to the given database.

## Determining the exact location of a failure and restoring up to that point

You sometimes have the problem where data loss is not necessarily caused by a server error, but by malicious SQL statements. If, for example, an accidental DROP statement deleted all of your data, then you will have to recover your database as well. In this situation, completely reprocessing the binary logs is a bad idea because this would also execute the DROP statement again, leaving you with a broken database again. In these cases, you will have to manually inspect the binary logs to find out about the specific statements that caused the problem.

To inspect the binary log files, you can create a SQL file from them with a simple `mysqlbinlog myhost.00000x > binlog.sql` command. You can then open the resulting `binlog.sql` file in an editor and scan through the commands. If your binary log files are too large to be opened with an editor, you could make use of the `split` tool (consider using the `--line-bytes` option; see `http://unxutils.sourceforge.net` for a Windows implementation) to break these files into smaller chunks.

As soon as you have found the first command that you do **not** want to include in the recovery process any more, note the number of the line before it, for example `# at 1174`. This denotes the end position at which processing should stop. To exclude any command henceforth from the binary log recovery, add a `--stop-position=1174` option to the `mysqlbinlog` command. This will apply to the last given file (in the above example: `myhost.000008`) and suppresses processing of all commands following the given binary log position. This should prevent repeating the same errors again, which lead to the problems in the first place.

## See also

▶ *Defining a specific user for backup*

# 5
# Managing Data

This chapter presents some proven approaches to managing your data beyond the basic SQL operations like `INSERT` or `DELETE` (which we assume the reader to be familiar with). The first few recipes will discuss ways of exporting data from and importing data into the database using different file formats. This covers the following topics:

- ▸ Exporting data to a simple CSV file
- ▸ Exporting data to a custom file format
- ▸ Using stored procedures to export repeatedly
- ▸ Importing data from a simple CSV file
- ▸ Importing data from custom file formats
- ▸ Inserting new data and updating data if it already exists
- ▸ Inserting data based on existing database content
- ▸ Deleting all data from large tables
- ▸ Deleting all but a fragment of a large table's data
- ▸ Deleting data incrementally from large tables

## Introduction

The basic set of SQL data manipulation commands (`SELECT`, `INSERT`, `UPDATE`, and `DELETE`) is a well understood means to handle the data stored in your database, and its concepts and basic usage are not difficult to learn. There are situations, however, that require more detailed knowledge about these commands' subtleties. This holds especially true when large amount of data need to be taken care of—you have to know what you are doing, otherwise you might run into serious performance problems.

Also, the task of exporting specifically formatted data from or importing external data into your database is a common challenge that can be quite tricky to address.

We are going to address these issues in the following recipes and we will also introduce ways of manipulating data in the database while taking the present contents of the database into account.

We will show solutions to real-world challenges when confronted with data manipulation tasks. It actually took us a while to figure out how to tackle these real-world problems the most efficient way when first faced with them. Because these strategies are not too obvious, a collection of tested methods for these topics might be useful.

# Exporting data to a simple CSV file

While databases are a great tool to store and manage your data, you sometimes need to extract some of the data from your database to use it in another tool (a spreadsheet application being the most prominent example for this). In this recipe, we will show you how to utilize the respective MySQL commands for exporting data from a given table into a file that can easily be imported by other programs.

## Getting ready

To step through this recipe, you will need a running MySQL database server and a working installation of a SQL client (like MySQL Query Browser or the mysql command line tool). You will also need to identify a suitable export target, which has to meet the following requirements:

- ► The MySQL server process must have write access to the target file
- ► The target file must not exist

 The export target file is located on the machine that runs your MySQL server, not on the client side!

 If you do not have file access to the MySQL server, you could instead use export functions of MySQL clients like *MySQL Query Browser*.

In addition, a user with FILE privilege is needed (we will use an account named sample_install for the following steps; see also Chapter 8 *Creating an installation user*).

Finally, we need some data to export. Throughout this recipe, we will assume that the data to export is stored in a table named `table1` inside the database `sample`. As export target, we will use the file `C:/target.csv` (MySQL accepts slashes instead of backslashes in Windows path expressions). This is a file on the machine that runs the MySQL server instance, so in this example MySQL is assumed to be running on a Windows machine. To access the results from the client, you have to have access to the file (for example, using a file share or executing the MySQL client on the same machine as the server).

## How to do it...

1.  Connect to the database using the `sample_install` account.

2.  Issue the following SQL command:

    ```
    mysql> SELECT * FROM sample.table1 INTO OUTFILE 'C:/target.csv'
    FIELDS ENCLOSED BY '"' TERMINATED BY ';' ESCAPED BY '"' LINES
    TERMINATED BY '\r\n';
    ```

Please note that when using a backslash instead of a slash in the target file's path, you have to use `C:\\target.csv` (double backslash for escaping) instead.

 If you do not give a path, but only a file name, the target file will be placed in the data directory of the currently selected schema of your MySQL server.

## How it works...

In the previous SQL statement, a file `C:/target.csv` was created, which contains the content of the table `sample.table1`. The file contains a separate line for each row of the table, and each line is terminated by a sequence of a carriage return and a line feed character. This line ending was defined by the `LINES TERMINATED BY '\r\n'` portion of the command.

Each line contains the values of each column of the row. The values are separated by semicolons, as stated in the `TERMINATED BY ';'` clause. Every value is enclosed by a double quotation mark ("), which results from the `FIELDS ENCLOSED BY '"'` option.

When writing the data to the target file, no character conversion takes place; the data is exported using the *binary* character set. This should be kept in mind especially when importing tables with different character sets for some of its values.

You might wonder why we chose the semicolon instead of a comma as the field separator. This is simply because of a greatly improved *Microsoft Excel* compatibility (you can simply open the resulting files), without the need to import external data from the files. But you can, however, open these files in a different spreadsheet program (like *OpenOffice.org Calc)* as well. If you think the usage of semicolons is in contradiction to the notion of a CSV file, think of it as a Character Separated File.

The use of double quotes to enclose single values prevents problems when field values contain semicolons (or generally the field separator character). These are not recognized as field separators if they are enclosed in double quotes.

## There's more...

While the previous `SELECT ... INTO OUTFILE` statement will work well in most cases, there are some circumstances in which you still might encounter problems. The following topics will show you how to handle some of those.

### Handling errors if the target file already exists

If you try to execute the `SELECT ... INTO OUTFILE` statement twice, an error `File 'C:/target.csv' already exists` occurs. This is due to a security feature in MySQL that makes sure that you cannot overwrite existing files using the `SELECT ... INTO OUTFILE` statement. This makes perfect sense if you think about the consequences. If this were not the case, you could overwrite the MySQL data files using a simple `SELECT` because MySQL server needs write access to its data directories. As a result, you have to choose different target files for each export (or remove old files in advance).

Unfortunately, it is not possible to use a non-constant file name (like a variable) in the `SELECT ... INTO OUTFILE` export statement. If you wish to use different file names, for example, with a time stamp as part of the file name, you have to construct the statement inside a variable value before executing it:

```
mysql> SET @selInOutfileCmd := concat("SELECT * FROM sample.table1 INTO
OUTFILE 'C:/target-", DATE_FORMAT(now(),'%Y-%m-%d_%H%i%s'), ".csv' FIELDS
ENCLOSED BY '\"' TERMINATED BY ';' ESCAPED BY '\"' LINES TERMINATED BY
'\r\n';");

mysql> PREPARE statement FROM @selInOutfileCmd;

mysql> EXECUTE statement;
```

The first `SET` statement constructs a string, which contains a `SELECT` statement. While it is not allowed to use variables for statements directly, you can construct a string that contains a statement and use variables for this. With the next two lines, you prepare a statement from the string and execute it.

# Handling NULL values

Without further handling, `NULL` values in the data you export using the previous statement would show up as "N in the resulting file. This combination is not recognized, for example, by Microsoft Excel, which breaks the file (for typical usage). To prevent this, you need to replace `NULL` entries by appropriate values. Assuming that the table `sample.table1` consists of a numeric column `a` and a character column `b`, you should use the following statement:

```
mysql> SELECT IFNULL(a, 0), IFNULL(b, "NULL") FROM sample.table1 INTO
OUTFILE 'C:/target.csv' FIELDS ENCLOSED BY '"' TERMINATED BY ';' ESCAPED
BY '"' LINES TERMINATED BY '\r\n';
```

The downside to this approach is that you have to list all fields in which a `NULL` value might occur.

# Handling line breaks

If you try to export values that contain the same character combination used for line termination in the `SELECT ... INTO OUTFILE` statement, MySQL will try to escape the character combination with the characters defined by the `ESCAPED BY` clause. However, this will not always work the way it is intended. You will typically define \r\n as the line separators. With this constellation, values that contain a simple line break \n will not cause problems, as they are exported without any conversion and can be imported to Microsoft Excel flawlessly. If your values happen to contain a combination of carriage return and line feed, the \r\n characters will be prepended with an escape character ("\r\n), but still the target file cannot be imported correctly. Therefore, you need to convert the full line breaks to simple line breaks:

```
mysql> SELECT a, REPLACE(b, '\r\n', '\n') FROM sample.table1 INTO OUTFILE
'C:/target.csv' FIELDS ENCLOSED BY '"' TERMINATED BY ';' ESCAPED BY '"'
LINES TERMINATED BY '\r\n';
```

With this statement, you will export only line breaks \n, which are typically accepted for import by other programs.

# Including headers

For better understanding, you might want to include headers in your target file. You can do so by using a `UNION` construct:

```
mysql> (SELECT 'Column a', 'Column b') UNION ALL (SELECT * FROM sample.
table1 INTO OUTFILE 'C:/target.csv' FIELDS ENCLOSED BY '"' TERMINATED BY
';' ESCAPED BY '"' LINES TERMINATED BY '\r\n');
```

The resulting file will contain an additional first line with the given headers from the first `SELECT` clause.

# Exporting data to a custom file format

You sometimes have the task to export data in a special format in order to fulfill the requirements of the recipient of the data. In this recipe, we will show you one way to export data in a format that is beyond the possibilities of the SELECT ... INTO OUTFILE format options.

In the following recipe, we will show you how to create an export file in a hypothetical format. This includes the name of the file, a time stamp, a short description of the file's content, and the number of data rows contained in the file in the first four lines. The data portion starts with a header line with names for all columns followed by the actual data rows. Every data row should start with a prefix consisting of the hash character (#), the line number, a colon, and a space. This prefix is followed by the data items separated by pipe (|) characters. Each line should end with a dollar sign ($) (and the line break, of course).

This format is used as an example, but the steps involved can be adapted to more complex file formats if necessary.

## Getting ready

As in the previous recipe, we will need an account with appropriate permissions (FILE), a SQL client, and a file name for the target file. Again, we will assume an account named sample_install and we will export data from table sample.table2 (which consists of three columns c1, c2, and c3) to a file C:/target.txt in the format mentioned previously. We also propose to create a file customExport.sql for the SQL commands using an editor to store the SQL commands.

## How to do it...

1. Create a new script named customExport.sql and add the following statements to it:

```
SET @filename := 'Filename: C:/target.txt';
SET @description := 'Description: This is a test export from
sample.table2 with columns c1, c2, and c3';
SELECT NOW() INTO @timestamp;
SELECT COUNT(*) FROM sample.table2 INTO @rowcount;
SET @rows := CONCAT('Row count: ', @rowcount);
SET @header := '#Row Nr: Column c1 | Column c2 | Column c3 $';
SET @counter := 0;
SELECT @filename
    UNION SELECT @description
    UNION SELECT @timestamp
    UNION SELECT @rows
    UNION SELECT @header
```

```
UNION SELECT CONCAT('#',
    @counter := @counter + 1,
    ': ',
    CONCAT_WS(' | ', c1, c2, c3),
    ' $')
FROM sample.table2
INTO OUTFILE 'C:/target.txt';
```

2. Connect to the database using the `sample_install` account.

3. Execute the SQL statements from `customExport.sql` (as an alternative to copying the statements to your SQL client, you could also execute the statements in the file using `mysql`'s `source` command)

4. The target file will look as follows:

```
Filename: C:/target.txt
Description: This is a test export from sample.table2 with columns
c1, c2, and c3
2009-06-14 13:25:05
Row count: 3
#Row Nr: Column c1 | Column c2 | Column c3 $
#1: 209 | Some text in my test data | Some more text $
#2: 308 | Next test text for testing | Text to test $
#3: 406 | The quick brown fox jumps | Really? $
```

## How it works...

Although this solution takes some commands, they are divided into a preparation part (the first seven commands that define the user variables) and the actual export command. Of course, you could minimize the number of statements by omitting the user variables, but the resulting statement would be somewhat bulky.

The preparation part simply defines some user variables for later reference. The final `SELECT` command consists of a `UNION` construct, which basically concatenates the rows that are required for the file header. The actual data from the table is prepared by the following `SELECT` clause:

```
SELECT CONCAT('#', @counter := @counter + 1, ': ', CONCAT_WS(' | ',
c1, c2, c3), ' $') FROM sample.table2
```

The `CONCAT` statement concatenates its parameters; so let us have a look at the statement's parts. The clause `'#', @counter := @counter + 1, ': '` forms the required line number portion of the rows. The variable `@counter` gets incremented for every row, which produces the intended line number. The following `CONCAT_WS` will also concatenate the given values, but the first parameter is used as a separator character (`_WS` stands for *with separator*). For every row, this will result in a string with the values of columns (`c1`, `c2`, and `c3`) separated by the pipe character. With a closing dollar sign as the final parameter, the first `CONCAT` is closed.

While this approach allows for the creation of rather complex file formats, it is not suitable for every situation. For advanced requirements, we encourage the use of other programming techniques beyond the SQL commands (for example, reading and processing the data using a scripting language). This holds especially true when the target file has to be in XML format.

 For advanced formatting capabilities, consider exporting your data in XML format (using `mysqldump --xml`) and processing the resulting file using an XSLT processor!

## There's more...

Please note that using parentheses on the UNION to clarify the separation of the different SELECT statements might lead to unexpected problems: the INTO OUTFILE clause has to be attached to the last SELECT statement of a UNION construct. A statement like SELECT (...) UNION (SELECT ...) INTO OUTFILE ... will **not** work, while SELECT (...) UNION (SELECT ... INTO OUTFILE) does. While this might not seem too intuitive, it is a well documented behavior and not a bug.

# Using stored procedures to export repeatedly

In some situations, you will need data exports on a regular basis, for example, to provide an external system with data for daily reports. One possibility is to define a scheduled task (for Windows) or a *cron* job (for Unix/Linux systems) to execute an appropriate export SQL script every day. The drawback of this is that if you need to change the internal data structures of your database, it is not sufficient to change only the database content, but you also have to adapt the export SQL script definition of your export job simultaneously.

To resolve this problem, you could define a stored procedure. This procedure defines a stable interface by which the external job can trigger the export. The definition of the actual steps necessary to perform the export is encapsulated by the stored procedure that is inside the database. Thus, all the necessary changes in case of structural changes are restricted to the database itself.

In this recipe, we will show you an example of how this works by defining a stored procedure that performs the same export task as in the previous recipe.

Stored procedures are only available since MySQL version 5.0. Earlier versions do not support this feature.

## Getting ready

To step through this recipe, you basically need the same prerequisites as in the previous recipe *Exporting data to a custom file format*. In addition, you need a user account that has the CREATE ROUTINE privilege to define a stored procedure. Finally, you have to make sure that the account used for the external job has the EXECUTE privilege. We will use the sample_install and sample_guest accounts here, assuming that they have the appropriate privileges.

## How to do it...

1. Create a stored procedure by connecting to MySQL (using mysql and the sample_install account) and entering the following statements:

```
mysql> delimiter //
mysql> CREATE PROCEDURE sample.export_table2() READS SQL DATA
    -> BEGIN
    ->    SET @filename := 'Filename: C:/target.txt';
    ->    SET @description := 'Description: This is a test export
          from sample.table2 with columns c1, c2, and c3';
    ->    SELECT NOW() INTO @timestamp;
    ->    SELECT COUNT(*) FROM sample.table2 INTO @rowcount;
    ->    SET @rows := CONCAT('Row count: ', @rowcount);
    ->    SET @header := '#Row Nr: Column c1 | Column c2 | Column
          c3 $';
    ->    SET @counter := 0;
    ->    SELECT @filename
    ->          UNION SELECT @description
    ->          UNION SELECT @timestamp
    ->          UNION SELECT @rows
    ->          UNION SELECT @header
    ->    UNION SELECT CONCAT('#',
    ->                @counter := @counter + 1,
    ->          ': ',
    ->             CONCAT_WS(' | ', c1, c2, c3),
```

```
      ->                      ' $')
      ->            FROM sample.table2
      ->                INTO OUTFILE 'C:/target.txt';
      -> END //
Query OK, 0 rows affected (0.00 sec)


mysql> delimiter ;
mysql>
```

2. Call the stored procedure by executing the following command using the `sample_guest` account:

```
mysql> CALL sample.export_table2();
Query OK, 0 rows affected (0.01 sec)
```

## How it works...

The steps discussed in the aforementioned section are pretty straightforward. In step 1, we create a stored procedure that consists of the very same commands as presented in the previous recipe *Exporting data to a custom file format*. In step 2, this newly created procedure is called from a different account.

The first and last command of step 1 is the `delimiter //` statement, which is necessary to define a stored procedure with more than one statement. It orders the `mysql` client not to interpret the semicolon as the end of a command, but to consider `//` as the end of a statement. With this we can use semicolons inside the procedure body, which would otherwise have caused `mysql` to send the (yet unfinished) command to the server, thus causing a syntax error. Because of the changed delimiter, we have to close the procedure definition by `END //` (instead of `END;`). Also, as we do not want to keep the changed delimiter longer than necessary, we revert this to the original form (semicolon) in the next line with the closing `delimiter ;` statement. The `READS SQL DATA` portion of the `CREATE TABLE` command is only instructive and has no implications for the way the procedure is executed.

One advantage of this approach is that Step 2 can be repeated often without having to enter rather complex export statements again and again.

Another benefit is that the changes made to the database structure can be hidden from the user of the procedure. If, for example, column `c1` needs to be renamed to `foo`, you simply need to adapt the stored procedure accordingly by replacing the `CONCAT_WS` portion by `CONCAT_WS(' | ', foo, c2, c3)`.

Finally, this solution makes it possible to provide the ability to export data to a file without having to grant the `FILE` privilege to the respective account. Granting the `FILE` privilege to normal users is widely considered a security issue, as this privilege allows access to the host file system from the context of the MySQL database server process. Using the aforementioned stored procedure, the account that calls the routine does not need to have the FILE privilege attached, as the statements are executed in the security context of the *creator* of the routine (in our example: sample_install).

 When defining a stored procedure in MySQL, the procedure is by default executed with the privileges of the definer of the procedure. If you want to apply the privileges of the invoker instead, you have to add a SQL SECURITY INVOKER clause to the CREATE PROCEDURE statement. The default value is SQL SECURITY DEFINER.

With this arrangement, sample_guest is able to export data to files (using predefined stored procedures), but is not allowed to execute SELECT ... INTO OUTFILE statements on its own.

## There's more...

The code example from the recipe exports data to a predefined file. Anyone who calls the routine has to make sure that the target file C:/target.txt does not exist. In some situations, this restriction is not acceptable. Using parameters, it is possible to pass the name of the target file as a parameter. Because the file name in the INTO OUTFILE clause has to be a literal value, we have to use the approach mentioned previously of constructing the command in a string value, preparing a statement from this, and executing it:

```
mysql> delimiter //
mysql> CREATE PROCEDURE sample.export_table2_FileAsParam(IN file
CHAR(255)) READS SQL DATA
    -> BEGIN
    ->    SET @filename := CONCAT('Filename: ', @file);
    ->    SET @description := 'Description: This is a test export from
             sample.table2 with columns c1, c2, and c3';
    ->    SELECT NOW() INTO @timestamp;
    ->    SELECT COUNT(*) FROM sample.table2 INTO @rowcount;
    ->    SET @rows := CONCAT('Row count: ', @rowcount);
    ->    SET @header := '#Row Nr: Column c1 | Column c2 | Column c3 $';
    ->    SET @command = CONCAT("SELECT @filename
    ">          UNION SELECT @description
    ">          UNION SELECT @timestamp
    ">          UNION SELECT @rows
    ">          UNION SELECT @header
    ">     UNION SELECT CONCAT('#',
    ">              @counter := @counter + 1,
```

```
">              ': ',
">                 CONCAT_WS(' | ', c1, c2, c3),
">                    ' $')
">              FROM sample.table2
">                 INTO OUTFILE '", file, "';");
->    SET @counter := 0;
->    PREPARE statement FROM @command;
->    EXECUTE statement;
->    END //
Query OK, 0 rows affected (0.00 sec)

mysql> delimiter ;
```

This routine allows passing the file name when calling it:

```
mysql> call sample.export_table2_FileAsParam("C:/data.out");
Query OK, 0 rows affected (0.00 sec)
```

# Importing data from a simple CSV file

A common task when working with databases is to import data from different sources. Unfortunately, this data will typically not be provided as a convenient set of well-formed SQL statements that you can simply run against your database. Therefore, here you will have to deal with data in a different format.

As a common denominator, **character-separated values (CSV)** are still a prevalent way of exchanging data. In this chapter, we will show you how to import data stored in CSV files. As a typical example, we will use the file format *Microsoft Excel* produces when storing files using the *.CSV file type.

This recipe is the counterpart of the *Exporting data to a simple CSV file* recipe in this chapter.

## Getting ready

To step through this recipe, we will definitely need a file to import (here: C:/source.csv) and a table to import the data into (here: sample.table1). The source file and target table have to have a matching format concerning the number of columns and the type of data stored in them. Furthermore, an account with INSERT and FILE privileges is required; we will assume an account sample_install in this recipe.

The source file has to be located on the machine that runs your MySQL server, not on the client side!

## How to do it...

1. Connect to the database using the `sample_install` account.
2. Issue the following SQL command:

```
mysql> LOAD DATA INFILE 'C:/source.csv' INTO TABLE sample.table1
FIELDS ENCLOSED BY '"' TERMINATED BY ';' ESCAPED BY '"' LINES
TERMINATED BY '\r\n';
Query OK, 20 rows affected (0.06 sec)
Records: 20  Deleted: 0  Skipped: 0  Warnings: 0
```

## How it works...

The `LOAD DATA INFILE` command works analogous to the `SELECT ... INTO OUTFILE` command discussed in the previous recipes, but as a means for importing data rather than exporting. The format options available for both commands are identical, so you can typically import data exported by a `SELECT ... INTO OUTFILE` statement using a `LOAD DATA INFILE` command with the same format options.

As most files consist of lines terminated by a sequence of a carriage return and a line feed character, we use the `LINES TERMINATED BY '\r\n'` option. The choice of the semicolon character—as a separator for different fields of every line (`TERMINATED BY ';'`)—is mainly due to the fact that *Excel* uses this format. If you happen to receive CSV files that, for example, use a comma instead, you have to adjust this accordingly.

The term `FIELDS ENCLOSED BY '"'` tells the import to look for double quotes at the start of every field imported. If there is one, the field is considered to end at the next double quote. To be able to have double quotes inside a field value, we define an escape character (`ESCAPED BY '"'`). With this constellation, a sequence of two double quotes is not treated as the end of the field, but as a double-quote character as part of the value.

## There's more...

The data is read from the file using the default character set of the database. If the file uses a different character encoding, you can specify this by adding a `CHARACTER SET` clause after the table definition (`LOAD DATA INFILE ... INTO TABLE sample.table1 CHARACTER SET utf8;`). Please note that the character sets `ucs2`, `utf16`, and `utf32` are not supported (as of MySQL version 5.1.35).

## See also

▸  *Exporting data to a simple CSV file*

# Importing data from custom file formats

In the previous recipe *Importing data from a simple CSV file*, we discussed a way of importing data from a nicely formatted file. Unfortunately, you sometimes have to deal with far less convenient data sources. In this recipe, we will present some more advanced topics of importing data from files with a less strict structure.

Obviously, it is not possible to present a universal recipe for every file format imaginable, so we will use an example that covers some of the common problems one has to tackle when importing data from custom files. For this, we will refer to the same hypothetical format as in *Export data to a custom file format*, which defines four initial lines (containing name of the file, a time stamp, a description, and the number of rows), a header line with the name of the columns, and subsequently the rows with the actual data to import. Each data row starts with a hash character (#), the line number, a colon, and a space. The data values that follow the row number are separated by a pipe (|) character and the row closes with a dollar sign ($).

## Getting ready

Again, the account used in the recipe needs the FILE privilege (besides the INSERT permission for the table the data should be imported into). With a SQL client, a file with the appropriate format, and a table as the import target, we are ready to go. As in previous recipes, we use `sample_install` as the account name, `C:/source.txt` as the source file, and `sample.table2` (consisting of three columns c1, c2, and c3) as the target table. We assume the source file to have the following content:

```
Filename: C:/source.txt
Description: This is a file for test import to sample.table2, columns
c1, c2, and c3
2009-06-14 13:25:05
Row count: 3
#Row Nr: Column c1 | Column c2 | Column c3 $
#1: 209 | Some text in my test data | Some more text $
#2: 308 | Next test text for testing | Text to test $
#3: 406 | "A water | pipe" | Really? $
```

## How to do it...

1.  Connect your favorite client (for example, the `mysql` command-line client) to your MySQL server using the `sample_install` account.

2. Execute the following SQL command:

```
mysql> LOAD DATA INFILE "C:/source.txt"
    ->    INTO TABLE sample.table2
    ->    FIELDS TERMINATED BY ' | '
    ->    OPTIONALLY ENCLOSED BY '"'
    ->    LINES STARTING BY ':'
    ->    TERMINATED BY '\r\n'
    ->    IGNORE 5 LINES
    ->    SET c3=TRIM(TRAILING ' $' FROM c3);
Query OK, 3 rows affected (0.05 sec)
Records: 3  Deleted: 0  Skipped: 0  Warnings: 0
```

## How it works...

Let us dissect the above statement by having a look at the source file: first of all, we want to import data from the file `C:\source.txt` into the table `sample.table2`, which is represented by the first two lines (`LOAD DATA INFILE … INTO TABLE …`).

At the top of the file, we have five lines (the initial four lines with information about the file plus the header) that should not be imported into the target table. To achieve this, the `IGNORE 5 lines` option is added.

The remaining lines are prefixed with a hash character, the row number, and a colon. This part of every line has to be ignored, which is what the `LINES STARTING BY ':'` option does: it tells MySQL to ignore the first colon of the line and any character before it. By doing this, the row number prefix is skipped.

After the prefix, the lines contain the actual values, separated by pipe characters. The `FIELDS TERMINATED BY ' | '` option tells MySQL how to identify a field separator. With the additional setting `OPTIONALLY ENCLOSED BY '"'`, the value itself might contain this field separator sequence—if the whole value is enclosed by double quotes (this is the case in the last row of the sample file).

At this point, there is only one problem left: the lines end with a dollar sign, which is not part of the last value. An intuitive approach would be to include this character in the line termination sequence, which means to use `$\r\n` as a line ending (instead of `\r\n`). Unfortunately, this definition of a line end does not work as expected for our example, as it would break the interpretation of the first five lines, which are not terminated the same way. As a result, the first six lines would be considered as one single line by the import because only the sixth line actually ends with a character sequence of `$\r\n`. To be able to explicitly exclude the header lines from the import, we have to rely on the "traditional" line ending defined by the `[LINES] TERMINATED BY '\r\n'` option.

Hence, the options for defining the field separators, and the beginning and termination of a line do not allow us to get rid of the closing dollar sign. Thus it is considered part of the last value, which is assigned to column $c3$. To finally get rid of this postfix, the `SET` clause of the `LOAD DATA INFILE` command comes in handy, which allows to clearly define the values that are assigned to the columns in the target table. The closing option `SET c3=TRIM(TRAILING ' $' FROM c3);` defines a way to strip the unwanted postfix from the last field.

If we put it all together, the import works as intended:

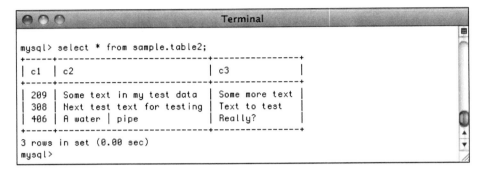

```
mysql> select * from sample.table2;
+-----+-----------------------------+----------------+
| c1  | c2                          | c3             |
+-----+-----------------------------+----------------+
| 209 | Some text in my test data   | Some more text |
| 308 | Next test text for testing  | Text to test   |
| 406 | A water | pipe              | Really?        |
+-----+-----------------------------+----------------+
3 rows in set (0.00 sec)
mysql>
```

## There's more...

As with exporting data, it is recommended to consider using an external programming language to import more complex data structures into MySQL. While it is possible to import rather sophisticated file formats using MySQL commands as well, it is often far more efficient to have a full-blown programming language at hand to solve the task of parsing input files. This is most notably the case when it comes to XML files.

 For importing data from XML files, consider using an XSLT processor to produce corresponding SQL commands!

## See also

- ▶ *Importing data from a simple CSV file*
- ▶ *Exporting data to a custom file format*

# Inserting new data and updating data if it already exists

Manipulating data in a database is part of everyday work and the basic SQL means of `INSERT`, `UPDATE`, and `DELETE` make this a pretty straightforward, almost trivial task—but is this always true?

When considering data manipulation, most of the time we think of a situation where we know the content of the database. With this information, it is usually pretty easy to find a way of changing the data the way you intend to. But what if you have to change data in circumstances where you do not know the actual database content beforehand?

You might answer: "Well, then look at your data before changing it!" Unfortunately, you do not always have this option. Think of distributed installations of any software that includes a database. If you have to design an update option for this software (and the respective databases), you might easily come to a situation where you simply do not know about the actual database content.

One example of a problem arising in these cases is the question of whether to insert or to update data: "Does the data in question already (partially) exist?" Let us assume a database table `config` that stores configuration settings. It holds key-value pairs, with `name` being the name (and thus the key) of the setting and `value` its value. This table exists in different database installations, one for every branch office of your company. Your task is to create an update package to set a uniform upper limit of 25% for the price discount that is allowed in your sales software. If no such limit has been defined yet, there is no respective entry in the `config` table, and you have to **insert** a new record. If the limit, however, has been set before (for example by the local manager), the entry does already exist, in which case you have to **update** it to hold the new value.

While the update of a potentially existing entry does not pose a problem, an `INSERT` statement that violates uniqueness constraints will simply cause an error. This is, however, typically not acceptable in an automated update procedure. The following recipe will show you how to solve this problem with only one SQL command.

## Getting ready

Besides a running MySQL server, a SQL client, and an account with appropriate user rights (`INSERT`, `UPDATE`), we need a table to update. In the earlier example, we assumed a table named `sample.config` with two character columns `name` and `value`. The `name` column is defined as the primary key:

```
CREATE TABLE sample.config (
    name VARCHAR(64) PRIMARY KEY,
    value VARCHAR(64));
```

## How to do it...

1.  Connect to your database using your SQL client

2.  Execute the following command:

```
mysql> INSERT INTO sample.config VALUES ("maxPriceDiscount",
"25%") ON DUPLICATE KEY UPDATE value='25%';

Query OK, 1 row affected (0.05 sec)
```

## How it works...

This command is easily explained because it simply does what it says: it inserts a new row in the table using the given values, as long as this does not cause a duplicate entry in either the primary key or another unique index. If a duplicate record exists, the existing row is updated according to the clauses defined after ON DUPLICATE KEY UPDATE.

While it is sometimes tedious to enter some of the data and columns two times (once for the INSERT and a second time for the UPDATE), this statement allows for a lot of flexibility when it comes to the manipulation of potentially existing data.

Please note that when executing the above statement, the result differs slightly with respect to the number of affected rows, depending on the actual data present in the database: When the record does not exist yet, it is inserted, which results in one affected row. But if the record is updated rather than inserted, it reports **two** affected rows instead, even if only one row gets updated.

## There's more...

The INSERT INTO … ON DUPLICATE UPDATE construct does not work when there is no UNIQUE or PRIMARY KEY defined on the target table. If you have to provide the same semantics without having appropriate key definitions in place, it is recommended to use the techniques discussed in the next recipe.

## See also

▶   *Inserting data based on existing database content*

# Inserting data based on existing database content

In the previous recipe *Inserting new data and updating data if it already exists*, we discussed a method to either insert or update records depending on whether the records already exist in the database. A similar problem arises when you need to insert data to your database, but the data to insert depends on the data in your database.

As an example, consider a situation in which you need to insert a record with a certain message into a table `logMsgs`, but the message itself should be different depending on the current system language that is stored in a configuration table (`config`).

It is fairly easy to achieve a similar behavior for an UPDATE statement because this supports a WHERE clause that can be used to only perform an update if a certain precondition is met:

```
UPDATE logMsgs SET message=
   CONCAT('Last update: ', NOW()) WHERE EXISTS
   (SELECT value FROM config WHERE
    name='lang' AND value = 'en');
UPDATE logMsgs SET message=
   CONCAT('Letztes Update: ', NOW()) WHERE EXISTS
   (SELECT value FROM config WHERE
    name='lang' AND value = 'de');
UPDATE logMsgs SET message=
   CONCAT('Actualisation derniere: ', NOW()) WHERE EXISTS
   (SELECT value FROM config WHERE
    name='lang' AND value = 'fr');
```

Unfortunately, this approach is not applicable to INSERT commands, as these do not support a WHERE clause. Despite this missing option, the following recipe describes a method to make INSERT statements execute only if an appropriate precondition in the database is met.

## Getting ready

As before, we assume a database, a SQL client (`mysql`), and a MySQL user with sufficient privileges (INSERT and SELECT in this case). Additionally, we need a table to insert data into (here: `logMsgs`) and a configuration table `config` (please refer to the previous recipe for details).

## How to do it...

1. Connect to your database using your SQL client.

2. Execute the following SQL commands:

```
mysql> INSERT INTO sample.logMsgs(message)
    -> SELECT CONCAT('Last update: ', NOW())
    -> FROM sample.config WHERE name='lang' AND value='en';
Query OK, 0 rows affected (0.00 sec)
Records: 0  Duplicates: 0  Warnings: 0


mysql> INSERT INTO sample.logMsgs(message)
    -> SELECT CONCAT('Letztes Update: ', NOW())
    -> FROM sample.config WHERE name='lang' AND value='de';
Query OK, 1 row affected (0.05 sec)
Records: 1  Duplicates: 0  Warnings: 0


mysql> INSERT INTO sample.logMsgs(message)
    -> SELECT CONCAT('Dernière actualisation: ', NOW())
    -> FROM sample.config WHERE name='lang' AND value='fr';
Query OK, 0 rows affected (0.00 sec)
Records: 0  Duplicates: 0  Warnings: 0
```

## How it works...

Our goal is to have an INSERT statement take into account the present language stored in the database. The trick to do so is to use a SELECT statement as input for the INSERT. The SELECT command provides a WHERE clause, so you can use a condition that only matches for the respective language. One restriction of this solution is that you can only insert one record at a time, so the size of scripts might grow considerably if you have to insert lots of data and/or have to cover many alternatives.

## There's more...

If you have more than just a few values to insert, it is more convenient to have the data in one place rather than distributed over several individual INSERT statements. In this case, it might make sense to consolidate the data by putting it inside a **temporary table**; the final INSERT statement uses this temporary table to select the appropriate data rows for insertion into the target table. The downside of this approach is that the user needs the CREATE TEMPORARY TABLES privilege, but it typically compensates with much cleaner scripts:

```
Terminal
mysql> CREATE TEMPORARY TABLE sample.temp_logMsgs
    -> (message VARCHAR(128), lang CHAR(2));
Query OK, 0 rows affected (0.03 sec)

mysql> INSERT INTO sample.temp_logMsgs VALUES
    -> (CONCAT('Last update: ', NOW()), 'en'),
    -> ('Version number: 2.1.0', 'en'),
    -> (CONCAT('Letztes Update: ', NOW()), 'de'),
    -> ('Versionsnummer: 2.1.0', 'de'),
    -> (CONCAT('Actualisation derniere: ', NOW()), 'fr'),
    -> ('Numero de version: 2.1.0', 'fr');
Query OK, 6 rows affected (0.01 sec)
Records: 6  Duplicates: 0  Warnings: 0

mysql> INSERT INTO sample.logMsgs
    -> SELECT message FROM sample.temp_logMsgs WHERE lang=
    -> (SELECT value FROM sample.config WHERE name='lang');
Query OK, 2 rows affected (0.05 sec)
Records: 2  Duplicates: 0  Warnings: 0

mysql> DROP TEMPORARY TABLE sample.temp_logMsgs;
Query OK, 0 rows affected (0.02 sec)

mysql> SELECT * FROM sample.logMsgs;
+---------------------------------+
| message                         |
+---------------------------------+
| Last update: 2009-06-14 23:52:47 |
| Version number: 2.1.0           |
+---------------------------------+
2 rows in set (0.00 sec)

mysql>
```

After creating the temporary table with the first statement, we insert data into the table with the following INSERT statement. The next statement inserts the appropriate data into the target table sample.logMsgs by selecting the appropriate data from the temporary data that matches the language entry from the config table. The temporary table is then removed again. The final SELECT statement is solely for checking the results of the operation.

## See also

▸   *Inserting new data and updating data if it already exists*

# Deleting all data from large tables

Almost everyone who works with databases experiences the constant growth of the data stored in their database and it is typically well beyond the initial estimates. Because of that you often end up with rather large data sets. Another common observation is that in most databases, there are some tables that have a special tendency to grow especially big.

If a table's size reaches a virtual threshold (which is hard to define, as it depends heavily on the access patterns and the data structures), it gets harder and harder to maintain and performance degradation might occur. From a certain point on, it is even difficult to get rid of data in the table again, as the sheer number of records makes deletion a pretty expensive task. This particularly holds true for storage engines with **Multi-Version Concurrency Control (MVCC)**: if you order the database to delete data from the table, it must not be deleted right away because you might still roll back the deletion. So even while the deletion was initiated, a concurrent query on the table still has to be able to see all the records (depending on the transaction isolation level). To achieve this, the storage engine will only mark the records as deleted, but the actual deletion takes place after the operation is committed and all other transactions that access this table are closed as well.

If you have to deal with large data sets, the most difficult task is to operate on the production system while other processes concurrently work on the data. In these circumstances, you have to keep the duration of your maintenance operations as low as possible in order to minimize the impact on the running system. As the deletion of data from a large table (typically starting at several millions of rows) might take quite some time, the following recipe shows a way of minimizing the duration of this operation in order to reduce side effects (like locking effects or performance degradation).

## Getting ready

Besides a user account with appropriate privileges (DELETE), you need a sufficiently large table to delete data from.

 For this recipe, we will use the employees database, which is an example database available from MySQL: http://dev.mysql.com/doc/employee/en/employee.html.

This database provides some tables with sensible data and some pretty large tables, the largest having more than 2.8 million records.

We assume that the Employees database was installed with an InnoDB storage engine enabled. To delete all rows of the largest table employees.salaries in a quick way, please read on.

## How to do it...

1. Connect to your database.
2. Enter the following SQL command:

```
mysql> TRUNCATE TABLE employees.salaries;
Query OK, 0 rows affected (0.16 sec)
```

## How it works...

The `TRUNCATE TABLE` command is a rather fast way of deleting all data from a table. For tables that are not referenced by Foreign key constraints (more on that later), the command basically drops the table temporarily and recreates the table with the same structure as before. This operation has basically a constant time characteristic—the amount of data stored inside the table does not have any effect in the time needed for the `TRUNCATE` command.

 Before MySQL 5.0.3, the `TRUNCATE TABLE` statement for InnoDB tables was always equivalent to a `DELETE` statement, regardless of whether Foreign key constraints exist or not. To take advantage of the speed improvements, you have to use MySQL 5.0.3 or later.

In comparison to a classical `DELETE FROM employees.salaries;` operation, the reduction in time needed is striking:

| Operation | Time needed |
| --- | --- |
| TRUNCATE TABLE | 0.16 sec |
| DELETE | 1 min 31.55 sec |

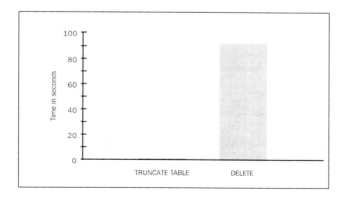

The TRUNCATE TABLE command takes only a fraction of the time needed for the DELETE. However, there are some caveats.

First of all, the TRUNCATE command will only have the speed advantage on InnoDB tables if the table is not referenced by any Foreign key constraints. But if the table *is* referenced by Foreign keys, the TRUNCATE TABLE command is equivalent to executing a DELETE statement with no WHERE clause, also eliminating all speed differences:

```
mysql> CREATE TABLE employees.salaries_referencer (
    -> emp_no       INT,
    -> from_date    DATE,
    -> CONSTRAINT   salaries_fk
    -> FOREIGN KEY (emp_no, from_date)
    -> REFERENCES   salaries (emp_no, from_date)
    -> ON DELETE RESTRICT);
Query OK, 0 rows affected (0.08 sec)


mysql> TRUNCATE TABLE employees.salaries;
Query OK, 0 rows affected (1 min 33.44 sec)
```

| Operation | Time needed |
|---|---|
| TRUNCATE TABLE (with foreign key ref) | 1 min 33.44 sec |
| DELETE | 1 min 32.96 sec |

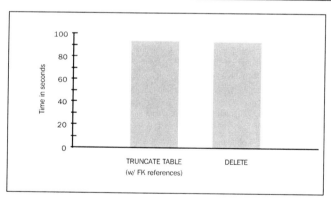

Furthermore, the TRUNCATE statement requires the DROP privilege (before MySQL 5.1.16, it only requires the DELETE permission), which forbids use of this command for some users.

And finally, TRUNCATE is not a transaction-safe command. If you execute a TRUNCATE statement, you will not be able to perform a rollback on this operation any more, and any open operation from the current transaction gets automatically committed as well. This is a characteristic that disqualifies this statement for situations in which the possibility of performing a rollback is mandatory; you will have to stick with the (much slower) DELETE in these cases.

## There's more...

As we have seen, TRUNCATE TABLE only has performance advantages if there is no Foreign key reference to the table that is to be deleted. Here we will discuss how to use the speed improvements even in case of existing references.

### Temporarily disabling Foreign key constraints

To make use of the increased speed of TRUNCATE TABLE although the target table is referenced via Foreign keys, you could temporarily remove the Foreign key constraints, use the TRUNCATE TABLE command, and reestablish the references afterwards. Using the above example of a table salaries_referencer that references salaries, you could use the following sequence:

```
mysql> ALTER TABLE employees.salaries_referencer
    -> DROP FOREIGN KEY salaries_fk;
Query OK, 0 rows affected (0.19 sec)
Records: 0  Duplicates: 0  Warnings: 0


mysql> TRUNCATE TABLE employees.salaries;
Query OK, 0 rows affected (0.44 sec)


mysql> ALTER TABLE employees.salaries_referencer
    -> ADD CONSTRAINT salaries_fk
    -> FOREIGN KEY (emp_no, from_date)
    -> REFERENCES salaries (emp_no, from_date)
    -> ON DELETE RESTRICT;
Query OK, 0 rows affected (0.14 sec)
Records: 0  Duplicates: 0  Warnings: 0
```

With this sequence, you temporarily disable the Foreign key constraints to have TRUNCATE TABLE use the faster deletion method. Beware, however, that this method might also lead to problems when the deletion of the table produces "loose ends". If the referencing table salaries.referencer holds records that referenced the now empty target table salaries, the creation of the Foreign key constraints will fail:

```
mysql> ALTER TABLE employees.salaries_referencer
    -> ADD CONSTRAINT salaries_fk
    -> FOREIGN KEY (emp_no, from_date)
    -> REFERENCES salaries (emp_no, from_date)
    -> ON DELETE RESTRICT;
ERROR 1452 (23000): Cannot add or update a child row: a foreign key constraint f
ails (`employees`.`#sql-828_8`, CONSTRAINT `salaries_fk` FOREIGN KEY (`emp_no`,
`from_date`) REFERENCES `salaries` (`emp_no`, `from_date`))

mysql>
```

Also, keep in mind that this situation might also occur because of concurrent processes, which are able (for the duration of the disabled constraints) to insert data into the tables that violate the intended referential integrity.

As an alternative, you might be tempted to temporarily disable the Foreign key checks by setting foreign_key_checks to zero. While this works regarding the TRUNCATE TABLE performance, it is strongly discouraged to use this option because the Foreign key integrity is not revalidated when the Foreign key checks are enabled again. So you risk inconsistent data with respect to the referential integrity.

# Deleting all but a fragment of a large table's data

In the previous recipe *Deleting all data from large tables*, we discussed a method of quickly removing all data from large tables while avoiding performance hits. But experience shows that you often must not delete all data, but have to retain some records and delete the rest. The TRUNCATE TABLE command does not allow any additional clauses to define which records to delete and which not; it always deletes all entries.

The intuitive solution to this would be to use a normal DELETE command with a WHERE clause that only matches the records to delete. For large tables, this might prove quite an expensive operation (in terms of duration). In this recipe, we will show you how to quickly remove most of the data from large tables while preserving some of the records.

## Getting ready

We again need a MySQL server up and running and a SQL client (like `mysql`). For this recipe, we also need a user account with `SELECT`, `INSERT`, `DELETE`, `DROP`, and `CREATE` privileges for the target database (we will use the `sample_install` user throughout this section). We will furthermore use the Employees sample database in an InnoDB context. This database was introduced in the previous recipe and is available for free on the MySQL website. We will use the largest table `salaries` (with more than 2.8 million records) as the table to delete from. In our example, we will delete all records having a `from_date` before the threshold of `'2002-01-01 00:00:00.0'`.

## How to do it...

1. Connect to the database using a SQL client and the `sample_install` account.
2. Execute the following commands:

```
mysql> use employees;
Database changed
mysql> CREATE TABLE salaries_part
    -> SELECT * FROM salaries
    -> WHERE from_date >= "2002-01-01 00:00:00.0";
Query OK, 140930 rows affected (11.47 sec)
Records: 140930  Duplicates: 0  Warnings: 0

mysql> TRUNCATE TABLE salaries;
Query OK, 0 rows affected (0.05 sec)

mysql> INSERT INTO salaries SELECT * from salaries_part;
Query OK, 140930 rows affected (4.63 sec)
Records: 140930  Duplicates: 0  Warnings: 0

mysql> DROP TABLE salaries_part;
Query OK, 0 rows affected (0.06 sec)
```

## How it works...

For speeding up the deletion of most of the data from a large table, we utilize the speed advantage of the TRUNCATE TABLE statement over a DELETE command. In detail, the steps are as follows:

The initial USE statement is for convenience only, so we do not have to give the employees prefix for every table.

With the next statement (CREATE TABLE ... SELECT * FROM ...), we simply copy the data that should **not** be removed to a newly created table salaries_part.

> Be careful to avoid errors when inverting conditions: to delete all entries before time X, you have to copy all records values later **or equal to** X! If you copy only records later than X, all records exactly at time X would get deleted as well

This table temporarily holds the data while we delete all data from the large salaries table using TRUNCATE in the next step. Afterwards, we simply copy the partial data from the salaries_part table back into the original (now emptied) salaries table. With the final step, we scrap the salaries_part table again, as it is not needed any more.

> You could also create salaries_part as a TEMPORARY table. In this case, you could also skip the final DROP statement. This method is discouraged because it might lead to data loss in case of an error. Think of an error that occurs right after all data was deleted from the original salaries table, but before the data from the temporary table is restored. If the connection is closed, the data from the temporary table is lost. A non-temporary table does not entail this risk.

# There's more...

We will not try to conceal that this approach has some caveats as well. First of all, the user who performs this operation needs some additional privileges like CREATE and DROP, which renders it unusable for many users with only basic permissions.

You should also keep in mind that the use of either CREATE TABLE or TRUNCATE causes an automatic commit of any transaction currently active, which basically means that this approach does not provide any transaction safety.

If concurrent database access is possible during the process of deletion, an additional problem comes up. In the period of time between the TRUNCATE and completion of the INSERT INTO ... SELECT FROM ... statements, the salaries table is empty for any other transaction. You have to make sure that this will not cause any problem. You should use the DELETE approach otherwise, as this will not produce intermediate states in which the database table is completely empty.

And finally, the performance benefit of this approach for InnoDB greatly depends on the speed of the TRUNCATE TABLE statement. However, if there are tables that reference the target table with a Foreign key, the TRUNCATE will be equivalent to a DELETE statement, thus destroying all performance improvements. A solution to this problem is to temporarily remove the Foreign key references. Please refer to the *Temporarily disabling Foreign key constraints* section of the previous recipe for a description of how to achieve this.

## Performance considerations

A comparison between the method presented in this recipe and the use of an ordinary DELETE statement shows that the advantages depend on the amount of data that is not deleted. The more data is copied to the provisional table, the longer the operation takes. The DELETE statement, however, behaves conversely: it gets faster if more data is deleted. From a certain threshold on, the normal deletion will even be faster than the Copy-and-Truncate approach. As a rule of thumb for InnoDB tables, if you delete two thirds of the data or more, you can use the Copy-and-Truncate method; otherwise, a simple DELETE might prove faster. This differs slightly for other storage engines: for MyISAM, the Copy-and-Truncate method typically works faster if more than half of the data is deleted. So when considering a partial deletion of data from large tables, you should take a second to think about which approach fits better for your particular circumstances.

The following two diagrams compare the times needed to partially delete data either using a simple DELETE statement or the Copy-and-Truncate solution for different numbers of rows that are left after the operation. The table originally contains about 2.8 million rows. The first figure shows the comparison for the InnoDB storage engine:

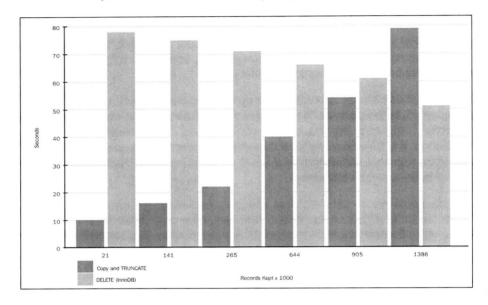

For MyISAM, the Copy-and-Truncate mechanism is faster even for larger numbers of remaining rows:

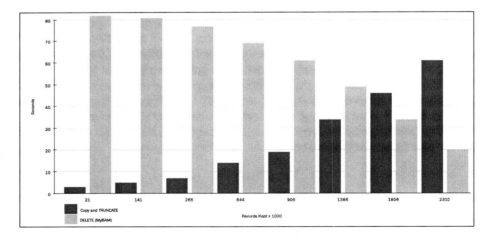

# Deleting all data incrementally from large tables

In the previous recipe *Deleting all but a fragment of a large table's data*, we discussed a method to quickly remove all but a small remainder of records from a large table. The downside of the approach presented there is the fact that during the process of deletion, the table temporarily appears completely empty to an observer. Unfortunately, this is often not acceptable, especially if your database is used in an environment with many parallel processes concurrently accessing the database, particularly the large table discussed here.

On the other hand, the alternative of simply using a DELETE statement is sometimes not acceptable either. A DELETE statement temporarily creates locks on the entries that are deleted. As a result, for the duration of the deletion, a major part of the table gets locked, thus preventing concurrent access to the table by other processes. This typically leads to timeout situations and other errors, as in the following example:

| SQL client 1 | SQL client 2 |
|---|---|
| `DELETE FROM employees.salaries WHERE emp_no < 485000;` | |
| | `INSERT INTO salaries VALUES(10001, 0, "2010-01-01", "2099-12-31");` |
| | `=> ERROR 1205 (HY000): Lock wait timeout exceeded; try restarting transaction` |
| `=> Query OK, 2702167 rows affected (1 min 11.85 sec)` | |

The following recipe shows an approach to deleting data from large tables without blocking access to the table's data for too long, so the deletion can happily be performed despite concurrent tasks simultaneously accessing the very same table.

## Getting ready

As the recipe uses a stored procedure, we again need a user account with the CREATE ROUTINE privilege as well as the DELETE permission for the target database. Throughout the following steps, we will again assume `sample_install` as the user. The example table for deletion is `salaries` from the `employees` sample database (see previous recipes) once more. In our example, we will delete all entries from the table with an employee number `emp_no` below `485000`.

## How to do it...

1. Connect to the database using the `sample_install` account.

2. Enter the following SQL statements:

```
mysql> delimiter //
mysql> CREATE PROCEDURE employees.delete_incrementally()
    -> MODIFIES SQL DATA
    -> BEGIN
    ->   REPEAT
    ->   DELETE FROM employees.salaries
    ->   WHERE emp_no < 485000
    ->   LIMIT 20000;
    ->   UNTIL ROW_COUNT() = 0 END REPEAT;
    -> END //
Query OK, 0 rows affected (0.00 sec)

mysql> delimiter ;

mysql> CALL employees.delete_incrementally();
Query OK, 0 rows affected, 137 warnings (3 min 58.09 sec)
```

## How it works...

The above steps simply create a stored procedure named `delete_incrementally()`, which can be used to delete certain records from the table `salaries`.

The `DELIMITER` statements at start and end of the script are necessary to define a stored procedure, as the statements would otherwise be executed right away. The procedure definition itself is pretty straightforward and basically consists of a `REPEAT ... UNTIL` loop that deletes data from the salaries table according to the given condition (`WHERE emp_no < 485000`). The special part of this `DELETE` statement is the `LIMIT` clause, which defines that no more than 20,000 rows should be deleted. This statement is executed by the loop as long as there are any records left to delete. As soon as the number of records affected by the `DELETE` statement (which can be retrieved using the `ROW_COUNT()` function) is zero, the loop ends.

The trick used by this approach is to distribute the period of time needed to delete the data from one block to multiple intervals.

In sum, the incremental deletion in steps of 20,000 actually is considerably slower than a single DELETE statement, but it is much more cooperative when it comes to concurrent write access to the same data.

The benefit lies within the fact that every single partial DELETE statement does not run very long, which drastically reduces the period of time in which locks are held for parts of the table. This basically eliminates the locking problems between deletion and other processes:

| SQL client 1 | SQL client 2 |
| --- | --- |
| `CALL delete_incrementally();` | |
| | `INSERT INTO salaries VALUES(10001, 0, "2010-01-01", "2099-12-31");` |
| | `=> Query OK, 1 row affected (0.67 sec)` |
| | `UPDATE salaries` |
| | `SET salary=salary+300` |
| | `WHERE emp_no < "490000";` |
| | `Query OK, 2669890 rows affected (59.63 sec)` |
| | `Rows matched: 2669890   Changed: 2669890  Warnings: 0` |
| `=> Query OK, 2702167 rows affected (1 min 11.85 sec)` | |

As you can see, even while the deletion still runs, the parallel modifications to the database work concurrently without lock wait timeout errors or similar problems.

## There's more...

While typically the incremental deletion is slower than one single delete operation, this can change under heavy load for InnoDB tables: parallel transactions work on a snapshot of the current data at the point in time when the transaction starts. This feature is provided by InnoDB's Multi-Version Concurrency Control (MVCC).

With many transactions and large amounts of data, the difference between the snapshots and the deleted data has to be maintained by MySQL. This housekeeping data is kept until the last transaction that was opened before the deletion was completed is closed. The administration of this delta might have negative impact on the overall MySQL performance. With incremental deletion, this delta data typically does not grow as big as with a long running delete statement, which often reduces the performance hit.

 Under heavy load, the incremental deletion approach might actually cause a gain in overall performance.

## See also

- ▸ *Deleting all but a fragment of a large table's data*
- ▸ *Deleting all data from large tables*

# 6
# Monitoring and Analyzing a MySQL Installation

In this chapter, we will discuss some recommendations on how to monitor your MySQL installation and how to analyze possible problems. In detail, the following topics will be covered:

- Checking free InnoDB tablespace
- Establishing alerting mechanisms for low remaining tablespace by using triggers
- Estimating tablespace requirements
- Identifying and changing MySQL variables
- Assessing the overall table count
- Finding the biggest tables
- Finding all columns with a certain name and/or type
- Finding all tables referencing each other

## Introduction

Even if MySQL is easy to set up and requires relatively little maintenance once it is up and running, there are situations in which it is necessary to check certain aspects of MySQL—either to identify and solve certain problems (for example performance problems), or preferably, to prevent trouble in the first place. This chapter will introduce some techniques that might prove useful for maintaining your database, so you have some tools at hand to ensure continuous, problem-free operation of your MySQL installation.

# Checking free InnoDB tablespace

One of the most common problems for database administrators is to deal with the constant data growth most databases will display. You have to keep an eye on the remaining space available to avoid the situation where no space is left to add new data. An out-of-space scenario typically leads to a de facto breakdown of your database.

The default storage engine of MySQL is MyISAM, which stores its data in plain files. For each table, a separate file is created. The file's size is adapted according to the data stored in it. If more data is written to the table, the file gets bigger. In case of data reduction, the freed space can be reclaimed by using the OPTIMIZE TABLE command, which results in a smaller file size. This way, it is a straightforward task to check how much space is left for further data growth: you just have to take a look at the space left on the drive your data (your MyISAM data, specifically) is stored in.

For the alternative storage engine InnoDB, this question is not so easy to answer. The following recipe will show you how to retrieve this information.

## Getting ready

For this recipe, we will need a MySQL user who has SELECT access to all schemata in the MySQL installation. We assume the admin4mysql account is used throughout the following steps.

## How to do it...

1.  Connect to the database using the admin4mysql account.

2.  Enter the following SQL statement:

    ```
    SELECT DATA_FREE/(1024*1024) AS FREE_MB, TABLE_SCHEMA, TABLE_NAME
    FROM  INFORMATION_SCHEMA.TABLES WHERE ENGINE="InnoDB";
    ```

3.  Read the remaining free tablespace (in MBytes) from the results:

```
 ● ● ●                          MySQL Cookbook
+----------+----------------+---------------+
| FREE_MB  | TABLE_SCHEMA   | TABLE_NAME    |
+----------+----------------+---------------+
|  19.0000 | empl3          | employees     |
| 134.0000 | employees      | departments   |
| 134.0000 | employees      | dept_emp      |
| 134.0000 | employees      | dept_manager  |
| 134.0000 | employees      | employees     |
| 134.0000 | employees      | salaries      |
| 134.0000 | employees      | titles        |
| 134.0000 | employees2     | departments   |
| 134.0000 | employees2     | dept_emp      |
| 134.0000 | employees2     | dept_manager  |
| 134.0000 | employees2     | employees     |
| 134.0000 | employees2     | salaries      |
| 134.0000 | employees2     | titles        |
| 134.0000 | sample         | a_table2_ref  |
| 134.0000 | sample         | bar           |
| 134.0000 | sample         | config        |
| 134.0000 | sample         | departments   |
| 134.0000 | sample         | logmsgs       |
| 134.0000 | sample         | table1        |
| 134.0000 | sample         | table1_copy   |
| 134.0000 | sample         | table2        |
| 134.0000 | test           | test1         |
+----------+----------------+---------------+
22 rows in set (1.31 sec)
```

## How it works...

The statement entered in step 2 simply reads the DATA_FREE column from the table INFORMATION_SCHEMA.TABLES and displays it in a convenient way (including a downscaling to show MBytes instead of bytes). For each table in each schema, the remaining free tablespace is shown (in MByte).

As you have noticed, most tables in the above example show the identical value of 134 MBytes. This is due to the fact that all these tables are stored in a shared MySQL tablespace (as defined by the innodb_data_home_dir variable). For most InnoDB installations, this will be the typical setup: all data is stored in a common tablespace, thus all tables will show the identical value for remaining tablespace.

In our example, however, the first table shows a different value. This is because this table was created in a table-specific tablespace, which can be achieved by using the innodb_file_per_table parameter in the MySQL configuration. All tables that are created with this setting are created in separate files. The files are extended in size as needed, but are not shrunk automatically if data is deleted from the table.

The value retrieved by the above recipe shows the size available with the current file sizes (both for shared and file-per-table tablespace). If autoextending tablespaces are used, the remaining space on the file system has to be added to this value to calculate the true available space.

Remaining autoextend space = Free tablespace + Remaining file system space

Autoextending tablespace is in place when the `innodb_file_per_table` setting is used or if the `innodb_data_home_dir` definition includes an autoextend suffix.

 Note that for `innodb_data_home_dir` the default value `ibdata1:10M:autoextend` is used, which means automatic extension is in place!

In these cases, the free tablespace value discussed above is not the only relevant value; you should additionally establish a monitoring for the available space on the disk device the tablespace files are stored on.

 Please note that for both `autoextend` and `innodb_file_per_table` the tablespace will be extended as needed, but once the space is allocated for InnoDB use, it will not be released automatically if less storage is needed.

With `innodb_file_per_table`, unused tablespace can be released by executing an `OPTIMIZE TABLE` command, resulting in smaller tablespace files.

## There's more...

The above approach will only work for MySQL version 5.1.28 or higher, as these versions expose the remaining InnoDB tablespace in the `DATA_FREE` column of `INFORMATION_SCHEMA.TABLES`. To retrieve the data from versions before that, you will have to take a look at the `TABLE_COMMENT` column:

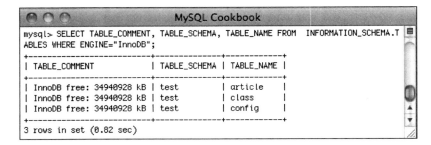

```
mysql> SELECT TABLE_COMMENT, TABLE_SCHEMA, TABLE_NAME FROM INFORMATION_SCHEMA.T
ABLES WHERE ENGINE="InnoDB";
+------------------------+--------------+------------+
| TABLE_COMMENT          | TABLE_SCHEMA | TABLE_NAME |
+------------------------+--------------+------------+
| InnoDB free: 34940928 kB | test       | article    |
| InnoDB free: 34940928 kB | test       | class      |
| InnoDB free: 34940928 kB | test       | config     |
+------------------------+--------------+------------+
3 rows in set (0.82 sec)
```

Note that the values are given in KB, not in bytes as in the `DATA_FREE` column.

An alternative way to retrieve this information without explicitly accessing INFORMATION_ SCHEMA is to use the SHOW TABLE STATUS command, which shows the status (including the comment) for each table in the currently selected schema.

## See also

▶ *Defining an alternative user for administrative tasks*

# Establishing alerting mechanisms for low remaining tablespace by using triggers

In the previous recipe, we introduced a way to read the remaining InnoDB tablespace. While it is important to have this information at hand, in a professional setting you will have to make sure that your database will not run out of tablespace. To avoid having to manually check the remaining tablespace on a regular basis (you have better things to do, especially on weekends and on vacation, right?), an automatic monitoring mechanism is needed.

It is not in the scope of this book to describe how to establish a working monitoring and alerting infrastructure. On most platforms you will have means to monitor for certain conditions and/or alert people or groups responsible for a particular issue. Typical examples for alerting solutions are third-party products like Nagios, Insight Manager, or OpenView, or even the good old e-mail. Alerts can be triggered for example by trigger files, certain system log entries, SNMP, or specific clients.

In this recipe, we will show you how to establish a monitoring mechanism for remaining InnoDB tablespace that can easily be adapted to use the alerting mechanism of your choice.

 Note that this recipe is targeted at installations with a fixed InnoDB tablespace size. Scenarios that rely on the *autoextend* feature of InnoDB have to take the available file system space into account as well.

## Getting ready

First of all, you will have to come up with a threshold value for your free tablespace; if the available free tablespace drops below this threshold, an alert will be raised.

 20 percent is a sensible starting point for a tablespace alert, but this value should be adapted according to your needs. Data fluctuation and response time for alerts have to be taken into account.

Throughout this recipe, we will assume a fixed size InnoDB tablespace of 10 GB and a threshold value of 2 GB.

We will additionally need a MySQL user with administrative privileges; for the following example, we will use the `admin4mysql` account again.

And finally, you will have to give a directory on your server's file system into which to write the trigger file that is not used by other applications (we will assume `C:/temp/MySQLMonitoring/` in the following steps).

 The recipe makes use of MySQL's scheduler feature, so it requires MySQL version 5.1 or greater.

## How to do it...

1. Connect to your MySQL database
2. Enter the following commands to create a stored procedure to check for low tablespace:

```
mysql> delimiter //
mysql> CREATE PROCEDURE mysql.check_innodb_ts()
    -> BEGIN
    ->   SELECT MIN(DATA_FREE) FROM INFORMATION_SCHEMA.TABLES
    ->         WHERE ENGINE="InnoDB" INTO @free;
    ->   SET @threshold := 2*1024*1024*1024;
    ->   SET @fileprefix := "C:/log/innodb_free_ts_alert_";
    ->   SELECT DATE_FORMAT(NOW(), "%Y_%m_%d_%H%i%s")
    ->         INTO @timestamp_suffix;
    ->   SELECT CONCAT(@fileprefix, @timestamp_suffix)
    ->         INTO @filename;
    ->   SELECT CONCAT(
    ->         "Free InnoDB table space (",
    ->         @free,
    ->         ") is below warning threshold (",
    ->         @threshold,
    ->         ").") INTO @warning;
    ->   SELECT CONCAT(
    ->         "SELECT @warning INTO OUTFILE '",
    ->         @filename,
    ->         "';") INTO @command;
    ->   IF @free < @threshold THEN
```

```
    ->              PREPARE statement FROM @command;
    ->              EXECUTE statement;
    ->   END IF;
    -> END //
Query OK, 0 rows affected (0.00 sec)
mysql> delimiter ;
```

3.  Use the following commands to schedule the tablespace check:

```
mysql> CREATE EVENT mysql.check_innodb_ts_event
    ->   ON SCHEDULE EVERY 15 MINUTE
    ->   DO CALL mysql.check_innodb_ts();
Query OK, 0 rows affected (0.00 sec)
```

4.  Configure your platform-specific monitoring/alerting mechanism to scan for files named `innodb_free_ts_alert_*` in the `C:/log/` directory—if a file exists, an alert should be raised.

## How it works...

In step 2, a stored procedure named `mysql.check_innodb_ts()` is created, which checks the remaining InnoDB tablespace against a threshold value (here: 2 GB, given as an arithmetic expression: `2 * 1024 * 1024 * 1024`). If the space is below the threshold value, a file with a given name prefix and the timestamp as a name suffix is written to the `C:/log/` directory. The file contains an alert message that states the actual as well as the threshold value.

Step 3 creates a scheduled event (named `mysql.check_innodb_ts_event`), which causes the stored procedure defined in step 2 to be executed automatically every 15 minutes (the MySQL scheduler has to be enabled, see *There's more* below). You should adapt this interval according to your needs, but keep in mind that longer intervals will increase the probability that a sudden peak in data growth might fill up your database before your alert fires. On the other hand, a shorter interval will be at the cost of an increased server load induced by the monitoring mechanism. You will have to balance these aspects to find the best solution for your environment.

Step 4 should be considered a placeholder for the respective steps required to produce an alert in your specific environment. If your monitoring tool is not able to check for the existence of files with a specific file pattern (`C:\log\innodb_free_ts_alert_*` in our example), you might have to introduce an intermediate layer that checks for the trigger files created by the MySQL event scheduler on a regular basis. An example for a Windows environment could be to define a scheduled task that executes a command-line script along the lines of:

```
IF EXIST "C:\log\innodb_free_ts_alert_*" (alert.exe "Table space
low!")
```

For Unix-like systems, a *bash* script like the following run by a *cron* job would have a similar effect:

```
files=$(ls /log/innodb_free_ts_alert_* 2> /dev/null)
if [ $files ]; then /etc/bin/alert "Table space low!"; fi
```

For these examples, `alert.exe` and `/etc/bin/alert` have to be replaced by the tools of your choice to raise an alert.

## There's more...

For the sake of brevity, some prerequisites and further options for improvement were not fully discussed in the above recipe. The following sections will show you how to make sure the prerequisites are given and how to ease future changes in configuration.

### Enabling the MySQL scheduler

The scheduled event from step 3 relies on a running MySQL scheduler.

> The scheduler feature has been available since version 5.1, so the recipe does not fully work with MySQL 5.0 or lower.

As the scheduler is not enabled by default even in MySQL 5.1, you should make sure that your configuration contains the setting `event_scheduler=ON` in the [mysqld] section of your MySQL configuration file. Alternatively, you can enable the scheduler using the `SET GLOBAL event_scheduler = ON;` command.

If you happen to work with a version of MySQL that does not support the scheduler or if for any reason you cannot enable the MySQL scheduler in your installation, you should consider establishing a scheduled task (for Windows) or a cron job (for Unix/Linux), which executes the `CALL mysql.check_innodb_ts();` command using the `-e` option of the *mysql* command-line client.

### Improving configuration

As the stored procedure defined in step 2 contains some hard-coded values (most importantly *threshold* and *fileprefix*), it is hard to adapt those values to changed needs, for example if the threshold should be changed. Thus you could consider reading the specific values from a configuration table using the `SELECT ... INTO @variable` notation. To change a configuration value, the stored procedure can be left unchanged; you only need to update the values in your configuration table.

# See also

▶  *Defining an alternative user for administrative tasks* (Chapter 8 *MySQL User Management*)

# Estimating tablespace requirements

When planning a database installation, one problem that comes up pretty soon is how much drive space should be reserved for the data. This is an important aspect to consider in terms of reliability because if the reserved space is too small, your database might grind to a halt if no space is left to store additional data. On the other hand, today's cost pressure will often not allow for demands that are not based on a traceable method of demand estimation. The following recipe will present an approach that allows for a realistic estimate of the storage requirements of your database.

# Getting ready

For the following recipe, you will need to have some information at hand:

▶  The table structure of your database

▶  An estimate of the maximum number of records for each table (take data growth into account)

▶  Representative sample records for each table (the more, the better)

**Choosing sample values for variable length columns carefully:**

When thinking about sample records for your tables, think about reasonable values for columns with data types of variable length (like VARCHAR or BLOB. The length of the values should match the average size of the expected values of the productive database. If you cannot give a valid estimate, we propose to use sample values half as long as the maximum.

For international operations, take Unicode encoding of VARCHAR values into account. If you have to deal with character sets like for example Cyrillic, Chinese, Japanese, Arabic, or Hebrew, use sample values for these as well, as these characters will require more space than an ASCII character.

The table structure of your database should already be present, which means all tables should be created, but not necessarily filled with data.

Furthermore, you will need an account with read and write privileges to the schema for which you want to calculate the space requirements estimate.

For the following recipe, we will assume the `sample_stduser` account is used. Furthermore, we will use a database `sample` with two tables—`table1` and `table2`—created using the following statements:

```
CREATE TABLE `table1` (
  `id` LONG,
  `name` varchar(255) DEFAULT NULL,
   INDEX `idx_name` (`name`)
) ENGINE=InnoDB DEFAULT CHARSET=utf8;

CREATE TABLE `table2` (
  `name` char(16) NOT NULL,
  `description` varchar(128) NOT NULL,
  PRIMARY KEY (`name`)
) ENGINE=InnoDB DEFAULT CHARSET=utf8;
```

We will assume that `table1` will have a maximum row count of one million, and `table2` will hold at most 20,000 records.

## How to do it...

1. Connect to your database using the `sample_stduser` account.

2. Insert as much sample data into your tables as possible:

```
INSERT INTO table1 values
(1,"John Doe"),
(2,"Mickey Mouse"),
(3,"Дмитрий Анатольевич Медведев"),
(4,"Jane Doe"),
(5,"Jeffrey \"The Dude\" Lebowksi"),
(6,"Walter Sobchak"),
(7,"Donny Kerabatsos"),
(8,"Neo"),
(9,"Trinity"),
(10,"Morpheus");

INSERT INTO table2 values
("Bit", "Smallest piece of binary logic: either 0 or 1"),
("Byte", "Consists of eight bits"),
("Nibble", "Half a byte, consists of four bits"),
("kB", "Kilobyte; either 1,000 or 1,024 bytes"),
("KiB", "Kibibyte; correct IEC term for 1,024 bytes"),
("MB", "Megabyte; either 1,000,000 or 1,048,576 bytes"),
("MiB", "Mebibyte; correct IEC term for 1,024 KiB");
```

3.  Calculate the tablespace requirements for each table by using the following statements:

```
mysql> SELECT 1000000 * (DATA_LENGTH + INDEX_LENGTH) /
    ->    (SELECT COUNT(*) FROM sample.table1) / (1024*1024)
    ->    AS REQUIRED_SPACE_MB
    ->    FROM INFORMATION_SCHEMA.TABLES
    ->    WHERE TABLE_SCHEMA="sample" AND
    ->    TABLE_NAME="table1";
```

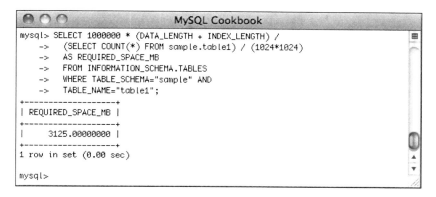

```
mysql> SELECT 20000 * (DATA_LENGTH + INDEX_LENGTH) /
    ->    (SELECT COUNT(*) FROM sample.table2) / (1024*1024)
    ->    AS REQUIRED_SPACE_MB
    ->    FROM INFORMATION_SCHEMA.TABLES
    ->    WHERE TABLE_SCHEMA="sample" AND
    ->    TABLE_NAME="table2";
```

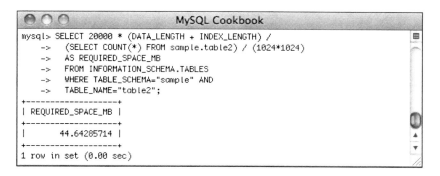

## How it works...

The statements in step 3 use the metadata available in INFORMATION_SCHEMA.TABLES to calculate the space requirements for the table. We retrieve the current space required for the current data and index information, and divide it by the number of records currently stored in the table, which gives the average size of a single record. We simply multiply this value with the target number of records in the table. For better readability, the value is scaled down to MBytes.

 Note that for a low number of sample records, these estimates are typically way too high. The more records are present in the tables, the more accurate the results are.

The following diagram shows how the sample data row count affects the results of the calculations:

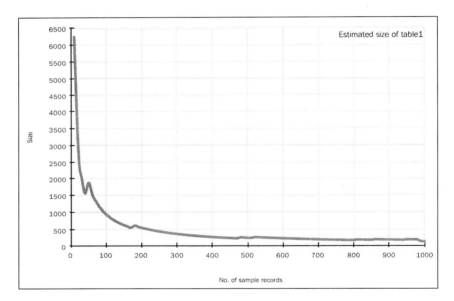

As you can see, the initial estimate was way too conservative. For low numbers of sample records, the estimated table size was extremely high. The more sample data is present, the lower (and more precise) the estimates get.

The reason for the inexact figures produced when too little sample data is used is due to the fact that storage space for data and index information is reserved in pages (a page consists of 16 KB). So for the first row, 32 KB of storage is reserved (one page for data, one page for the index). Based on this, one million rows of this size would require roughly 32 GB of storage. But the next row will fit into the very same page that was already reserved as well, thus reducing the calculated estimate for the space requirements by 50 percent. This is why with very small sets of sample data, a realistic estimate of how much space is going to be required for a large row count is hardly possible. The advantage is that this effect protects you against estimates that are too low.

Note that simply multiplying the AVG_ROW_LENGTH value by the number of rows is not sufficient because this does not take the storage requirements for the index information into account. In some cases, the indexes are bigger than the actual data!

**See also**

> ▸ *Creating a basic user*

# Identifying and changing MySQL variables

The behavior of MySQL installations can be widely configured using variables. You will probably have come across some of these variables, as they are defined in your MySQL configuration file (my.ini). But there are many variables that you will probably not know of because they have sensible default values and are rarely modified.

The typical way to adapt MySQL variables is to edit the MySQL configuration and restart your database server. But if you want to know whether a setting in your MySQL configuration was in fact accepted or if you want to know which setting is in place in the currently running MySQL instance without having to resort to the MySQL startup configuration, this recipe will show you how to do this.

We will also show you how to change certain settings during server runtime, which allows performing certain changes without the need for a MySQL restart.

**Getting ready**

All we need is any MySQL client (like the mysql command-line client) and a MySQL user account. To read a variable setting, any user that allows you to connect to the server is sufficient. If you want to change the value of a MySQL system variable, you will need the SUPER privilege. For the following example, we will assume an administration account named admin4mysql.

## How to do it...

1. Connect to your MySQL database with the SQL client of your choice using the `admin4mysql` account.

2. Show all variables by entering the following command (you will have to scroll through the results to see all values):

```
mysql> SHOW VARIABLES;
```

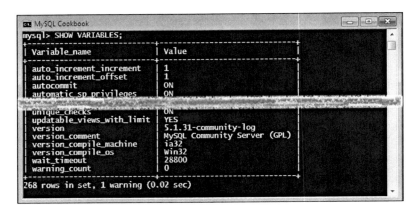

3. To display the value of a certain variable, execute the following statement:

```
mysql> SHOW VARIABLES LIKE "version";
```

4. To display a group of variables with a common name, you can also use SQL wildcard characters:

```
mysql> SHOW VARIABLES LIKE "version%";
```

5. To modify a variable **for your connection only**, use the SET command:

   ```
   mysql> SET auto_increment_increment=2;
   Query OK, 0 rows affected (0.00 sec)
   ```

   ```
   ⊖ ⊙ ⊙                    MySQL Cookbook
   mysql> SET auto_increment_increment=2;
   Query OK, 0 rows affected (0.00 sec)
   mysql> SHOW VARIABLES like "auto_increment_increment";
   +--------------------------+--------+
   | Variable_name            | Value  |
   +--------------------------+--------+
   | auto_increment_increment | 2      |
   +--------------------------+--------+
   1 row in set (0.00 sec)
   ```

6. To globally modify a variable, use set SET GLOBAL statement:

   ```
   mysql> SET GLOBAL auto_increment_increment=3;
   Query OK, 0 rows affected (0.00 sec)
   ```

## How it works...

Steps 2 through 4 show different ways to retrieve variable settings, which is pretty straightforward. Step 5 changes a server variable to a new value (in the above example, we modify auto_increment_increment to a value of 2). This setting takes effect immediately, but it only affects your own connection. Any other connection will use the previous value! And as soon as you drop your connection and reconnect to the server, the variable is reset to the old value again.

Step 6 shows you how to apply a change not only to your current connection. With the SET GLOBAL syntax, the setting is applied to other connections as well. However, note that not all changes are applied to other connections immediately: some changes will only affect **new** connections. The reason for this is that there are basically three kinds of MySQL variables:

1. Variables that apply to your connection (called **session variables**).
2. Variables that are defined globally and affect all connections alike (**global variables**).
3. Variables that exist both globally and for your current session, and which can be changed independently for each context.

If a variable that is solely defined globally is changed, then the change will affect all connections, both existing and new ones. For variables that are both session and global variables (auto_increment_increment is an example for this), any change will only affect **new** connections. The variable values for connections that already exist will be left unchanged. This behavior is due to the fact that on connection creation the value from the global variable is copied to the session variable. Any change to the global variable will not affect the session variable afterwards.

Note that all changes made using the SET GLOBAL command will be lost on the next MySQL startup! To make permanent changes to the MySQL configuration, you will have to edit the startup configuration (typically the my.ini file) as well.

## There's more...

The following sections will introduce some additional options, which can be used to specifically read information from the MySQL variables.

### Displaying more than one named variable at a time

You can also display the values for more than one named variable in one statement using the following syntax:

```
mysql> SHOW VARIABLES
    -> WHERE variable_name IN ("wait_timeout", "autocommit")
    -> OR variable_name LIKE "version%";
```

```
MySQL Cookbook
mysql> SHOW VARIABLES
    -> WHERE variable_name IN ("wait_timeout", "autocommit")
    -> OR variable_name LIKE "version%";
+----------------------------+-------------------------------+
| Variable_name              | Value                         |
+----------------------------+-------------------------------+
| autocommit                 | ON                            |
| version                    | 5.1.31-community-log          |
| version_comment            | MySQL Community Server (GPL)  |
| version_compile_machine    | ia32                          |
| version_compile_os         | Win32                         |
| wait_timeout               | 28800                         |
+----------------------------+-------------------------------+
6 rows in set (0.00 sec)
```

### Displaying global settings

If you have changed any of the settings of your connection and you want to find out about the global setting of this variable, use the SHOW GLOBAL statement:

```
mysql> SHOW GLOBAL VARIABLES like "auto_increment_increment";
```

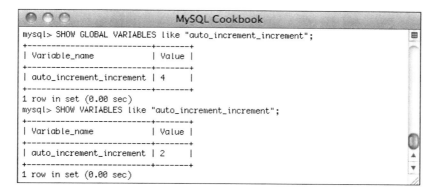

```
mysql> SHOW GLOBAL VARIABLES like "auto_increment_increment";
+--------------------------+-------+
| Variable_name            | Value |
+--------------------------+-------+
| auto_increment_increment | 4     |
+--------------------------+-------+
1 row in set (0.00 sec)
mysql> SHOW VARIABLES like "auto_increment_increment";
+--------------------------+-------+
| Variable_name            | Value |
+--------------------------+-------+
| auto_increment_increment | 2     |
+--------------------------+-------+
1 row in set (0.00 sec)
```

## See also

▸  *Defining an alternative user for administrative tasks* (Chapter 8. *MySQL User Management*)

# Assessing the overall table count

In some MySQL installations, you will have a lot of databases (of schemata) in place. To keep track of the databases, it sometimes comes in handy to get an overview of the tables that reside in each schema. The following recipe will show you how to achieve this.

## Getting ready

You will need a MySQL account to reproduce the following recipe. To get an overview of all databases of your installations, you need at least SELECT privileges on all databases, which is why we assume the administrative user account named admin4mysql is used. The above mentioned methods will work for more restricted accounts as well, but will produce results only for the databases accessible to the user.

## How to do it...

1. Connect to your MySQL database using the `admin4mysql` account.

2. Execute the following command:

```
mysql> SELECT TABLE_SCHEMA, COUNT(*) AS TABLE_COUNT
    ->    from INFORMATION_SCHEMA.TABLES
    ->    GROUP BY TABLE_SCHEMA WITH ROLLUP;
```

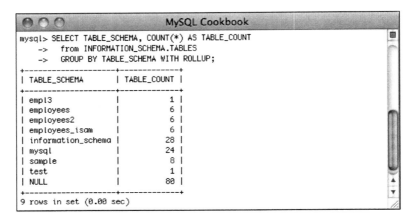

```
                                 MySQL Cookbook
mysql> SELECT TABLE_SCHEMA, COUNT(*) AS TABLE_COUNT
    ->    from INFORMATION_SCHEMA.TABLES
    ->    GROUP BY TABLE_SCHEMA WITH ROLLUP;
+--------------------+-------------+
| TABLE_SCHEMA       | TABLE_COUNT |
+--------------------+-------------+
| empl3              |           1 |
| employees          |           6 |
| employees2         |           6 |
| employees_isam     |           6 |
| information_schema |          28 |
| mysql              |          24 |
| sample             |           8 |
| test               |           1 |
| NULL               |          80 |
+--------------------+-------------+
9 rows in set (0.00 sec)
```

## How it works...

The result from step 2 displays an overview of the databases that are present in our installation and the number of tables defined for each database. The last line shows the overall table count of all databases.

## See also

▸ *Defining an alternative user for administrative tasks*

# Finding the biggest tables

On the quest for performance during the daily struggle against uncontrolled data growth, the biggest tables are often the most promising candidates for optimization. This recipe shows you how to get an overview of the largest tables in your installation.

## Getting ready

You will only need an appropriate MySQL user account to perform the steps of this recipe. To retrieve the information for all databases, an administrative user like `admin4mysql` (which we will use here) is best. To get an overview of the tables in your database, a user with access only to the respective database can be used as well.

## How to do it...

1. Connect to your MySQL database using the `admin4mysql` account.
2. Perform the following SQL statement:

```
mysql> SELECT TABLE_SCHEMA,
    -> TABLE_NAME,
    -> (INDEX_LENGTH+DATA_LENGTH)/(1024*1024) AS SIZE_MB,
    -> TABLE_ROWS
    -> FROM INFORMATION_SCHEMA.TABLES
    -> WHERE TABLE_SCHEMA NOT IN("mysql", "information_schema")
    -> ORDER BY SIZE_MB DESC;
```

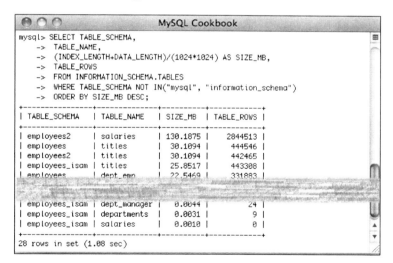

## How it works...

The above statement simply makes use of the table metadata available from the table `INFORMATION_SCHEMA.TABLES` and displays it in a readable way. It is sorted by the size of the table (according to the storage reserved by this table). If the number of records is more of interest to you, you could of course adapt the above statement accordingly:

```
SELECT TABLE_SCHEMA,
     TABLE_NAME,
     TABLE_ROWS,
     (INDEX_LENGTH+DATA_LENGTH)/(1024*1024) AS SIZE_MB
     FROM INFORMATION_SCHEMA.TABLES
     WHERE TABLE_SCHEMA NOT IN("mysql", "information_schema")
     ORDER BY TABLE_ROWS DESC;
```

In both cases, the `WHERE TABLE_SCHEMA NOT IN("mysql", "information_schema")` clause helps to filter out any results from the `mysql` and `information_schema` schemata, which are typically not in the focus of interest.

## See also

▶  *Defining an alternative user for administrative tasks*

# Finding all columns with a certain name and/or type

In large databases, it often makes sense to agree on some kind of data modeling standards to avoid unnecessary effort. For example, you decide to standardize that all columns containing a name should be of type `VARCHAR(64)`. If, however, the situation comes up that the standard type for name columns should be changed to, say, `VARCHAR(128)` to allow for very long names, the question arises how many columns or tables have to be adapted—for large installations, this is not a trivial question to answer. This recipe will show you how to retrieve this information.

## Getting ready

You will need a MySQL user with `SELECT` rights for the databases that are to be checked for matching columns. We will use the `sample_guest` user here.

And, of course, you will have to know what data type and column name you are looking for. In the following steps, we will be looking for `name` columns and columns of data type `VARCHAR(64)`.

## How to do it...

1. Connect to your MySQL database using the `sample_guest` user.
2. Execute the following query to find all name columns:

```
mysql> SELECT TABLE_SCHEMA,
     ->     TABLE_NAME,
     ->     COLUMN_NAME,
```

```
->     DATA_TYPE,
->     CHARACTER_MAXIMUM_LENGTH AS SIZE
->     FROM INFORMATION_SCHEMA.COLUMNS
->     WHERE COLUMN_NAME="name" AND
->     TABLE_SCHEMA NOT IN ("mysql", "information_schema");
```

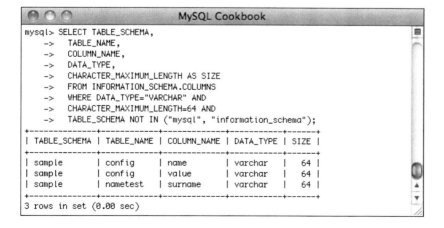

3. To find all columns with data type VARCHAR(64), execute this command:

```
mysql> SELECT TABLE_SCHEMA,
->     TABLE_NAME,
->     COLUMN_NAME,
->     DATA_TYPE,
->     CHARACTER_MAXIMUM_LENGTH AS SIZE
->     FROM INFORMATION_SCHEMA.COLUMNS
->     WHERE DATA_TYPE="VARCHAR" AND
->     CHARACTER_MAXIMUM_LENGTH=64 AND
->     TABLE_SCHEMA NOT IN ("mysql", "information_schema");
```

```
000                      MySQL Cookbook
mysql> SELECT TABLE_SCHEMA,
    ->     TABLE_NAME,
    ->     COLUMN_NAME,
    ->     DATA_TYPE,
    ->     CHARACTER_MAXIMUM_LENGTH AS SIZE
    ->     FROM INFORMATION_SCHEMA.COLUMNS
    ->     WHERE DATA_TYPE="VARCHAR" AND
    ->     CHARACTER_MAXIMUM_LENGTH=64 AND
    ->     TABLE_SCHEMA NOT IN ("mysql", "information_schema");
+--------------+------------+-------------+-----------+------+
| TABLE_SCHEMA | TABLE_NAME | COLUMN_NAME | DATA_TYPE | SIZE |
+--------------+------------+-------------+-----------+------+
| sample       | config     | name        | varchar   | 64   |
| sample       | config     | value       | varchar   | 64   |
| sample       | nametest   | surname     | varchar   | 64   |
+--------------+------------+-------------+-----------+------+
3 rows in set (0.00 sec)
```

## How it works...

The preceding statements simply make use of the information available in the `INFORMATION_SCHEMA.COLUMNS` metadata table. It helps you identify columns with certain attributes. The `mysql` and `information_schema` schemata are filtered out using the `WHERE TABLE_SCHEMA NOT IN ("mysql", "information_schema")` clause to display only results of interest.

## There's more...

If the data type you are looking for is a numeric data type, you will have to adapt the queries to take the `NUMERIC_PRECISION` and `NUMERIC_SCALE` attributes into account:

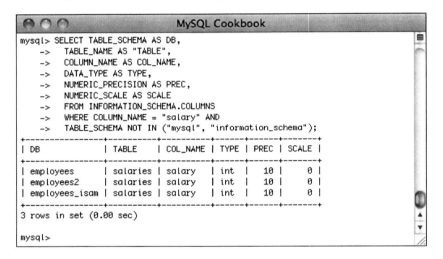

```
mysql> SELECT TABLE_SCHEMA AS DB,
    ->     TABLE_NAME AS "TABLE",
    ->     COLUMN_NAME AS COL_NAME,
    ->     DATA_TYPE AS TYPE,
    ->     NUMERIC_PRECISION AS PREC,
    ->     NUMERIC_SCALE AS SCALE
    ->     FROM INFORMATION_SCHEMA.COLUMNS
    ->     WHERE COLUMN_NAME = "salary" AND
    ->     TABLE_SCHEMA NOT IN ("mysql", "information_schema");
+----------------+-----------+----------+------+------+-------+
| DB             | TABLE     | COL_NAME | TYPE | PREC | SCALE |
+----------------+-----------+----------+------+------+-------+
| employees      | salaries  | salary   | int  | 10   | 0     |
| employees2     | salaries  | salary   | int  | 10   | 0     |
| employees_isam | salaries  | salary   | int  | 10   | 0     |
+----------------+-----------+----------+------+------+-------+
3 rows in set (0.00 sec)

mysql>
```

You can also narrow down the results to columns with a specific precision or scale:

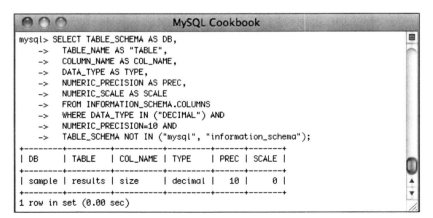

```
mysql> SELECT TABLE_SCHEMA AS DB,
    ->     TABLE_NAME AS "TABLE",
    ->     COLUMN_NAME AS COL_NAME,
    ->     DATA_TYPE AS TYPE,
    ->     NUMERIC_PRECISION AS PREC,
    ->     NUMERIC_SCALE AS SCALE
    ->     FROM INFORMATION_SCHEMA.COLUMNS
    ->     WHERE DATA_TYPE IN ("DECIMAL") AND
    ->     NUMERIC_PRECISION=10 AND
    ->     TABLE_SCHEMA NOT IN ("mysql", "information_schema");
+--------+---------+----------+---------+------+-------+
| DB     | TABLE   | COL_NAME | TYPE    | PREC | SCALE |
+--------+---------+----------+---------+------+-------+
| sample | results | size     | decimal | 10   | 0     |
+--------+---------+----------+---------+------+-------+
1 row in set (0.00 sec)
```

## See also

▸ *Creating a read-only account*

# Finding all tables referencing each other

For both manual data modifications and changes to the table structure, it is important to know whether the referential integrity of the database is affected. For complex data models, it is often the case that the details about which table references are in place are not known. This recipe helps you to make the dependencies between tables visible.

## Getting ready

Again, we only need a user who has the privileges to access the database in question (SELECT privileges are sufficient). We will use an account named employees_guest account here, which has SELECT privileges for the employees database.

## How to do it...

1. Connect to your MySQL database using the sample_guest user.

2. To display all tables referencing the employees table, execute the following statement:

```
mysql> SELECT TABLE_NAME,
    ->     CONSTRAINT_NAME,
    ->     UPDATE_RULE AS "UPDATE",
    ->     DELETE_RULE AS "DELETE"
    ->     FROM INFORMATION_SCHEMA.REFERENTIAL_CONSTRAINTS
    ->     WHERE REFERENCED_TABLE_NAME="employees";
```

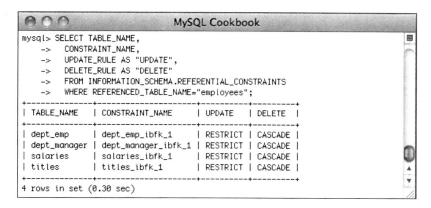

3. Use the following query to retrieve information about the tables referenced by the `salaries` table:

```
mysql> SELECT REFERENCED_TABLE_NAME,
    ->    CONSTRAINT_NAME,
    ->    UPDATE_RULE AS "UPDATE",
    ->    DELETE_RULE AS "DELETE"
    ->    FROM INFORMATION_SCHEMA.REFERENTIAL_CONSTRAINTS
    ->    WHERE TABLE_NAME="salaries";
```

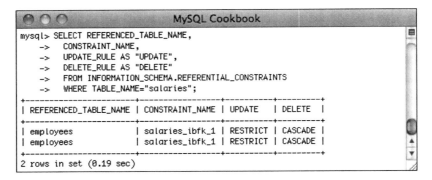

```
mysql> SELECT REFERENCED_TABLE_NAME,
    ->    CONSTRAINT_NAME,
    ->    UPDATE_RULE AS "UPDATE",
    ->    DELETE_RULE AS "DELETE"
    ->    FROM INFORMATION_SCHEMA.REFERENTIAL_CONSTRAINTS
    ->    WHERE TABLE_NAME="salaries";
+----------------------+-----------------+----------+---------+
| REFERENCED_TABLE_NAME | CONSTRAINT_NAME | UPDATE   | DELETE  |
+----------------------+-----------------+----------+---------+
| employees            | salaries_ibfk_1 | RESTRICT | CASCADE |
| employees            | salaries_ibfk_1 | RESTRICT | CASCADE |
+----------------------+-----------------+----------+---------+
2 rows in set (0.19 sec)
```

## How it works...

This recipe uses the information available in the `REFERENTIAL_CONSTRAINTS` metadata table in the `INFORMATION_SCHEMA` schema. The information retrieved in step 2 means that updating information in the employees table might become difficult, as it is referenced by four other tables, and an `ON UPDATE RESTRICT` policy is in place. Deletion of data, however, will be easy, as the deletion rules for all four dependencies are marked as `ON DELETE CASCADE`. Because of this, you should be even more careful, however, not to delete the wrong data.

Especially, the information delivered by step 2 is often very important to get an overview of the dependencies of large data models that evolved over a longer period of time and with many people involved.

## See also

▶ *Creating a read-only account*

# 7
# Configuring MySQL

In this chapter, we will shed some light on MySQL configuration settings. There is an abundance of dials and knobs available for both the MySQL server and the different storage engines underneath it. Covering them all would by far exceed the limitations of any book, so we will just go for a selection of some of the most important ones:

- ▸ Setting up a fixed InnoDB tablespace
- ▸ Setting up an auto-extending InnoDB tablespace
- ▸ Storing InnoDB data in one file per table
- ▸ Decreasing InnoDB tablespace
- ▸ Enabling and configuring binary logging
- ▸ Configuring the InnoDB redo log
- ▸ Understanding and configuring important MySQL and InnoDB timeout options
- ▸ Adjusting table and database name letter case handling for better platform independence
- ▸ Installing MySQL as a Windows service with custom options
- ▸ Running multiple MySQL server instances in parallel on a Linux server
- ▸ Preventing invalid date values from being stored in `DATE` or `DATETIME` columns

# Introduction

Installing a MySQL server is one thing that is fairly easy to do. Setting up the vast amount of configuration options available can be far more challenging, as there is no one-fits-all combination of settings. MySQL comes with some presets that can serve as a starting point for different server sizes. They are called `my-large.cnf`, `my-huge.cnf`, `my-medium.cnf`, and `my-innodb-heavy-4G.cnf`. On Ubuntu Linux they can be found in compressed form in the `/usr/share/doc/mysql-server-5.0/examples` directory. On Windows, the same examples exist but have file names ending in `.ini` and are located in the MySQL program directory.

In this chapter, we will delve into a selection of the most relevant configuration options, focusing on important InnoDB settings, as this is the storage engine most relevant to enterprise applications.

Please refer to the appendix for a description of how to set up the `innodb_buffer_pool_size` setting and make the best use of the available memory.

# Setting up a fixed InnoDB tablespace

When using the InnoDB storage engine of MySQL, the data is typically not stored in a per-database or per-table directory structure, but in several dedicated files, which collectively contain the so-called **tablespace**. By default (when installing MySQL using the configuration wizard) InnoDB is configured to have one small file to store data in, and this file grows as needed. While this is a very flexible and economical configuration to start with, this approach also has some drawbacks: there is no reserved space for your data, so you have to rely on free disk space every time your data grows. Also, if your database grows bigger, the file will grow to a size which makes it hard to handle—a dozen files of 1 GB each are typically easier to manage than one clumsy 12 GB file.

Large data files might, for example, cause problems if you try to put those files into an archive for backup or data transmission purposes. Even if the 2 GB limit is not present any more for the current file systems, many compression programs still have problems dealing with large files.

And finally, the constant adaptation of the file in InnoDB's default configuration size will cause a (small, but existent) performance hit if your database grows.

The following recipe will show you how to define a fixed tablespace for your InnoDB installation, by which you can avoid these drawbacks of the InnoDB default configuration.

## Getting ready

To install a fixed tablespace, you will have to reflect about some aspects: how much tablespace should be reserved for your database, and how to size the single data files which in sum constitute the tablespace.

> Note that once your database completely allocates your tablespace, you will run into *table full* errors (error code 1114) when trying to add new data to your database.

Additionally, you have to make sure that your current InnoDB tablespace is completely empty. Ideally, you should set up the tablespace of a freshly installed MySQL instance, in which case this prerequisite is given.

> To check whether any InnoDB tables exist in your database, execute the following statement and delete the given tables until the result is empty:
>
> ```
> SELECT TABLE_SCHEMA, TABLE_NAME FROM information_
> schema.tables WHERE engine="InnoDB";
> ```

> If your database already contains data stored in InnoDB tables that you do not want to lose, you will have to create a backup of your database and recover the data from it when you are done with the recipe. Please refer to the chapter *Backing Up and Restoring MySQL Data* for further information on this.

And finally, you have to make sure that the InnoDB data directory (as defined by the `innodb_data_home_dir` variable) features sufficient free disk space to store the InnoDB data files.

For the following example, we will use a fixed tablespace with a size of 500 MB and a maximal file size of 200 MB.

## How to do it...

1. Open the MySQL configuration file (`my.ini` or `my.cnf`) in a text editor.
2. Identify the line starting with `innodb_data_file_path` in the `[mysqld]` section. If no such line exists, add the line to the file.
3. Change the line `innodb_data_file_path` to read as follows:

   ```
   innodb_data_file_path=ibdata1:200M;ibdata2:200M;ibdata3:100M
   ```

4. Save the changed configuration file.

5. Shut down your database instance (if running).

6. Delete previous InnoDB data files (typically called `ibdata1`, `ibdata2`, and so on) from the directory defined by the `innodb_data_home_dir` variable.

7. Delete previous InnoDB logfiles (named `ib_logfile0`, `ib_logfile1`, so on) from the directory defined by the `innodb_log_group_home_dir` variable.

If `innodb_log_group_home_dir` is not configured explicitly, it defaults to the `datadir` directory.

8. Start your database.

9. Wait for all data and log files to be created.

Depending on the size of your tablespace and the speed of your disk system, creation of InnoDB data files can take a significant amount of time (several minutes is not an uncommon time for larger installations). During this initialization sequence, MySQL is started but it will not accept any requests.

## How it works...

Steps 1 through 4—and particularly 3—cover the actual change to be made to the MySQL configuration, which is necessary to adapt the InnoDB tablespace settings. The value of the `innodb_data_file_path` variable consists of a list of data file definitions that are separated by semicolons. Each data file definition is constructed of a file name and a file size with a colon as a separator. The size can be expressed as a plain numeric value, which defines the size of the data file in bytes. If the numeric value has a K, M, or G postfix, the number is interpreted as Kilobytes, Megabytes, or Gigabytes respectively. The list length is not limited to the three entries of our example; if you want to split a large tablespace into relatively small files, the list can easily contain dozens of data file definitions.

If your tablespace consists of more than 10 files, we propose naming the first nine files `ibdata01` through `ibdata09` (instead of `ibdata1` and so forth; note the zero), so that the files are listed in a more consistent order when they are displayed in your file browser or command line interface.

Step 5 is prerequisite to the steps following after it, as deletion of vital InnoDB files while the system is still running is obviously not a good idea. In step 6, old data files are deleted to prevent collision with the new files. If InnoDB detects an existing file whose size differs from the size defined in the `innodb_data_file_path` variable, it will not initialize successfully. Hence, this step ensures that new, properly saved files can be created during the next MySQL start.

Note that deletion of the InnoDB data files is only sufficient if all InnoDB tables were deleted previously (as discussed in the *Getting ready* section).

Alternatively, you could delete all `*.frm` files for InnoDB tables from the MySQL data directory, but we do not encourage this approach (clean deletion using `DROP TABLE` statements should be preferred over manual intervention in MySQL data directories whenever possible).

Step 7 is necessary to prevent InnoDB errors after the data files are created, as the InnoDB engine refuses to start if the log files are older than the tablespace files. With steps 8 and 9, the new settings take effect.

 When starting the database for the first time after changes being made to the InnoDB tablespace configuration, take a look at the MySQL error log to make sure the settings were accepted and no errors have occurred.

The MySQL error log after the first start with the new settings will look similar to this:

```
InnoDB: The first specified data file E:\MySQL\InnoDBTest\ibdata1 did
not exist:
InnoDB: a new database to be created!
091115 21:35:56  InnoDB: Setting file E:\MySQL\InnoDBTest\ibdata1 size
to 200 MB
InnoDB: Database physically writes the file full: wait...
InnoDB: Progress in MB: 100 200
...
InnoDB: Progress in MB: 100
091115 21:36:19  InnoDB: Log file .\ib_logfile0 did not exist: new to
be created
InnoDB: Setting log file .\ib_logfile0 size to 24 MB
InnoDB: Database physically writes the file full: wait...
...
InnoDB: Doublewrite buffer not found: creating new
InnoDB: Doublewrite buffer created
InnoDB: Creating foreign key constraint system tables
InnoDB: Foreign key constraint system tables created
091115 21:36:22  InnoDB: Started; log sequence number 0 0
091115 21:36:22 [Note] C:\Program Files\MySQL\MySQL Server 5.1\bin\
mysqld: ready for connections.
Version: '5.1.31-community-log'  socket: ''  port: 3306  MySQL
Community Server (GPL)
```

## There's more...

If you already use a fixed tablespace, and you want to increase the available space, you can simply append additional files to your fixed tablespace by adding additional data file definitions to the current `innodb_data_file_path` variable setting. If you simply append additional files, you do not have to empty your tablespace first, but you can change the configuration and simply restart your database. Nevertheless, as with all changes to the configuration, we strongly encourage creating a backup of your database first.

## See also

► *Backing Up and Restoring MySQL Data*
► *Estimating tablespace requirements*

# Setting up an auto-extending InnoDB tablespace

The previous recipe demonstrates how to define a tablespace with a certain fixed size. While this provides maximum control and predictability, you have to block disk space based on the estimate of the maximum size required in the foreseeable future. As long as you store less data in your database than the reserved tablespace allows for, this basically means some disk space is wasted. This especially holds true if your setting does not allow for a separate file system exclusively for your MySQL instance, because then other applications compete for disk space as well. In these cases, a dynamic tablespace that starts with little space and grows as needed could be an alternative. The following recipe will show you how to achieve this.

## Getting ready

When defining an auto-extending tablespace, you should first have an idea about the minimum tablespace requirements of your database, which will set the initial size of the tablespace. Furthermore, you have to decide whether you want to split your initial tablespace into files of a certain maximum size (for better file handling).

If the above settings are identical to the current settings and you only want to make your tablespace grow automatically if necessary, you will be able to keep your data. Otherwise, you have to empty your current InnoDB tablespace completely (please refer to the previous recipe *Setting up a fixed InnoDB tablespace* for details).

As with all major configuration changes to your database, we strongly advise you to create a backup of your data first. If you have to empty your tablespace, you can use this backup to recover your data after the changes are completed. Again, please refer to the chapter *Backing Up and Restoring MySQL Data* for further information on this.

And as before, you have to make sure that there is enough disk space available in the `innodb_data_home_dir` directory—not only for the initial database size, but also for the anticipated growth of your database.

The recipe also requires you to shut down your database temporarily; so you have to make sure all clients are disconnected while performing the required steps to prevent conflicting access.

As the recipe demands changes to your MySQL configuration file (`my.cnf` or `my.ini`), you need write access to this file.

For the following example, we will use an auto-extending tablespace with an initial size of 100 MB and a file size of 50 MB.

## How to do it...

1. Open the MySQL configuration file (`my.ini` or `my.cnf`) in a text editor.
2. Identify the line starting with `innodb_data_file_path` in the `[mysqld]` section. If no such line exists, add the line to the file.
3. Change the line `innodb_data_file_path` to read as follows:

   ```
   innodb_data_file_path=ibdata1:50M;ibdata2:50M:autoextend
   ```

 Note that no file definition except the last one must have the `:autoextend` option; you will run into errors otherwise.

4. Save the changed configuration file.
5. Shut down your database instance (if running).
6. Delete previous InnoDB data files (typically called `ibdata1`, `ibdata2`, and so on) from the directory defined by the `innodb_data_home_dir` variable.
7. Delete previous InnoDB logfiles (named `ib_logfile0`, `ib_logfile1`, and so on) from the directory defined by the `innodb_log_group_home_dir` variable.

 If `innodb_log_group_home_dir` is not configured explicitly, it defaults to the `datadir` directory.

8. Start your database.
9. Wait for all data and log files to be created.

Depending on the size of your tablespace and the speed of your disk system, creation of InnoDB data files can take a significant amount of time (several minutes is not an uncommon time for larger installations). During this initialization sequence, MySQL is started but will not accept any requests.

 When starting the database for the first time after changes being made to the InnoDB tablespace configuration, take a look at the MySQL error log to make sure the settings were accepted and no errors have occurred.

## How it works...

The above steps are basically identical to the steps of the previous recipe *Setting up a fixed InnoDB tablespace*, the only difference being the definition of the innodb_data_file_path variable. In this recipe, we create two files of 50 MB size, the last one having an additional :autoextend property.

 If the innodb_data_file_path variable is not set explicitly, it defaults to the value ibdata1:10M:autoextend.

As data gets inserted into the database, parts of the tablespace will be allocated. As soon as the 100 MB of initial tablespace is not sufficient any more, the file ibdata2 will become larger to match the additional tablespace requirements.

 Note that the :autoextend option causes the tablespace files to be *extended* automatically, but they are not automatically *reduced* in size again if the space requirements decrease. Please refer to the *Decreasing InnoDB tablespace* recipe for instructions on how to free unused tablespace.

## There's more...

The recipe only covers the basic aspects of auto-extending tablespaces; the following sections provide insight into some more advanced topics.

### Making an existing tablespace auto-extensible

If you already have a database with live data in place and you want to change your current fixed configuration to use the auto-extension feature, you can simply add the :autoextend option to the last file definition.

Let us assume a current configuration like the following:

```
innodb_data_file_path=ibdata1:50M;ibdata2:50M
```

The respective configuration with auto-extension will look like this:

```
innodb_data_file_path=ibdata1:50M;ibdata2:50M:autoextend
```

In this case, do not empty the InnoDB tablespace first, you can simply change the configuration file and restart your database, and you should be fine. As with all configuration changes, however, we strongly recommend to back up your database before editing these settings even in this case.

## Controlling the steps of tablespace extension

The amount by which the size of the auto-extending tablespace file is increased is controlled by the `innodb_autoextend_increment` variable. The value of this variable defines the number of Megabytes by which the tablespace is enlarged. By default, 8 MB are added to the file if the current tablespace is no longer sufficient.

## Limiting the size of an auto-extending tablespace

If you want to use an auto-extending tablespace, but also want to limit the maximum size your tablespace will grow to, you can add a maximum size for the auto-extended tablespace file by using the `:autoextend:max:[size]` option. The `[size]` portion is a placeholder for a size definition using the same notation as the size description for the tablespace file itself, which means a numeric value and an optional K, M, or G modifier (for sizes in Kilo-, Mega-, and Gigabytes). As an example, if you want to have a tiny initial tablespace of 10 MB, which is extended as needed, but with an upper limit of 2 GB, you would enter the following line to your MySQL configuration file:

```
innodb_data_file_path=ibdata1:10M:autoextend:max:2G
```

[

Note that if the maximum size is reached, you will run into errors when trying to add new data to your database.
]

## Adding a new auto-extending data file

Imagine an auto-extending tablespace with an auto-extended file, which grew so large over time that you want to prevent the file from growing further and want to append a new auto-extending data file to the tablespace. You can do so using the following steps:

1.  Shut down your database instance.
2.  Look up the _exact_ size of the auto-extended InnoDB data file (the last file in your current configuration).

3. Put the exact size as the tablespace file size definition into the `innodb_data_file_path` configuration (number of bytes without any K, M, or G modifier), and add a new auto-extending data file.

4. Restart your database.

As an example, if your current configuration reads `ibdata1:10M:autoextend` and the `ibdata1` file has an actual size of 44,040,192 bytes, change configuration to `innodb_data_file_path=ibdata1:44040192;ibdata2:10M:autoextend:max:2G`.

## See also

▶ *Backing Up and Restoring MySQL Data*
▶ *Estimating tablespace requirements*
▶ *Setting up a fixed InnoDB tablespace*
▶ *Decreasing InnoDB tablespace*

# Storing InnoDB data in one file per table

In the previous recipes, we presented a way to define a common tablespace in which the InnoDB storage engine stores all data for InnoDB tables. While this has some advantages (for example, dynamic reuse of free space across tables), this approach is completely different from the MyISAM technique that stores the data for each table in a separate file. The following recipe will show you how to configure InnoDB to store data in separates files, one for each table.

## Getting ready

The following steps include a database downtime, so you have to prepare a maintenance window for your database that allows you to complete the steps without interfering with clients still accessing the database.

## How to do it...

1. Create a SQL dump of your entire database.
2. Shut down your database.
3. Open the MySQL configuration file (`my.ini` or `my.cnf`) in a text editor.

4. Add the following line to the `[mysqld]` section:

   `innodb_file_per_table`

5. Save the changed configuration file.

6. Start your database instance.

7. Recover all data from the SQL dump created in step 1.

## How it works...

This recipe is pretty straightforward: create a backup, add the `innodb_file_per_table` option to the `[mysqld]` configuration, and recover data from the backup (please refer to the chapter _Backing Up and Restoring MySQL Data_ for details). But why the recovery?

After the restart of the database in step 6, you will not notice any changes to the database. At this point, all data is still stored in the InnoDB tablespace. This is because the file per table setting only applies to newly created tables! Step 7 takes care of this: during recovery, every table is dropped and created again (this time in a separate file) before the original data is inserted.

The `innodb_file_per_table` setting allows you to use the operating system's means to map tables to different physical disks or to back up and recover certain tables on the file level.

 However, note that with this approach, each table has its own auto-extending tablespace—extension yes, but no reduction!

If you delete data from a table, the file size will not reduce automatically. As each table uses its own tablespace, this means that the space that gets freed by deleting from one table cannot be reused by another table, as is the case for the "classical" shared InnoDB tablespace. There is a way to free unused space again: please refer to the following recipe _Decreasing InnoDB tablespace_ for instructions on how to do this.

## See also

▸ _Backing Up and Restoring MySQL Data_

▸ _Decreasing InnoDB tablespace_

# Decreasing InnoDB tablespace

The previous recipes enable you to define a tablespace; and for the `autoextend` and `innodb_file_per_table` approaches, the tablespace will grow until you run out of disk space (or you hit a file size boundary set by your operating system). The opposite direction, however, does not work as easily: InnoDB lacks an automatic shrink option if you happen to delete data from your database. The following recipe will introduce ways to reduce the size of your InnoDB tablespace if your storage requirements decrease.

## Getting ready

As the following recipe involves creation of a backup dump of your database, you have to reserve enough disk space to temporarily store the dump file. Furthermore, if you want to establish a shared tablespace with a reduced size, you have to decide about the size of the tablespace and how to split it into separate files. For a fixed size tablespace, you additionally have to calculate the space requirements of your current data (please refer to the *Estimating tablespace requirements* recipe in Chapter 6 for details) to decide about the new size of the fixed tablespace.

The recipe also requires you to shut down your database temporarily, so you have to make sure you have a maintenance interval in which the database is not accessed by any clients.

## How to do it...

1. Create a full backup of your database (for further instructions please see the *Backing Up and Restoring MySQL Data* chapter).

2. Drop all databases (except for the `mysql` and `information_schema` databases).

3. Shut down your database.

4. Open the MySQL configuration file (`my.ini` or `my.cnf`) using a text editor.

5. Configure the InnoDB tablespace according to your new reduced space requirements (please refer to the previous recipes for further details).

6. Save the changed configuration file.

7. Delete the old InnoDB data files (typically called `ibdata1`, `ibdata2`, and so on) from the directory defined by the `innodb_data_home_dir` variable.

8. Delete previous InnoDB logfiles (named `ib_logfile0`, `ib_logfile1`, and so on) from the directory defined by the `innodb_log_group_home_dir` variable.

If `innodb_log_group_home_dir` is not configured explicitly, it defaults to the `datadir` directory.

9.  Start your database instance.
10. Wait for all data and log files to be created.
11. Recover all data from the SQL dump created in step 1.

## How it works...

This recipe is basically a slight modification of the previous recipes to set up a shared tablespace. The additional steps are backing up your database and subsequently dropping all databases initially, and the recovery from the backup as the final step.This ensures that data directory entries for all InnoDB tables are removed flawlessly, and (in the case of the file per table option) all storage files are removed. The shared tablespace is created when starting the MySQL instance after the configuration changes. If the `innodb_file_per_table` option is used, the table files are created during the data recovery. In case of an auto-extending shared tablespace, the restoration of the data might cause the tablespace to increase in size, but only to the size actually needed by the current data.

As this approach might require a significant downtime for any client, we propose performing a tablespace reduction only if absolutely necessary—with thorough planning of your storage requirements, your disk structure, and your tablespace sizing, you hopefully will not need to resize your tablespace on a regular basis.

## There's more...

If you use the `innodb_file_per_table` feature and you want to reduce the size of the separate files to the currently needed size, you have an alternative that does not include the full dump, deletion, and recovery procedure:

 To free unused tablespace with `innodb_file_per_table` in place, you can execute an empty `ALTER TABLE` statement:
`ALTER TABLE example_table ENGINE=InnoDB;`

You have to execute this command for each InnoDB table whose storage file you want to resize. However, note that this temporarily creates a copy of the whole table and locks the table during the process.

Due to potential locking conflicts, try to avoid freeing unused tablespace (using the `ALTER TABLE` command) with large and/or heavily used tables in a running system.

## See also

▶ *Backing Up and Restoring MySQL Data*

▶ *Estimating tablespace requirement*

▶ *Setting up a fixed InnoDB tablespace*

▶ *Setting up an auto-extending InnoDB tablespace*

▶ *Storing InnoDB data in one file per table*

# Enabling and configuring binary logging

Binary logging (or binlogging for short), describes a feature of MySQL that will write a transcript of all statements issued that actually modified or could have modified data. This includes `UPDATE`, `INSERT`, and `DELETE` statements, regardless of whether they actually matched any rows on the server, as well as data definition language statements (`CREATE TABLE`, `DROP TABLE`, and the like).

This protocol is written in a special format that contains metadata about transactions, server settings, and more, which makes it suitable as a basis for both replication, backups, and even change auditing, with the former two being the most important ones.

 Generally, we do not recommend running MySQL without binlogging, as the performance penalty is very low—the MySQL manual speaks of a speed degradation of about 1%—and the benefits clearly outweigh this.

You can find detailed information about the binary log in section 5.2.4 *The Binary Log* of the online manual at `http://dev.mysql.com/doc/refman/5.1/en/binary-log.html`.

In this recipe, we will show you how to make sure your MySQL servers are configured to write binary logs in the first place and also keep them maintainable in terms of file sizes.

## Getting ready

As the binary log setup is a part of the server configuration, you will need an operating system user account and sufficient rights to modify the server's configuration file. Moreover, it is recommended to have sufficient rights to restart the MySQL service because binlogging cannot be reconfigured on the fly.

## How to do it...

1.  Open the MySQL configuration file, typically `my.cnf` or `my.ini` (on Windows).

2.  Locate the `[mysqld]` section in the file.

3.  Add the following settings or edit them if they are already present. Adapt the path after `log_bin` and fill in a path valid on your server. Substitute your server's machine name for `HOSTNAME`:

    ```
    log_bin=/var/log/mysql/HOSTNAME-bin
    expire_logs_days=10
    max_binlog_size=200M
    ```

4.  Save the file.

5.  Restart the MySQL service.

6.  Check the directory you specified for `log-bin`. You should see a file called `HOSTNAME-bin.000001` there and a corresponding `HOSTNAME-bin.index` file.

## How it works...

The first parameter `log_bin` tells the server which directory is intended to store the binary logs. This should be a storage volume with sufficient space and ideally on a different physical disk than the data directory for better performance. The amount of disk space required depends on the amount of write access to your databases.

 All databases of one server share the same binlog files, meaning you have to consider this in your space estimation.

The `expire_logs_days` setting is meant to prevent excessive disk space usage by older binlogs. A setting of 10 means that any binary log file older than 10 days will be deleted the next time a new binary log is started. You can use the `PURGE BINARY LOGS` command to force a new binary log to be started manually.

`max_binlog_size` is meant to keep the binlog files manageable by automatically splitting and rotating them once they exceed the configured size threshold. Please note that each file might in fact become slightly larger than the configured limit because transactions are always written as a whole. This means that when a binlog file has almost reached its size limit and a large transaction is then committed, it will still be written to that file, pushing it past the configured threshold.

## There's more...

Binary logs are very important for point-in-time backup and recovery. Make sure you configure the `expire_logs_days` to a value that is large enough to span the time between two full backups. Otherwise there would be a chance that you cannot do a complete disaster recovery when the binlogs have already been deleted before you have taken the next full backup. To completely switch off the automatic deletion of old binlog files, set the `expire_logs_days` parameter to `0` or remove it from the configuration file.

Even though it is possible, it is not recommended to delete older binlogs manually from the file system. Depending on the server version you are using, MySQL might fail to start when its index file and the binlogs actually present do not match.

To prevent problems of this kind, we recommend always using the `PURGE BINARY LOGS` command. For details on its options, see the MySQL online manual at `http://dev.mysql.com/doc/refman/5.1/en/purge-binary-logs.html`.

# Configuring the InnoDB redo log

In order to prevent the transactional nature of InnoDB from completely thwarting its performance, it implements what is called the **redo log**.

In this recipe, we will present the relevant settings to (re-)configure a database server's redo log.

## Getting ready

As the redo log setup is a part of the server configuration, you will need an operating system user account and sufficient rights to modify the server's configuration file. You will also need rights to restart the MySQL service because the redo log cannot be reconfigured on the fly.

Moreover, an administrative MySQL user account is required to prepare the server for the shutdown, necessary as part of the procedure.

**Caution**:

As this recipe will modify the configuration of parameters critical to data integrity, you should make a backup copy of the configuration file before editing it!

## How to do it...

1. Connect to the server using your administrative account.

2. Issue the following command:

   ```
   mysql> SET GLOBAL innodb_fast_shutdown=0;

   Query OK, 0 rows affected (0.00 sec)
   ```

3. Verify the setting like this:

   ```
   mysql> SHOW VARIABLES LIKE 'innodb_fast_shutdown';
   ```

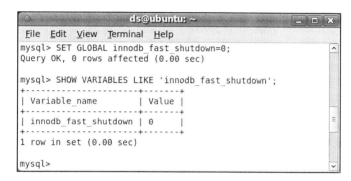

4. Log off from MySQL and stop the MySQL server.

5. Locate the MySQL configuration file, usually called `my.cnf` or `my.ini` (on Windows) and open it in a text editor.

6. Locate the following parameters in the `[mysqld]` section (you values will vary, of course):

   ```
   [mysqld]
   . . .
   innodb_log_group_home_dir=/var/lib/mysql/redolog
   innodb_log_file_size=32M
   innodb_log_buffer_size=64M
   innodb_log_files_in_group=2
   . . .
   ```

7. Edit the above configuration settings to their new values. If you require help on how to find suitable values, see the *There's more...* section of this recipe.

8. Save the configuration file.

9. Navigate to the directory configured for `innodb_log_group_home_dir`. If there is no such setting in your configuration file, navigate to MySQL's data directory that is then taken as the default.

10. Move the files whose names start with `ib_logfile` to a backup location. Do not copy them; they must be removed from their original location.

11. Restart the MySQL server.

12. Verify that new files are created as you configured them:

```
$ ls -l /var/lib/mysqld/redolog
```

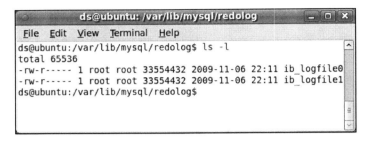

```
ds@ubuntu:/var/lib/mysql/redolog$ ls -l
total 65536
-rw-r----- 1 root root 33554432 2009-11-06 22:11 ib_logfile0
-rw-r----- 1 root root 33554432 2009-11-06 22:11 ib_logfile1
ds@ubuntu:/var/lib/mysql/redolog$
```

If you do not see the new files appear and the server does not start up correctly, check the MySQL error log for messages. Usually, the only thing that can go wrong here is that you either mistyped the directory name or did not actually remove the previous `ib_logfile` files.

To restore everything back to the original configuration, restore your configuration file from the backup and restore the `ib_logfile` files you moved out to the backup to their original location.

## What just happened...

By setting `innodb_fast_shutdown` to 0, you told the server to finish writing any pending changes to the disk before actually exiting. This makes sure there are no remaining transactions in the current redo logs that could get lost when these files are replaced.

After that you could change the configuration to new values, possibly using a different number of files and different sizes.

Then, before restarting, you could move the old redo log files out of the way. This is important because otherwise MySQL would complain about a mismatch between the settings file and the actual situation on disk. When it comes up finding no redo log files, it will create new ones with the settings just configured.

## There's more...

Often when talking about transactions, the word **rollback** comes up. It means that if something goes wrong in the middle of a possibly complex data manipulation operation and it has to be aborted, the database server will safely restore everything back to the state it was in when that operation began, not leaving any data only partially deleted or modified.

The opposite term—**rollforward** or **redoing**—is less commonly used. It means that whenever the complex operation mentioned earlier completes successfully, you are guaranteed that nothing short of actual hardware failure could lead to these changes being lost again. This might appear obvious because one would expect the database server not to report anything as successful unless it was actually completely done. However, if that were so, write operations would become painfully slow, as the underlying I/O subsystem (generally meaning hard disks) is very often the bottleneck component.

To evade this potential performance problem, most transactional databases, InnoDB being no different, uses the concept of a transaction—or redo—log that allows it to more efficiently handle write operations without risking data integrity. The redo log works as a sort of scratch pad, containing information on what remains to be done to the data files. With its help, the server can optimize disk access to improve performance.

The ideal size for the redo log depends on the size and number of transactions the server has to process. Generally speaking, the log should be large enough to store any single transaction plus about 10 percent. As a rule of thumb, the total log size (the number of log files times their individual size) need not exceed about 50% of the InnoDB buffer pool size.

For more information on redo logs and how to determine a sensible size setting, visit `http://mysqldump.azundris.com/archives/78-Configuring-InnoDB-An-InnoDB-tutorial.html` for a detailed description of InnoDB log configuration.

# Understanding and configuring important MySQL and InnoDB timeout options

MySQL's configuration file can contain a variety of different timeout settings, each responsible for a specific kind of operation or connection. In this recipe, we present a selection of these timeout settings and a suggested value to go along with each. The *How it works...* section has details on each value presented.

 In general, the values suggested here should be appropriate for both MySQL versions 5.0 and 5.1. However, please note that any of these options may well vary for your environment, depending on what the requirements are; so please do not simply use these values verbatim.

## Getting ready

To apply timeout configuration settings, you will need access to the MySQL configuration file—typically `my.cnf` or `my.ini` (on Windows)—and the rights to restart the server to have any changes made to the configuration take effect.

## How to do it...

1. Locate the MySQL configuration file and open it in a text editor.

2. In the `[mysqld]` section, set up the following values. Some of the options may already be present; others will likely have to be added. Make sure each option only appears once.

```
[mysqld]
. . .
innodb_rollback_on_timeout
innodb_lock_wait_timeout=50

interactive_timeout=1200
wait_timeout=28800

net_read_timeout=30
net_write_timeout=120
. . .
```

3. Save the file.

4. Restart the MySQL server.

## How it works...

By setting the values as described in the above section, you tell MySQL to use different values than the defaults for the options mentioned. The new settings take effect with the server restart.

### Setting values for innodb_rollback_on_timeout / innodb_lock_wait_timeout

These two settings are probably the most important as regards the locking behavior in any MySQL setup. Starting with version 5.0.13, MySQL changed the rollback behavior in case a timeout occurred because a transaction could not acquire a lock for a row. This usually happens when another transaction is still working on that row, and this is to be expected in normal database operations. The database server rolls back the entire transaction in this case. Applications should be designed to respond to such conditions by retrying the entire transaction.

Prior to 5.0.13, this was the default behavior, maintaining the rule that a transaction either succeeds or fails and is rolled back completely *as an atomic entity*. In 5.0.13 and newer versions, the default was modified to roll back only the very last statement of the failing transaction instead, keeping the transaction open. While there is a reason behind that change (for long transactions, it can be faster to just retry the very last statement than wait for the rollback and try again from the start), it requires special precautions taken on the application level to be able to handle this very MySQL-specific scenario.

 Setting the `innodb_rollback_on_timeout` option in the configuration file restores the more standard way of rolling back the whole transaction in case of a lock wait timeout. We strongly recommend enabling this option unless you are perfectly sure your application is aware of the MySQL-specific behavior configured as the default.

`innodb_lock_wait_timeout` defines the number of seconds a transaction will wait to acquire a necessary lock when a second transaction is working concurrently on the same records. The default value is 50 seconds and if the lock could not be acquired by then, a timeout error will occur and the transaction will be rolled back. Depending on how long the transactions in your setup typically take, this value often needs to be adjusted. If you regularly have bulk data operations that affect a lot of rows, you will want to increase this value. If on the other hand your system normally uses very short transactions, reducing this value may help you find out about problems with lock contention earlier.

## Setting values for interactive_timeout / wait_timeout

`interactive_timeout` defines how long an interactive client connection can be idle before the server closes it automatically. 'Idle' in this context refers to the time between two statements being executed with no activity in between.

We recommend reducing this from the default value of 28,800 seconds (8 hours) to a much lower value like 1,200 seconds (20 minutes). This allows the server to close idle connections and conserve some resources.

The counterpart variable for non-interactive sessions, such as those from an application server's connection pool, is called `wait_timeout` and has the same semantics. Depending on your application, you might want to leave this setting on a higher value as most connection pools can be configured to release connections automatically depending on current load conditions.

## Setting values for net_read_timeout / net_write_timeout

The protocol MySQL uses to handle communication between server and clients is rather limited in design, allowing only one operation to be carried out at a time. A side effect of this is that once a data transfer in either direction has started, there is no way for it to be interrupted in a controlled manner.

The `net_read_timeout` controls how long a piece of information can be sent from the client to the server, before the connection is aborted. This is usually not a problem—the default setting is 30 seconds. Under no regular circumstances will a communication in that direction take so long.

The `net_write_timeout` is more problematic because for large result sets, the default value of 60 seconds might be too short. This is especially true for clients that fetch the result in streaming mode, potentially performing time-consuming operations on each row retrieved, thereby making the overall operation take longer than the timeout.

The exact value required for your setup depends on how clients fetch data and work with it; so you will need to experiment and find a suitable value.

One caveat to consider with `net_write_timeout` is that it may lead to seemingly random failures of `mysqldump` like this:

```
mysqldump: Error 2013: Lost connection to MySQL server during query
when dumping table `tablename` at row: 935578
```

This can happen if the following conditions apply:

▶ `net_write_timeout` is set to a low value
▶ `max_allowed_packet` is set to a large value

Depending on the speed of the network over which `mysqldump` has connected and the size of the rows being dumped, it may be necessary to increase `net_write_timeout` much higher, at least to as long as it takes to transmit `max_allowed_packet` bytes over the network and write it to the output.

`mysqldump` is a regular client program and subject to the `net_write_timeout` setting. When the server sends rows to be dumped to `mysqldump` in chunks of up to `max_allowed_packet` bytes, depending on the network connection in between, this might take longer than `net_write_timeout` allows, making the server cut the connection even though nothing is really wrong. Increasing `net_write_timeout` for the `mysqldump` tool's session would remedy this, but unfortunately as of the time of writing there is no such setting for `mysqldump`. A workaround, if you encounter this problem, is to temporarily increase the global server `net_write_timeout` value:

```
$ mysql -uroot -e "SELECT @@GLOBAL.net_write_timeout AS oldvalue;
  SET GLOBAL net_write_timeout=600;"
$ mysqldump ...
$ mysql -e "SET GLOBAL net_write_timeout=oldvalue;"
```

The first command will display the current value for `net_write_timeout` and then set it to 10 minutes. After that the `mysqldump` can take place. Finally, the old value is reset (just make sure you fill in the correct old value).

See MySQL Bug #46103 at `http://bugs.mysql.com/bug.php?id=46103` for more details.

# Adjusting table and database name letter case handling for better platform independence

MySQL is available for a variety of platforms—the major ones being Windows and Linux. Even though data files are compatible and can be transferred between platforms, and configuration mostly follows the same general principles, there is an important caveat to know about how different operating systems handle file names.

In this recipe, we will show you how to set up MySQL in a way such that it is much less likely to run into problems when moving data files between platforms. Because MySQL databases and tables correlate to file system objects (directories and files), differences in how the operating system (or rather the file system) handles file and directory names can lead to undesired effects, especially when working in heterogenous environments.

We generally recommend setting up all your MySQL servers as described in this recipe to prevent any problems.

## Getting ready

You will need an operating system user account and sufficient rights to modify the server's configuration file. You will also need rights to restart the MySQL service because the name handling cannot be reconfigured on the fly.

Please note that for best results this setting should be applied before you start creating databases and tables on that server.

## How to do it...

1. Make sure MySQL is not running.

2. Locate the MySQL configuration file, usually called `my.cnf` or `my.ini` (on Windows) and open it in a text editor.

3. Locate the following parameter in the `[mysqld]` section. If it is not there, add it, otherwise edit it to match the value shown here:

```
[mysqld]
...
lower_case_table_names = 1
...
```

4.  Save the configuration file.

5.  Restart the MySQL server.

## How it works...

MySQL table and database names are mapped to file system names. Most Unix-like platform file systems are case sensitive, meaning that the two files `TableA` and `tablea` are different from each other. On Windows, these two names will refer to the very same file.

Setting the `lower_case_table_names` configuration to 1 tells MySQL to always convert any database or table names to lowercase letters, both when creating and using them in SQL statements. This will ensure that no matter what casing any SQL statements use, it will always affect the same tables.

This is especially useful in replication scenarios where you replicate between master and slave machines using different operating systems.

 Manually configuring this setting is highly recommended because depending on which platform MySQL is run on, the default setting will vary!

The only downside of setting up MySQL in this way is that the output of SHOW TABLES or SHOW DATABASES commands do not preserve the casing in which databases or tables were created, but this is merely a cosmetic issue.

## See also...

▸  *MySQL online manual on identifier case sensitivity, the relevant options and consequences*, section 8.2.2 at `http://dev.mysql.com/doc/refman/5.1/en/identifier-case-sensitivity.html`.

# Installing MySQL as a Windows service with custom options

While for development purposes it can be very handy to have MySQL run as a console application on Windows, for regular operations a background service is the option to go for. It has the advantage of starting up and shutting down automatically with Windows without the need for a user to log in to the machine.

In this recipe, we will show you how to install MySQL as a Windows service manually from the ZIP distribution available from the MySQL homepage and specify a custom configuration file.

# Getting started

Naturally, this is a Windows-only recipe. You will need a Windows user account with administrative privileges to register a new Windows service. Moreover, we assume you have already downloaded the MySQL distribution called *"Without installer (unzip in* C:\*)"*.

Make sure you choose the release matching your operating system (32 or 64 bit). In this recipe we will be using MySQL 5.1 from http://dev.mysql.com/downloads/mysql/5.1.html.

Be advised that security software on your computer might interfere with the installation of a Windows service, as some malicious software may try to hook into the system that way. If you encounter problems, you may have to disable anti-virus programs and other security products for the duration of the process. Do not forget to re-enable them when you are finished with the MySQL service setup!

# How to do it...

1. Unpack the downloaded ZIP file. Put the contents in c:\mysql\5.1.xx\service (replacing xx with the actual release number you are using).

2. On a command prompt (cmd.exe) enter the following commands to install the service. Make sure to enter the full path, instead of changing the working directory with the cd command:

   ```
   c:\> c:\mysql\5.1.xx\service\bin\mysqld.exe --install MySQL51
   --defaults-file=c:\mysql\5.1.xx\service\my.ini
   ```

```
Administrator: Command Prompt                                    _ □ X

c:\>c:\mysql\5.1.40\service\bin\mysqld.exe --install MySQL51 --defaults-file=c:\
mysql\5.1.40\service\my.ini
Service successfully installed.

c:\>
```

3. Edit the my.ini configuration file specified in the command above to meet your requirements.

4. Start the service and verify its status using these commands:

```
c:\> sc start MySQL51
```

```
c:\> sc query MySQL51
```

```
Administrator: Command Prompt

c:\>sc start MySQL51

SERVICE_NAME: MySQL51
        TYPE               : 10  WIN32_OWN_PROCESS
        STATE              : 2   START_PENDING
                             (NOT_STOPPABLE, NOT_PAUSABLE, IGNORES_SHUTDOWN)
        WIN32_EXIT_CODE    : 0   (0x0)
        SERVICE_EXIT_CODE  : 0   (0x0)
        CHECKPOINT         : 0x0
        WAIT_HINT          : 0x7d0
        PID                : 648
        FLAGS              :

c:\>sc query MySQL51

SERVICE_NAME: MySQL51
        TYPE               : 10  WIN32_OWN_PROCESS
        STATE              : 4   RUNNING
                             (STOPPABLE, PAUSABLE, ACCEPTS_SHUTDOWN)
        WIN32_EXIT_CODE    : 0   (0x0)
        SERVICE_EXIT_CODE  : 0   (0x0)
        CHECKPOINT         : 0x0
        WAIT_HINT          : 0x0

c:\>
```

You should see **STATE: 4 RUNNING** in the status output of the second command.

## How it works...

The MySQL server binary executable file `mysqld.exe` contains the necessary functionality to register itself with Windows as a background service. There are two options you should provide: `--install` and `--defaults-file`. The first one will specify the name of the new service to be created, MySQL51 in this case. The latter is used to define which configuration file the service will read its settings from.

Note that after the `--install` parameter, only a single parameter may follow. While this could be any parameter the MySQL server accepts, using the `--default-file` gives you the greatest flexibility, as you can put all other required settings there.

## There's more...

Apart from being able to run without a user having to log in to the server machine, services can define dependencies; so, for example, you could make sure your application server only gets started when the database is ready. For details on how to do this, refer to Microsoft Knowledge Base article #193888 at `http://support.microsoft.com/kb/193888`.

As services do not have access to a console or the graphical user interface in general, any problems encountered while starting the service will not tell you anything about the cause. On Windows, MySQL will report problems to the system event log, viewable from the control panel, and to the MySQL error log file, usually located in the data directory with a name composed from the machine name and a `.err` extension.

Should your service fail to start, inspect that log file to get an idea of what is wrong. To make sure your configuration file is OK, we recommend you to start the MySQL daemon once from the command line like this:

```
c:\> c:\mysql\5.1.xx\service\bin\mysqld.exe --defaults-file=c:\
mysql\5.1.xx\service\my.ini --console
```

This will allow you to see any potential problems right away before installing the service.

# Running multiple MySQL server instances in parallel on a Linux server

On most Linux setups, MySQL comes as a readymade installation package, making it easy to get started. It is, however, a little more complicated to run multiple instances in parallel, often a setup handy for development. This is because in contrast to Windows, MySQL is usually not installed in a self-contained directory, but most Linux distribution packages spread it across the appropriate system folders for programs, configuration files, and so on. You can, however, also install MySQL in its own directory, for example, if you need to use a version not available as a prepared package for your Linux distribution. While this gives you the greatest flexibility, as a downside you will have to take care of wiring up your MySQL server with the operating system manually. For example, you will need to hook up the startup and shutdown scripts with the appropriate facilities of your distribution.

In more recent distributions, you can make use of a tool called `mysqld_multi`, a solution that lets you set up multiple instances of MySQL daemons with varying configurations. In this recipe, we will show you how to set up two parallel MySQL servers, listening on different TCP ports and using separate data directories for their respective databases.

## Getting ready

This recipe is based on an Ubuntu Linux machine with the 8.04 LTS version. `mysqld_multi` comes with the MySQL packages for that operating system. If you are using other distributions, you need to make sure you have `mysqld_multi` installed to be able to follow along. Refer to your distribution's package repositories for information on which packages you need to install.

You will also need an operating system user with sufficient privileges to edit the MySQL configuration file—typically `/etc/mysql/my.cnf` on Ubuntu—and restart services. As for AppArmor or SELinux, we assume these have been disabled before you start to simplify the process.

## How to do it...

1. Locate and open the `my.cnf` configuration file in a text editor.

2. Create the following two sections in the file:

```
# mysqld_multi test, instance 1
[mysqld1]
server-id=10001
socket=/var/run/mysqld/mysqld1.sock
port=23306
pid-file=/var/run/mysqld/mysqld1.pid
datadir=/var/lib/mysql1
log_bin=/var/log/mysql1/mysql1-bin.log

# mysqld_multi test, instance 2
[mysqld2]
server-id=10002
socket=/var/run/mysqld/mysqld2.sock
port=33306
pid-file=/var/run/mysqld/mysqld2.pid
datadir=/var/lib/mysql2
log_bin=/var/log/mysql2/mysql2-bin.log
```

3. Save the configuration file.

4. Issue the following command to verify the two sections are found by `mysqld_multi`:

```
$ sudo mysqld_multi report
```

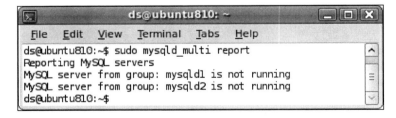

5. Initialize the data directories:

```
$ sudo mysql_install_db --user=mysql --datadir=/var/lib/mysql1
$ sudo mysql_install_db --user=mysql --datadir=/var/lib/mysql2
```

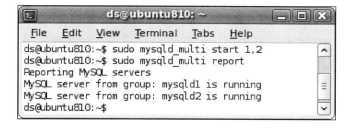

6. Start both instances and verify they have been started:

```
$ sudo mysqld_multi start 1
$ sudo mysqld_multi report
```

7. Connect to both instances and verify their settings:

```
$ mysql -S /var/run/mysqld/mysql1.sock
mysql> SHOW VARIABLES LIKE 'server_id';

$ mysql -S /var/run/mysqld/mysql2.sock
mysql> SHOW VARIABLES LIKE 'server_id';
```

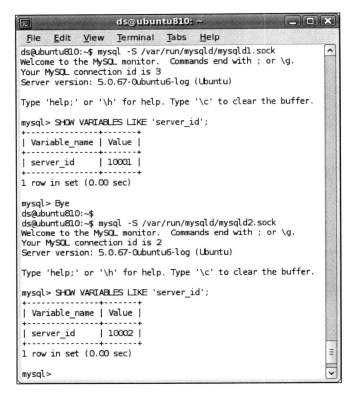

## How it works...

`mysqld_multi` uses a single configuration file for all MySQL server instances, but inside that file each instance has its individual `[mysqld]` section with its specific options. `mysqld_multi` then takes care of launching the MySQL executable with the correct options to use the options from its corresponding section.

The sections are distinguished by a positive number directly appended to the word `mysqld` in the section header. You can specify all the usual MySQL configuration file options in these sections, just as you would for a single instance. Make sure, however, to specify the minimum set of options as in the recipe steps previously stated, as these are required to be unique for every single instance.

## There's more...

Some special preparation might be needed, depending on the particular operating system you are using.

### Turning off AppArmor / SELinux for Linux distributions

If your system uses the AppArmor or SELinux security features, you will need to make sure these are either turned off while you try this out, or configured (for permanent use once your configuration has been finished) to allow access to the newly defined directories and files. See the documentation for your respective Linux distribution for more details on how to do this.

### Windows

On Windows, running multiple server instances is usually more straightforward. MySQL is normally installed in a separate, self-contained folder. To run two or more independent server instances, you only need to install a Windows service for each of them and point them to an individual configuration file. For information on how to set up MySQL as a Windows service and how to specify which settings file to use, see the relevant recipe in this chapter.

### Considering the alternative MySQL Sandbox project

As an alternative to `mysqld_multi` you might want to have a look at MySQL Sandbox, which offers a different approach to hosting multiple independent MySQL installations on a single operating system. While `mysqld_multi` manages multiple configurations in a single file, MySQL Sandbox aims at completely separating MySQL installations from each other, easily allowing even several MySQL releases to run side by side. For more details, visit the project's website at `http://mysqlsandbox.net`.

## See also

- ▸ *Installing MySQL as a Windows service with custom options*
- ▸ *Ubuntu Linux Wiki on AppArmor at* `https://wiki.ubuntu.com/AppArmor`
- ▸ *Fedora Wiki on SELinux* `http://fedoraproject.org/wiki/SELinux`

# Preventing invalid date values from being stored in DATE or DATETIME columns

In this recipe, we will show you how to configure MySQL in a way such that invalid dates are rejected when a client attempts to store them in a DATE or DATETIME column using a combination of flags for the SQL mode setting.

See the *There's more...* section of this recipe for some more detailed information on the server mode setting in general and on how to use it on a per-session basis.

## Getting ready

The configuration options shown in this recipe can be applied to individual sessions or as server-wide defaults. For production systems, we recommend specifying them in the MySQL configuration file. You will need the necessary operating system level privileges to edit it, and then restart the service to activate the settings.

The final step in the recipe is the attempt to insert some invalid dates. You can safely skip this step. If you want to try it, you will need a table set up like this in the *test* database:

```
CREATE TABLE table_a (
  test_date DATE NOT NULL
);
```

## How to do it...

1. Locate the MySQL configuration file, typically my.cnf or my.ini (on Windows), and open it in a text editor.

2. In the [mysqld] section make sure the following line is present, adding it if needed:

   ```
   [mysqld]
   . . .
   sql-mode=STRICT_ALL_TABLES,NO_ZERO_DATE,NO_ZERO_IN_DATE
   . . .
   ```

3. Save the file.

4. Restart the MySQL server.

5. Verify whether the setting was applied using this statement from a MySQL client:

```
mysql> SELECT @@GLOBAL.sql_mode;
```

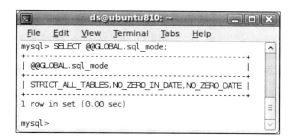

6. Optionally try to insert some false values:

```
mysql> INSERT INTO table_a VALUES ('2009-02-31');
mysql> INSERT INTO table_a VALUES ('2009-00-31');
mysql> INSERT INTO table_a VALUES ('0000-00-00');
```

## Getting ready

Setting the SQL mode to STRICT_ALL_TABLES will enable validation on all tables (as opposed to only those in transactional storage engines if you were to use STRICT_TRANS_TABLES). While setting up the SQL mode like this would already prohibit the insertion of values like Feb 31st, one could still insert all zero dates or dates with zero fields in them. This is what the other two options NO_ZERO_DATE and NO_ZERO_IN_DATE take care of.

## There's more...

Starting with MySQL 5.0, the concept of *SQL modes* was introduced to provide granular control over the degree of leniency the server will apply for invalid values. MySQL has traditionally been very forgiving when receiving invalid values to be inserted into its tables. There are truncation and approximation rules on what will happen when, for example, you try to insert a value that exceeds the maximum length of a column's definition.

For enterprise systems, this clearly is unwanted behavior. Whenever an application tries to store values in the database that do not meet the previously defined criteria of length and value ranges, an error must be thrown to prevent silent data corruption. One might argue that data validation must be done at the application level and invalid data never be stored to the database anyway. But we are strong believers in the database being the "last line of defense". Of course, any decent application will reject invalid inputs, but in reality there can be bugs or an administrator accessing the database independently might just make a mistake. Setting up MySQL to verify incoming data (again) can be invaluable in these situations. Even though you take a slight performance hit, data integrity should be considered as an even higher priority.

The so-called **strict mode** enables the general use of MySQL server-side data validation. The remaining options described in the MySQL online manual section 5.1.8 at `http://dev.mysql.com/doc/refman/5.1/en/server-sql-mode.html` allow a somewhat granular control over what exactly get validated and how.

We recommend going through all the SQL mode options to see if there are any that you would like to enable on your servers.

### Configuring SQL mode for the current session only

For experimenting with the different SQL modes, it is often easier to configure them for your current session only. The following statement disables the global settings configured above for the current session only:

```
mysql> SET @@session.sql_mode='';
```

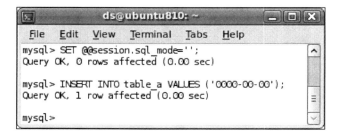

This can also come in handy for maintenance scripts that need to temporarily disable certain restrictions that are set up for normal operations.

# 8
# MySQL User Management

In this chapter, we will cover the basic tasks related to MySQL user management. You will learn about the following topics:

- ▶ Configuring MySQL Administrator to display global privileges and hosts
- ▶ Defining an alternative user for administrative tasks
- ▶ Disabling the default accounts
- ▶ Creating a basic user
- ▶ Creating an installation user
- ▶ Creating a read-only account
- ▶ Defining a specific user for backup
- ▶ Defining a specific user for replication
- ▶ Allowing access from specific hosts only
- ▶ Synchronizing user permissions across servers
- ▶ Regaining access to your database in case of lost account information
- ▶ Avoiding plain text passwords in administrative scripts

## Introduction

While MySQL has a reputation for being easy to set up in the first place (and rightly so), one has to keep in mind that the initial configuration, for example, as provided by the Windows installation wizard, needs some more tweaking for production use. This particularly holds true for the default user configuration.

Whenever you connect to a MySQL server, the connection is associated with a specific user (even if you do not specify the user explicitly, in which case a default account is selected). If you tell MySQL Windows installer to create an anonymous user, the resulting configuration allows for full local access to the database without having to provide any kind of credentials. Whoever is able to access the machine that runs your database will be able to play havoc with your data—which is not something you typically want for your production systems.

 Do NOT use an anonymous user on production systems!

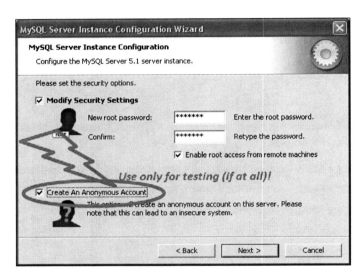

The definition of users and their respective access privileges is often considered a downstream configuration task that can be tackled shortly before production use. We strongly recommend defining the basic roles for database users in advance. This often helps to structure the way the database is accessed, which in turn might improve the systems architecture and prevent certain development flaws.

In this chapter, we will have a look at some typical user roles found in MySQL production environments. First of all, we will discuss how to create a hardened administration account that is not accessible anonymously, and then how to get rid of the default users provided by the MySQL installation. Additionally, we will introduce accounts for basic operations and guest access, and refer to technical users for replication, backup, and recovery.

Besides this, we will also cover how to restrict database access for certain users to specific clients. This makes for an additional line of defense because knowledge of a username and password are not sufficient to connect to the database. A potential attacker would also have to take control of the defined client address.

As MySQL installations with more than one database server are not an exotic configuration any more, the sometimes tedious task of keeping the user definitions in synch throughout all instances will be addressed as well. And finally, we will not conceal the downside of improved security: if a potential attacker will not be able to access the database without knowing the username and password, you will not, either. We will show you how to access your database even if the sticky notes with your credentials are lost.

The recipes in this chapter will primarily focus on MySQL Administrator as the tool of choice when manipulating the user accounts and their privileges.

 MySQL Administrator is an administration client provided by MySQL as part of the MySQL GUI Tools Bundle, which is available for free at http://dev. mysql.com/downloads/gui-tools/5.0.html.

However, in some situations a graphical user interface just does not fit the requirements. This is particularly the case if scripting is required, for example, for automated and unattended changes. For these situations, we will also show alternative ways to change the user rights without the help of MySQL Administrator.

While the recipes in this chapter will give you an overview of a typical role configuration, we encourage you to adapt this proposal according to your needs. And from our experience, it is typically a good idea to discuss the possible user configuration with your IT security department—if your company happens to have one—well in advance, so as to prevent lengthy discussions later on.

# Configuring MySQL Administrator to display global privileges and hosts

Throughout the following recipes, we will use MySQL Administrator as the main tool to manage user rights. Some of the privileges, however, are not visible in MySQL Administrator in its default configuration. This recipe will show you how to change the relevant options, so we will be able to manage even the global privileges.

## Getting ready

To step through this recipe, you will need a running MySQL database server and a working installation of MySQL Administrator. No other prerequisites are required.

## How to do it...

1. Start MySQL Administrator. Connect to your database server using any account.

2. Select the entry **Options...** from the **Tools** menu.

3. Make sure the options **Show Global Privileges** and **Show hosts in user list** are selected.

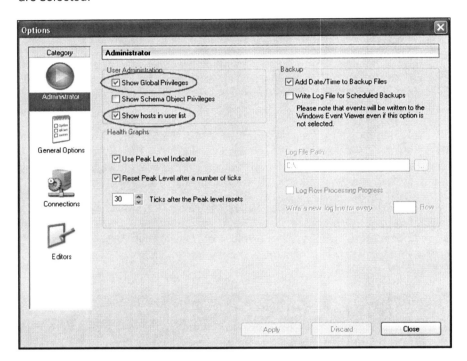

4. Select **Close**. If a **Save changes?** dialog comes up, press the **Yes (Apply these changes permanently)** button.

## How it works...

With the options selected throughout this recipe, MySQL Administrator will allow you to view and change not only the schema privileges that define the operations allowed on certain schemata, but also the global privileges.

The available global privileges are partially identical to the schema privileges, for example, **SELECT** or **UPDATE**, but there are also some additional privileges, such as **SHUTDOWN**, that affect the whole database regardless of specific schemata.

The options affect the **User Administration** view of MySQL Administrator. You will notice an additional tab **Global Privileges**, and when you select a user account in the list to the lower left, the hosts for which the specific rights were defined are listed.

# Defining an alternative user for administrative tasks

During MySQL installation, an account for user _root_ is created. This account receives all privileges without any exceptions. In most installations, this configuration is basically left unchanged, which makes the _root_ account a very rewarding target for attacks. An attacker will not have to guess a username and a corresponding password—the password alone will do because it is a safe bet to assume the existence of a username _root_. This is why we recommend that you create an administration account with a different name.

This recipe will show you how to create a user account that can act as a replacement for the _root_ user.

## Getting ready

You are going to need a catchy username for your administration account and a corresponding password. When making up the password, keep in mind the typical password recommendations for good passwords (hard to guess, but easy to remember; should contain upper and lower case letters, numbers, and special characters). Throughout this recipe, we will assume a username _admin4mysql_ and a password _As,ysp4M_ ("A simple, yet strong password for MySQL") throughout this recipe.

 The _admin4mysql_ user is only used as an example. For security reasons, please do NOT use this account name (or any of the other users introduced in this chapter) for real-world installations! We strongly suggest using your own, individual usernames instead.

Additionally, you will have to make sure that manipulation of global privileges is enabled in MySQL Administrator options. Please refer to the _Configuring MySQL Administrator to display global privileges and hosts_ recipe if in doubt.

Finally, you have to think about from which host you are going to connect to your MySQL instance to perform administrative tasks. In most cases, this will be `localhost`, which we assume as host in the following recipe. In some situations, however, this might differ, for example, if you have no login rights on the database host itself. In these situations, you should define a certain host as your base for administrative tasks. Have its host name or IP address ready for the following tasks.

The steps below will guide you through the process of creating an alternative administration account.

## How to do it...

1. Start MySQL Administrator. Connect to your database server using the *root* account.

2. Select the **User Administration** entry either from the list on the left or from the **View** menu.

3. Click on the **Add new user** button.

4. Enter the basic user information (username, password, contact information), followed by a click on the **Apply changes** button.

5. Right-click on the new user *admin4mysql* (in the user list on the lower left) and choose the option **Add host from which the user can connect**.

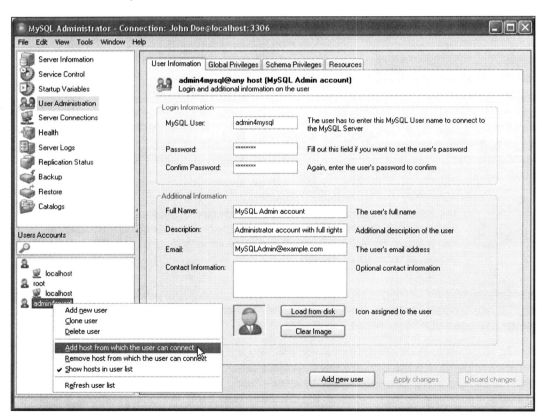

6.  In the following form, enter the host from which you are going to perform your administration tasks (typically `localhost`).

7.  Select the tab **Global Privileges**. Choose the **<<** button to grant all global rights to the user, followed by a click on the **Apply changes** button:

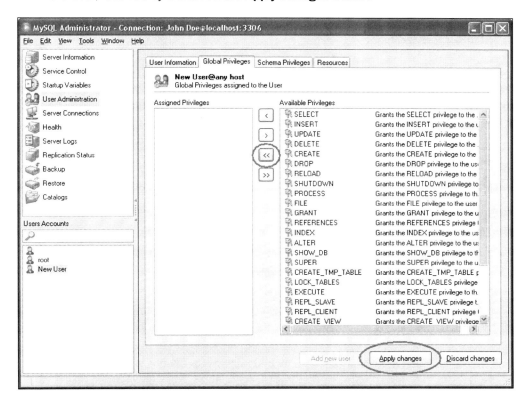

8.  Right-click on the **admin4mysql** entry on the user list and select **Remove host from which the user can connect** from the context menu.

9.  Confirm the message box indicating **The any-host (%) entry has been deleted**, followed by the **Apply changes** button.

## How it works...

Let's take a look at what we did throughout the above recipe. In steps 1 through 4, we created a new user named *admin4mysql*. At this point, this user could connect to the database server from any host, but as new users have no initial rights whatsoever, he or she would not be able to actually do anything. With steps 5 and 6, we defined a specific host from which the user will be allowed to log on. Step 7 finally assigns all rights to the newly-created user.

With steps 8 and 9, the user *admin4mysql* is no longer able to connect from any host other than `localhost`. This makes it necessary for a possible attacker to log in on the host itself before he or she can try to gain access to the database. This in turn ensures brute force attacks on the MySQL server via the network from a random host for this user will not be successful.

## There's more...

MySQL Administrator features a graphical user interface—it is not the tool of choice in some situations such as if scripting capabilities are needed. In these circumstances, a single SQL script will perform the same changes as the above recipe. This script could be executed, for example, by using the *mysql* command-line client and connecting with a privileged MySQL user like your current *root* account:

```
GRANT ALL PRIVILEGES ON *.* TO 'admin4mysql'@'localhost'
IDENTIFIED BY 'As,ysp4M' WITH GRANT OPTION;
```

The values for password and maybe host name have to be adapted according to your choices.

## See also

▶ *Configuring MySQL Administrator to display global privileges and hosts*

▶ *Avoiding plain text passwords in administrative scripts*

# Disabling the default accounts

In the previous recipe, we created a new user for administration tasks as a replacement for the default *root* user. If and only if another user with full rights is available, we can discard the default users that were created during MySQL installation. This helps harden your MySQL installation against possible intruders who will not be able to attack well-known account names.

## Getting ready

You have to assure yourself that you have a second user with full rights (in addition to the *root* user) at your disposal. By deleting the *root* account, you risk a database with no means of basic administration—unless there is an equivalent user available. This is why MySQL Administrator won't let you delete this user and hence we will have to resort to the command-line client to delete the *root* account.

The following steps will show you how to remove the default accounts.

## How to do it...

1.  Connect to your database server with the `mysql` command-line client using the additional administration account (*admin4mysql*).

2.  To delete the *root* user, issue the following commands:

    ```
    DROP USER 'root'@'localhost';
    DROP USER 'root'@'%';
    ```

3.  To delete the anonymous user, execute these commands:

    ```
    DROP USER ''@'localhost';
    DROP USER ''@'%';
    ```

## How it works...

MySQL creates up to four default accounts, depending on the choices made during the installation. These four accounts use two usernames, namely *root*, and the anonymous user with an empty username. For each username the two hosts—`localhost` and `%`—are defined, with the latter being the place holder for any host. Thus the default accounts are as follows:

► `'root'@'localhost'`

► `'root'@'%'`

► `''@'localhost'`

► `''@'%'`

 The first account `'root'@'localhost'` is always available, while the other three are only created in certain installation scenarios.

With the commands in the above steps, all possible default accounts will be deleted. If these users do not exist, you will receive an error message (*error code 1396 "operation failed"*) indicating that the account does not exist. After having executed all of these commands, you can be sure that no unwanted default accounts are left.

You can test the effect of the steps performed by using MySQL Administrator. The entries of the *root* user and the anonymous user (with the empty name) will be gone in the **User Administration** view if you reconnect to your database server.

## See also

► *Regaining access to your database in case of lost account information*

# Creating a basic user

If installed from scratch, MySQL does not provide a default user suitable for everyday use. You could of course use the *root* user or an alternative administrative user (for example: *admin4mysql*) with full rights. However, this is strongly discouraged for security reasons, especially if you have different users and/or applications that need access to your MySQL database. In the following recipe, we will show you how to create a typical user that has full access to a certain database (schema).

## Getting ready

You will need some information before stepping through this recipe:

In the first place, you will need a username and a password. If the user is a person who is going to use the database interactively, you will mostly use his or her real name as the login name. For accounts that will be used by applications, it is typically a good idea to include the application (and—if applicable—the role for which the account will be used) in the account name. Examples would be *john_doe*, *hotelbooking*, or *carrental_stdusr*. Keep in mind, however, that the length of the username (as of MySQL 5.1) is limited.

[  The length of a MySQL username must not exceed 16 characters! ]

Second, you should find out about which database of your MySQL installation has to be accessed by your user. This database has to exist already, otherwise you will not be able to assign the respective rights using MySQL Administrator (however, the script solution in the *There's more...* section would even work without an existing target schema).

Throughout this recipe, we will show you how to create a basic user *sample_stduser* with read-write access to a database named *sample* and a password *S4mpl3-Pw*. As a prerequisite, we assume that the database *sample* already exists.

## How to do it...

1. Start MySQL Administrator. Connect to your database server using the *admin4mysql* account.

2. Select the entry **User Administration** either from the list on the left or from the **View** menu.

3. Click on the **Add new user** button.

4. Enter the basic user information (username, password, contact information), followed by a click on the **Apply changes** button.

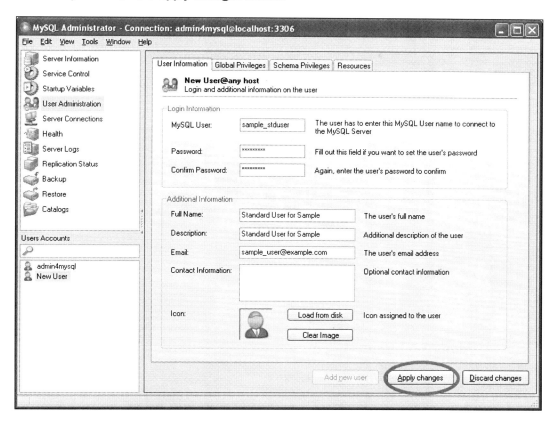

5. Select the tab **Schema Privileges** and select the schema *sample* from the Schemata list on the left. Select the privileges **SELECT**, **INSERT**, **UPDATE**, **DELETE**, **CREATE TEMPORARY TABLES**, **LOCK TABLES**, and **EXECUTE** from the **Available Privileges** list on the right, and for each selected privilege press the **<** button. Choose the **Apply changes** button afterwards.

To select and assign more than one privilege at once, hold down the *Ctrl* key while selecting the privileges.

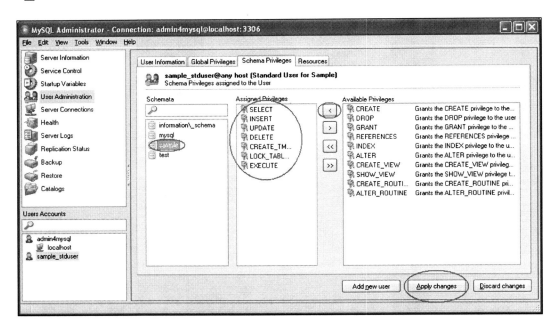

## How it works...

Step 4 creates a new user who is allowed to connect from any host, but has no privileges whatsoever. By assigning the privileges in step 5, the user is granted the rights to read (SELECT) and change (INSERT, UPDATE, DELETE) data from any table in the *sample* schema. These are the most basic rights that are typically necessary for a basic user.

Additionally, we grant the CREATE TEMPORARY TABLE privilege. This sometimes comes in handy for complex statements and the corresponding risks are typically acceptable. Temporary tables are not visible to other users and are limited to the database connection by which they are created. Moreover, they are purged as soon as the connection is closed. So typically, it is not a problem to grant this right. However, as with all privileges the basic security rule holds true for this rights as well.

 Don't assign unnecessary privileges!

If you are sure that this privilege will not be used, it is recommended not to assign it to the user you created.

The LOCK TABLES privilege allows the user to completely lock tables. This is sometimes helpful to coordinate concurrent access to data by different sessions and is needed by some applications that make use of LOCK TABLES statements to prevent concurrent data modifications. On the other hand, this privilege enables a user to block read and write access to all tables at discretion, which might basically render the database useless to other users in case of extensive or incautious use of of LOCK TABLES statements. If you are sure that your user won't need such statements, it is recommended not to assign this privilege.

Finally, the EXECUTE privilege gives the user the right to call stored routines. As the user is not granted the rights to create or change such routines, granting this privilege does not pose a noteworthy additional risk even if there are no stored routines to execute. If there are any, the EXECUTE privilege has to be assigned for the user to be able to call these stored routines. Some applications make use of stored routines, so this right was included for typical users. But as stored procedures and functions are still a fairly new feature of MySQL, they are not very widely used yet. So in many cases, you can do without this privilege.

With this set of privileges, we created a user that has full access to all tables in our schema. This account is a reasonable compromise between rights granted and restrictions still in place. However, you will need a corresponding installation user that can be used to set up the schema in the first place. The creation of this user is described in the following recipe.

## There's more...

If you want (or need) to avoid using MySQL Administrator for creating the basic user account, you can alternatively issue a single SQL statement instead (the values for password and database name have to be adapted according to your choices):

```
GRANT SELECT, INSERT, UPDATE, DELETE, CREATE TEMPORARY TABLES, LOCK
TABLES, EXECUTE ON sample.* TO 'sample_stduser'@'%' IDENTIFIED BY
'S4mpl3-Pw';
```

This is helpful if you need a scripting solution for user definitions, but it also gives you the possibility to create the user before the target database schema exists. With MySQL administrator, you have to define the schema first because it will only let you assign rights for existing databases. This script could be executed, for example, by using the MySQL command-line client.

## See also

▶  *Defining an alternative user for administrative tasks*
▶  *Avoiding plain text passwords in administrative scripts*
▶  *Creating an installation user*

# Creating an installation user

In the previous recipe *Creating a basic user*, we discussed how to define a typical user for accessing a certain database schema. Additionally, there is an administration user account with full rights. For installations that are managed by one single administrator, this might be sufficient. But often you do not want to perform all administrative tasks by yourself. For example, you might want to delegate the task of defining the database structure to a different person. Some applications also have their own installation routines that require rights to set up a database schema. For these tasks, you should consider creating a specific installation user for certain databases. This user should not have global rights, but should be restricted to make changes to one specific database. This way, you can delegate certain administration tasks without the risk of users tampering with other databases that are not their business.

Even if you manage your database installation all by yourself, it might be a good idea to use a specific account to perform these tasks, as this helps prevent accidental changes to other databases.

This recipe will guide you through the steps of creating such an installation user for a certain database (schema).

## Getting ready

For this recipe, you will again need to come up with a username (remember the 16 character length limit), a password, and the name of the database that will be accessible to the user. As before, this database should already exist, otherwise you will have to resort to the scripting solution from the *There's more...* section of this recipe.

We will assume *sample_install* as the username, *sample* as the database, and *1n5t4llPw* as the password.

## How to do it...

1. Start MySQL Administrator. Connect to your database server using the administration account (*admin4mysql*).

2. Select the entry **User Administration** either from the list on the left or from the **View** menu.

3. Click on the **Add new user** button.

4. Enter the basic user information (username, password, contact information), followed by a click on the **Apply changes** button.

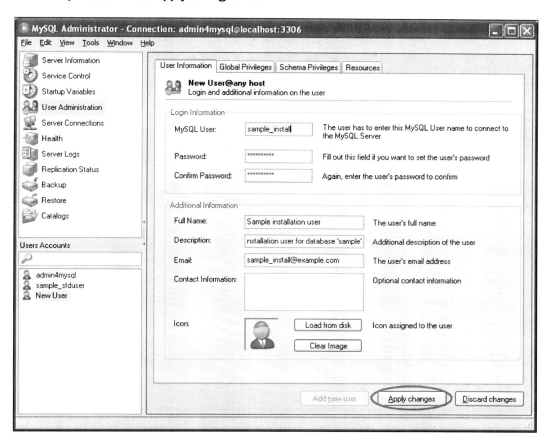

5. Select the tab **Schema Privileges** and select the schema *sample* from the Schemata list on the left. Press the **<<** button to assign all privileges for the sample database. Next, select the **GRANT** privilege from the **Assigned Privileges** list and press the **>** button to exclude the **GRANT** right. Choose the **Apply changes** button afterwards.

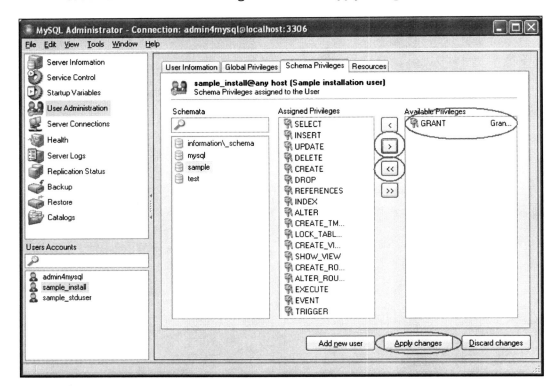

## How it works...

The new user is created in steps 1 through 4, while step 5 assigns all rights on the *sample* database to the user, with the **GRANT** privilege being the only exception (also see the *There's more...* section of this recipe).

This user has basically full rights for the whole database schema. This account can be used to set up the database, which might, for example, involve creation, deletion, or making changes to tables, management of stored routines, or definition of views. However, it is not recommended to use such a powerful account for normal operations. You should preferably stick to a basic user for this instead, as we have defined in the previous recipe.

## There's more...

In this section, we will discuss some advanced aspects of the user creation, such as scripted solutions to the problem and granting rights to create users to certain accounts.

### Creating the account without using MySQL Administrator

You can also create the account without having to use MySQL Administrator by issuing the following SQL command (adapt the values for password and database schema name accordingly):

```
grant ALL PRIVILEGES on sample.* to 'sample_install'@'%' identified by
'1n5t4ll-Pw';
```

As mentioned before, this allows for scripting as well as defining the account without having to create the database beforehand. For example, you could use the MySQL command-line client to execute this script.

### Permitting management of user rights

Some applications feature highly sophisticated installation routines, which try to perform many tasks automatically. In some cases, they also try to define MySQL user rights themselves to make sure they have the correct set of privileges. If this is the case, you might need to permit privilege management for the installation user.

As another example, you might want to delegate not only the responsibility of managing a database, but also the (sometimes tedious) task of maintaining the privileges of the corresponding user accounts.

In both situations, you should consider assigning the GRANT privilege to the installation user. This right allows granting those rights to other users (or revoking them from them) that you are granted yourself. As a result, the GRANT privilege will not allow the installation user to extend his or her rights.

To assign the GRANT privilege using MySQL Administrator, select the *sample_install* user in the **User Administration** view, switch to the **Schema Privileges** tab, select the sample schema, and assign the privilege by selecting it and pressing the **<** button, followed by the **Apply Changes** button.

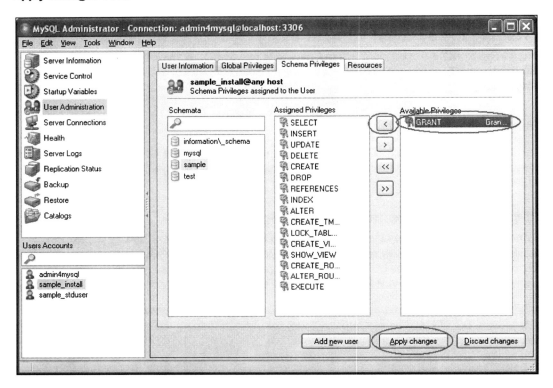

Alternatively, you could issue the following SQL command:

```
GRANT ALL PRIVILEGES ON sample.* TO 'sample_install'@'%' IDENTIFIED BY
'1n5t4ll-Pw' WITH GRANT OPTION;
```

 Please note that the GRANT privilege itself does not allow you to create users!

For being able to create users, an administration user has to have write access to the *mysql* database. Unfortunately, this allows for manipulation of *all* user accounts regardless of their scope; so a user with *mysql* write access is not restricted to managing one separate database any more. Because of this, we recommend leaving the creation or deletion of the accounts to the main administrative user. The installation user is then able to assign the specific rights for the database he or she is responsible for to the user.

Example: Let the *admin4mysql* account create a user with:

```
GRANT USAGE ON *.* to 'john_doe'@'%' IDENTIFIED BY 'Confidential';
```

The installation user *sample_install* (if he or she has the GRANT privilege) can then assign specific rights to the user at his or her own discretion:

```
GRANT SELECT ON sample.* to 'john_doe'@'%';
```

## See also

- ▸ *Defining an alternative user for administrative tasks*
- ▸ *Avoiding plain text passwords in administrative scripts*
- ▸ *Creating a basic user*

# Creating a read-only account

In the previous recipes, we presented how to define users for different roles: global administration, setting up a specific database, and basic access. Another typical role for users is the guest user, which typically is limited to read-only operations. Credentials for such an account can be passed on to different people without risking accidental or deliberate data manipulation. In this recipe, we will show you how to define such a read-only user account.

## Getting ready

Think of a catchy username, password, and the name of the database schema for which the user will have read access. In addition, this schema should already exist. You will have to use the SQL statement alternative from the *There's more...* section of this recipe otherwise.

We will assume *sample_guest* as the username, *sample* as the database, and *R34d-Only* as the password.

## How to do it...

1. Start MySQL Administrator. Connect to your database server using the administration account (*admin4mysql*).

2. Select the entry **User Administration** either from the list on the left or from the **View** menu.

3. Click on the **Add new user** button.

4. Enter the basic user information (username, password, contact information), followed by a click on the **Apply changes** button.

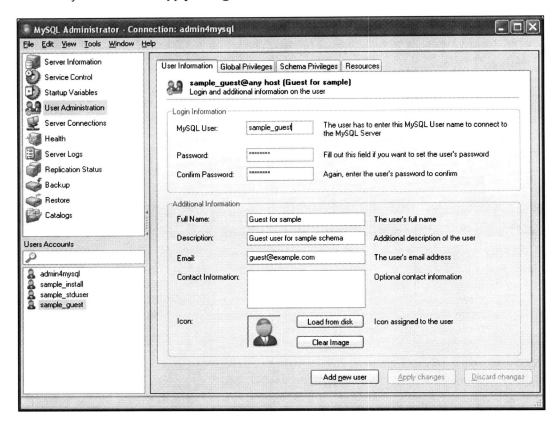

5.  Select the tab **Schema Privileges** and select the schema *sample* from the Schemata list on the left. Click on the **SELECT** privilege from the **Available Privileges** list on the right, and press the **<** button to assign this privilege. Choose the **Apply changes** button afterwards.

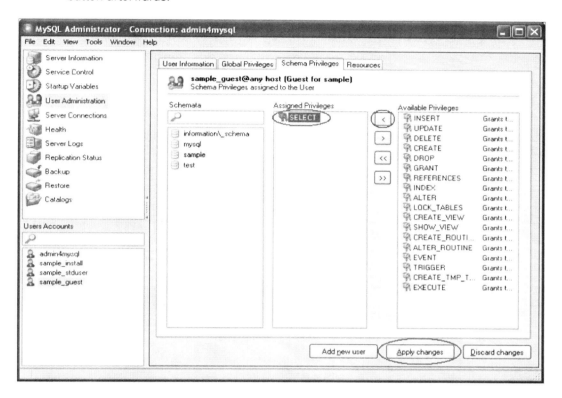

## How it works...

Steps 1 through 4 create the user without any privileges; step 5 assigns the **SELECT** right on the *sample* database to the user.

With these settings, this user is not able to make any changes to the database. Nevertheless, we strongly recommend not communicating the username and the password for this guest account too laxly. In many cases, a database contains valuable or sensitive information. If the credentials of a guest user account are common knowledge (or too easy to guess, like the infamous username 'guest' with exactly the same password), your data will be an easy prey for any possible intruder.

## There's more...

In this section, we will discuss some advanced aspects of the user creation, such as scripted solutions to the problem and granting rights to create users to certain accounts.

### Creating the account without using MySQL Administrator

To create the guest account without using MySQL Administrator, execute the following SQL command:

```
GRANT SELECT ON sample.* TO 'sample_guest'@'%' IDENTIFIED BY
'R34d-Only';
```

This command will also work if the sample database was not created in advance.

### Allowing stored procedure calls

Some database designers try to encapsulate complex statements in stored routines (functions or procedures). Some of these routines could also be very helpful for a guest user, so he or she can resort to predefined logic, and does not have to try to construct complex queries by him- or herself. For this reason, it might make sense to also assign the EXECUTE privilege to the guest user. But please note that assigning this privilege might have an unexpected side effect:

 A guest user with EXECUTE rights can perform changes to the database!

If a stored routine performs changes to the database, like an UPDATE or a DELETE operation, it will execute flawlessly even if the user who calls this routine does not have any other rights but EXECUTE. This does not typically pose a serious risk because the guest user is not able to define new routines on his or her own. But as soon as there are stored procedures in place that perform changes to the database, the EXECUTE privilege should be granted with care.

## See also

- ▶ *Defining an alternative user for administrative tasks*
- ▶ *Avoiding plain text passwords in administrative scripts*

# Defining a specific user for backup

Even though many people have a tendency to ignore the possibility of unpleasant future events, one of your duties as a database administrator is to take reasonable precautions to minimize the negative effects of a disaster. In short, it is your job to perform backups.

There are some strategies on how to best back up your database and there are also different tools on the market that promise to help you do so. Basically, the different backup strategies can be divided into two groups: hot and cold backup. While cold backups can simply be done by copying and saving files, hot backups are not as easy to perform.

There are some tools available that promise file-based hot backups. However, if you want or need to resort to the MySQL tools, you will typically have to do a database dump (for example, using *myqsldump*) to back up your data during normal operations (if all your tables are MyISAM tables, you could use the *mysqlhotcopy* tool instead).

To perform a database dump, you will need a user to connect to your database. We recommend defining a user that is specifically suited for this task. This allows you to quickly identify connections used for backups and you can be sure that these connections will not be able to change any data. The following recipe will show you how to create such an account.

 Please note that this user is suited for backup purposes only. The recovery task should be performed by an administrator user because you typically need full access to the database for this.

## Getting ready

Again, you are going to need a username and a password. We will use *backup_usr* as the username and *B4ckM3Up!* as the password.

## How to do it...

1.  Start MySQL Administrator. Connect to your database server using the *admin4mysql* account.

2.  Select the entry **User Administration** either from the list on the left or from the **View** menu.

3.  Click on the **Add new user** button.

4.  Enter the basic user information (username, password, contact information), followed by a click on the **Apply changes** button.

5. Right-click on the new user *backup_usr* (in the user list on the lower left) and choose the option **Add host from which the user can connect**.

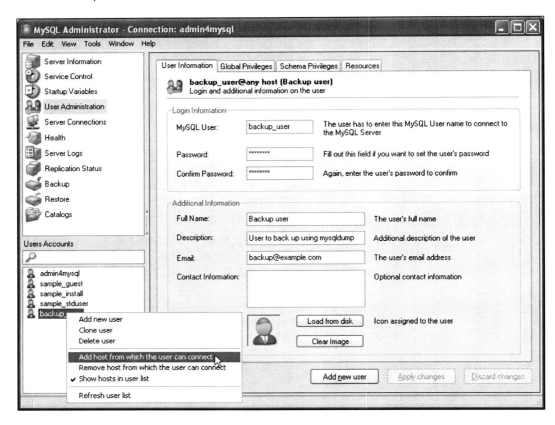

6. In the following form, enter the host from which you are going to perform your backups (typically `localhost`).

7.  Select the tab **Global Privileges**. Choose the **SELECT**, **RELOAD**, **LOCK_TABLES**, and **REPL_CLIENT** privileges from the **Available Privileges** list on the right, press the **<** button for each of them, and click on the **Apply changes** button.

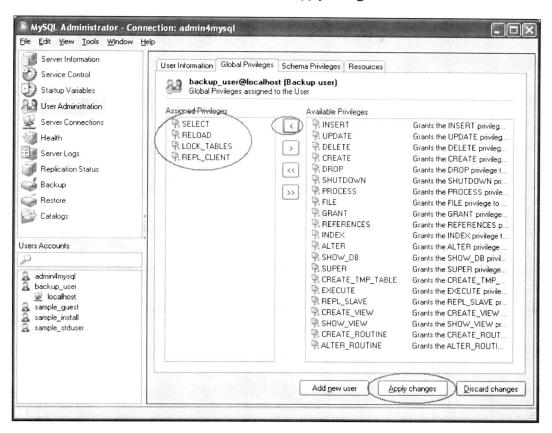

8. Right-click on the *backup_usr* entry on the user list and select **Remove host from which the user can connect** from the context menu.

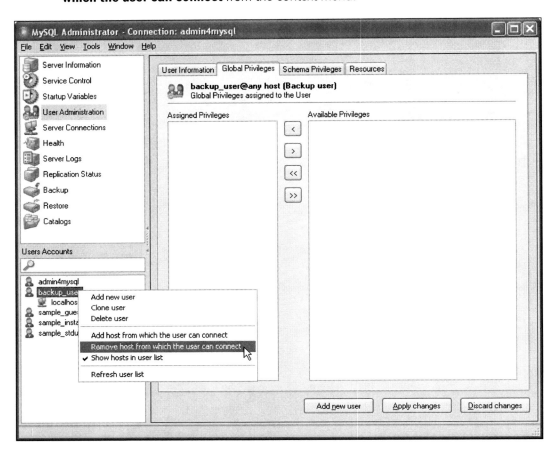

9. Confirm the message box indicating **The any-host (%) entry has been deleted**, then click the **Apply changes** button.

## How it works...

Let's take a look at the steps of this recipe. By following steps 1 through 4, a new user named *backup_usr* is created. At this point, this user does not have any rights, but could successfully connect from any host. Steps 5 and 6 define a specific host (`localhost`) from which the user will be allowed to log on. Step 7 finally assigns the rights that are necessary to perform backups using the *mysqldump* command.

With steps 8 and 9, the user is no longer able to connect from any host other than `localhost`. This makes an attack harder because a possible intruder would first have to log in to the host itself before he or she can access the database.

The first (and most important) privilege that was assigned is the **SELECT** privilege, which is used to read the data; otherwise we would not be able to write it to the dump file. As this user is allowed to read all data from all databases, you should not forward the user credentials of this user.

The second privilege is `LOCK_TABLES`. It is needed because *mysqldump* locks the tables before dumping their data. This privilege is not required when the *mysqldump* options `--single-transaction` or `--master-data` are used, but it is recommended to assign this right just in case a dump without one of these options has to be done.

Finally, the privileges `RELOAD` and `REPLICATION_CLIENT` are required for the *mysqldump* option `--master-data`. This option is used frequently, if you have to recover databases that are configured as replication clients; assigning these privileges allows you to use this option as well.

## There's more...

MySQL Administrator is not always the proper tool for user definition (for example, in a scripted environment). An alternative route to constitute an account for backup tasks is the execution of the following SQL command:

```
GRANT SELECT, LOCK TABLES, RELOAD, REPLICATION CLIENT ON *.* TO
'backup_user'@'localhost' IDENTIFIED BY 'B4ckM3Up!';
```

## See also

- ▸ *Defining an alternative user for administrative tasks*
- ▸ *Configuring MySQL Administrator to display global privileges and hosts*
- ▸ *Avoiding plain text passwords in administrative scripts*

# Defining a specific user for replication

In some cases, the MySQL replication mechanism is a very helpful feature, for example, to horizontally scale your read loads or to provide redundancy for improved robustness. If you plan to use this feature, you have to define a user on the replication master for this. This recipe will show how to create this user.

## Getting ready

To step through the recipe, you will need a username, a password, and the host on which the replication slave will be located. We will use *repl_user* as the username with *Pw_4_R3pl* as the corresponding password and we will assume that the replication slave will be located on host `bluebox`.

## How to do it...

1. Start MySQL Administrator. Connect to your database server using the *admin4mysql* account.

2. Select the entry **User Administration** either from the list on the left or from the **View** menu.

3. Click on the **Add new user** button.

4. Enter the basic user information (username *repl_user*, password *Pw_4_R3pl*, contact information), followed by a click on the **Apply changes** button.

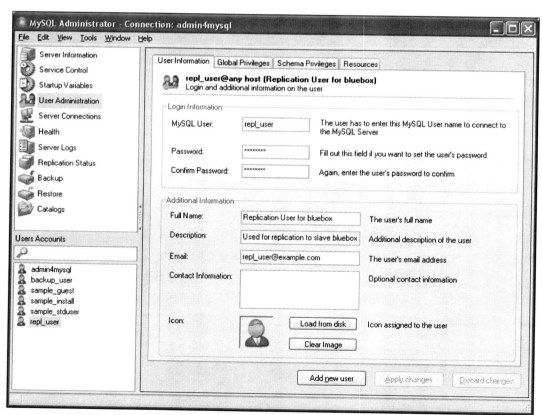

5. Right-click on the new user *repl_user* (in the user list on the lower left) and choose the option **Add host from which the user can connect**:

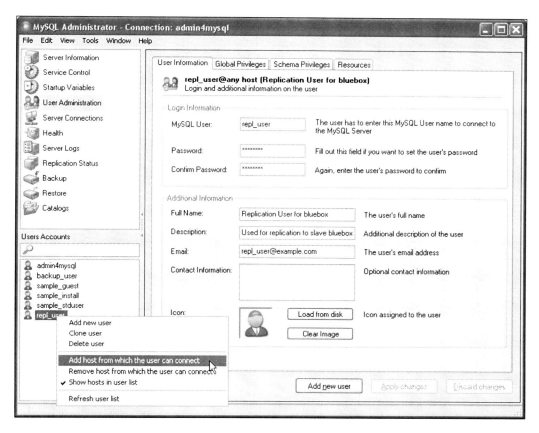

6. In the following form, enter the host from which you are going to perform your backups (here: `bluebox`).

7. Select the tab **Global Privileges**. Choose the **REPL_SLAVE** privilege from the **Available Privileges** list on the right, press the **<** button, and subsequently click on the **Apply changes** button.

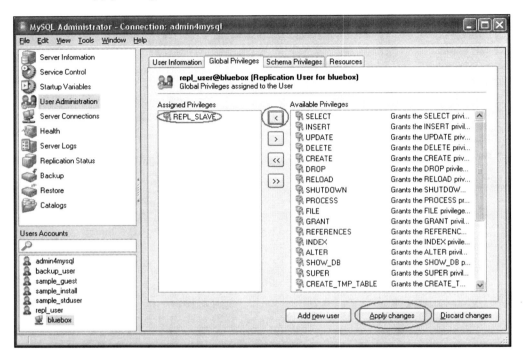

8. Right-click on the *backup_usr* entry on the user list and select **Remove host from which the user can connect** from the context menu.

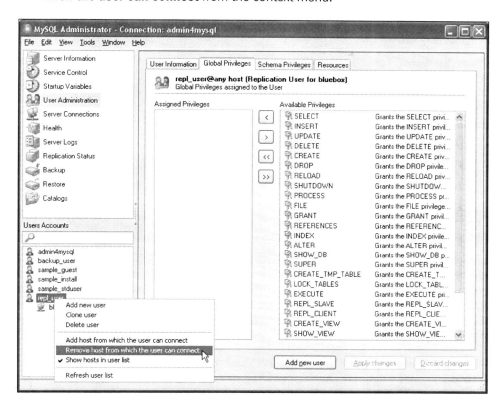

9. Confirm the message box indicating **The any-host (%) entry has been deleted**, then click the **Apply changes** button.

## How it works...

Let's inspect the steps of the above recipe. In steps 1 through 4, we defined a new account named *repl_user*, which at this point has no privileges at all, but could connect to the MySQL server from any host. With steps 5 and 6, we define the specific host from which the user will be allowed to log on (in this case this is the host that runs the replication slave). Step 7 assigns the privilege necessary for the replication slave to the new account.

With steps 8 and 9, the account *repl_user* is changed in such a way that it can no longer be used from any host (actually, the account *repl_user*@% is removed, while a second account *repl_user*@*bluebox* stays intact). A possible attacker would have to log in to the replication slave host to make use of this account.

## There's more...

To create the replication account without resorting to a GUI tool, you can alternatively use the following SQL command:

```
GRANT REPLICATION SLAVE ON *.* TO 'repl_user'@'bluebox' IDENTIFIED BY
'Pw_4_R3pl';
```

## See also

- Defining an alternative user for administrative tasks
- Configuring MySQL Administrator to display global privileges and hosts
- Avoiding plain text passwords in administrative scripts

# Allowing access from specific hosts only

When creating a user account using MySQL Administrator, the user is by default entitled to log in from any host. If the account will be used on specific clients only, it is advisable to modify the account in such a way that login is restricted to these clients. This helps to reduce the chance of successful attacks against your database server because a possible intruder will not only have to get hold of (or guess) the proper credentials, but also has to seize control of one of the registered clients.

The following recipe will guide you through the steps of restricting a user account to a specific host.

## Getting ready

For the following steps, we assume that an account with username *example* has already been defined and that this account is enabled for login from any host. We furthermore assume that this account should be changed in such a way that it can only be used to log in from host `client1.mycompany.com`.

## How to do it...

1. Start MySQL Administrator. Connect to your database server using the *admin4mysql* account.
2. Select the entry **User Administration** either from the list on the left or from the **View** menu.

3. Right-click on the user account you want to change in the **Users Accounts** list on the left and choose the option **Add host from which the user can connect**.

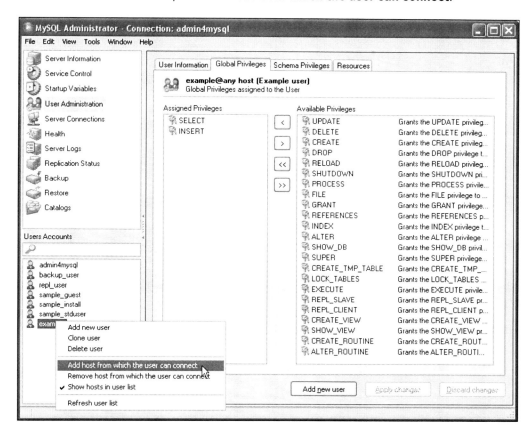

4. In the following form, enter the host from which the user will be able to connect (here: `client1.mycompany.com`).

5. Save the changes by clicking on the **Apply changes** button.

6.  Select the tab **Global Privileges**. Left-click on the user entry *example* on the list on the lower left. Note the privileges that are listed in the **Assigned Privileges** list (in the example screen, we assume that global privileges **SELECT** and **CREATE TEMPORARY TABLE** are assigned to the user).

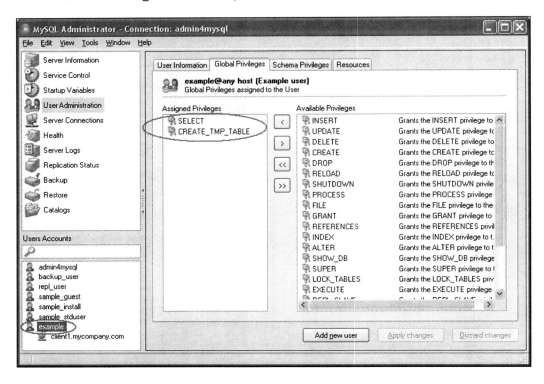

7.  Switch back to the new host by clicking on the host name client1.mycompany. com on the left. Assign the same privileges noted in the previous step (in this example: **SELECT** and **CREATE TEMPORARY TABLE**) by selecting them from the list of available privileges on the right and selecting the < button, followed by the **Apply changes** button.

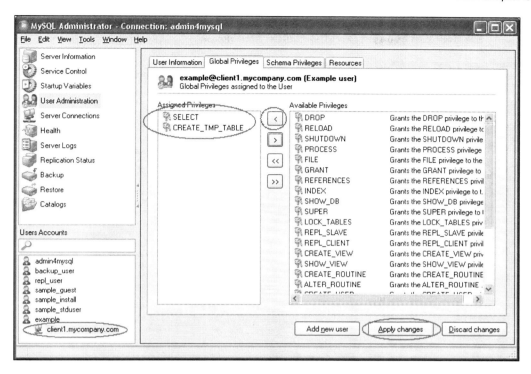

8. Choose the tab **Schema Privileges** and select the first schema from the Schemata list.

9. Select the entry *example* from the **Users Accounts** list on the lower left. Note the privileges that are assigned for the selected schema.

10. Switch to the new user by selecting the host name `client1.mycompany.com` on the left. Assign the privileges noted in the previous step (by selecting them from the list on the right and clicking the **<** button), then choose **Apply changes**.

11. Select the next schema and repeat steps 9 and 10 for every entry in the Schemata list.

12. Right-click on the **example** entry on the user list and select **Remove host from which the user can connect** from the context menu.

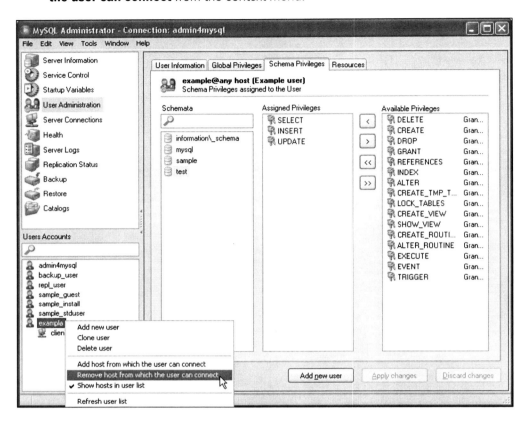

13. Confirm the message box indicating **The any-host (%) entry has been deleted**, then click the **Apply changes** button.

## How it works...

Let's have a look at what we did throughout this recipe.

In steps 1 through 5, we added the new host to which the account should be restricted (to be precise, we created a new account *example@client1.mycompany.com*).

Steps 6 and 7 are performed to copy the existing global privileges, while steps 8 through 11 do the same for the schema-level privileges. With these operations, the user will be granted the same permissions when logging in from the newly-defined specific host (this recipe does not take into account any schema object privileges).

Within steps 12 and 13, the permission to log in from any host is withdrawn by deleting the host from the account (technically speaking, the user *example@%* is deleted).

With these steps, we created a copy of the existing *example* account, which is restricted to a specific host, and disabled the possibility to log in from any other machine.

## There's more...

The preceding recipe can be used interactively only and it describes definition of single hosts only. Next, we will show you how to create a user by using a script and how to introduce multiple hosts.

### Creating the account without using MySQL Administrator

If you want to restrict access of an account to a client machine, but you do not want to use MySQL administrator for this, the following steps lead to identical results:

1. Connect to your database server as an administrative user (*admin4mysql*) using your favorite SQL client (for example, MySQL Query Browser).

2. Find out about the current privileges by issuing the following command:

   ```
   mysql> show grants for 'example'@'%';
   ```

3. The result of the above query will be a list of one or more SQL statements. Modify these statements by replacing the username `'example'@'%'` by the new name `'example'@'client1.mycompany.com'`.

4. Execute each of the modified statements from the previous step (you will have to put a semicolon at the end of each statement).

5. To deny login from any host, execute the following command:

   ```
   mysql> drop user 'example'@'%';
   ```

### Allowing access from a group of hosts

The above recipe is suited for accounts that are restricted to log in from a specific client machine. In some cases, however, you do not want to allow access from any host, but it is not possible to restrict connections to a single client machine either.

As long as the number of clients is reasonably low, it is possible to individually register the respective machines. For this, the mechanism outlined in the above recipe can be used. You will have to adapt steps 6 and 9 by selecting the appropriate template user and you typically will skip steps 12 and 13.

As soon as the number of clients exceeds a certain limit, it is no longer feasible to register them separately. For these cases, the wildcard feature of MySQL might be a valid alternative for you.

MySQL allows the use of wildcard operators when defining host names of user accounts. Let's assume you have a set of client machines `client01.mycompany.com` through `client99.mycompany.com`. These clients should be able to access the database, but you do not want to allow access from any other machine. In this case, you would restrict the access of your account to host `client%.mycompany.com` (note the `%` character). The percent sign acts as a wildcard that can be replaced by any character string. With this definition, login from host `client57.mycompany.com` will be successful, but a connection attempt from `alien1.mycompany.com` will be refused.

Please note that the use of wildcards does not necessarily allow for the exact restrictions you might want to define. In the above example, there are some unwanted machines that are still able to access the database: a machine named `clientfake.mycompany.com` would match the host definition as well. To minimize the wrong matches, you could use the host definition `client__.mycompany.com` instead (with `_` being a placeholder for exactly one arbitrary character), but a machine `clientXY.mycompany.com` would still be able to establish a connection.

The host definition for MySQL user accounts can also be used to provide IP addresses instead of machine names. If you are able to assign similar IP addresses to all machines that should be able to access your host, you can provide a host name like `192.168.1.%`. This example value would enable access for all clients with an IP address from 192.168.1.0 through 192.168.1.255.

The use of the single character wildcard is possible with IP addresses as well. A host value of `192.168.1.1__` will allow login from clients with IP addresses 192.168.1.100 through 192.168.1.199.

An alternative to wildcards is to group possible clients in a common subnet. You can then make use of a notation that allows defining IP ranges using the base address of the range combined with the corresponding netmask. If you set the host of a MySQL account to `<subnet prefix>/<subnet mask>`, connections from any IP address within this subnet will be accepted by MySQL.

If, for example, you want to allow login from four client machines whose IP addresses range from 192.168.1.100 to 192.168.1.103, you could set up an account with the host set to `192.168.1.100/255.255.255.252`, which will enable login for just the range you intended to.

This behavior is somewhat contradictory to the MySQL manual, which states:

> *"The netmask can only be used to tell the server to use 8, 16, 24, or 32 bits of the address." (See* `http://dev.mysql.com/doc/refman/5.1/en/account-names.html`.)

If this statement were true, the only possible subnet masks would be 255.0.0.0, 255.255.0.0, 255.255.255.0, and 255.255.255.255 (in the latter case the subnet mask would be skipped for the sake of brevity). However, experience shows that other subnet masks work just as well, but you have to make sure that the IP address given before the subnet mask is the pure subnet prefix. Any address from within the subnet would not work, as all connections would be refused.

To clarify that, we will inspect the example from the MySQL manual, which tries to prove that different netmasks do not work. The manual states that a host value `192.168.0.1/255.255.255.240` (28 bits) will not work, which is basically correct! But the reason for that is **not** that handling of a 28 bit netmask (255.255.255.240) is generally unsupported, but that the IP address 192.168.0.1 is an address from the subnet and not the subnet prefix itself. The correct subnet prefix would be 192.168.0.0, and with a host of `192.168.0.0/255.255.255.240`, every client from the subnet—with an IP address from 192.168.0.0 to 192.168.0.15—would be accepted for connections.

Generally, if you define the host with the `<subnet prefix>/<subnet mask>` notation, any client address is tested against this value according to the following rule (the operator "&" stands for the bitwise AND operation).

If the following equation is true, the client address is accepted: `<client address> & <subnet mask> = <subnet prefix>`.

## See also

▸ *Defining an alternative user for administrative tasks*

▸ *Configuring MySQL Administrator to display global privileges and hosts*

▸ *Avoiding plain text passwords in administrative scripts*

# Regaining access to your database in case of lost account information

Of course, you want to protect your database against attacks in every possible way. However, from time to time you might find yourself in a situation in which you have to act as an attacker yourself—for example, if you forgot the user credentials for the administration user or if you accidentally deleted the root user account without having created an equivalent user beforehand. But do not worry. We will show you a way to regain control of your database without losing any data (not even your existing user accounts).

## Getting ready

This recipe involves steps to edit the MySQL configuration files and to restart your MySQL server. Therefore, you will need access to the host your database runs on. You also need the rights to start and stop the MySQL instance at your own discretion. Furthermore, you should know the location of the MySQL configuration file (typically `my.ini`) and you should have the rights to change this file.

This recipe allows you to both create a new user and to change the password of a user that already exists. In our example, we will change the password of the user *admin4mysql* to *As,ysp4M* and we will create a new user *root* with *r00t_pw* as the password.

 Before executing the following instructions, you should make sure that no users or processes can access your database server.

## How to do it...

1. Open a text editor and create a file with the following content:

   ```
   SET PASSWORD FOR 'admin4mysql'@'localhost' =
       PASSWORD('As,ysp4M');
   GRANT ALL PRIVILEGES ON *.* TO 'root'@'localhost' IDENTIFIED
       BY 'r00t_pw' WITH GRANT OPTION;
   ```

    Make sure that the SET command and the GRANT command are each written on a single line.

2. Save the file in a location of your choice (for example: `C:\temp\mysql-init.sql`).

3. Open the MySQL configuration file (for example: `C:\Program Files\MySQL\ MySQL Server 5.1\my.ini`) in a text editor. Find the line that reads `[mysqld]` and add the following line below (if a line starting with `init-file=` already exists, change it accordingly):

   ```
   init-file="C:/temp/mysql-init.sql"
   ```

4. Use the location of the file you saved in step 2. Please note the use of simple forward slashes instead of backslashes.

5. Save the MySQL configuration file.

6. Restart your running MySQL instance (for example, by restarting the Windows service:

   ```
   net stop MySQL & net start MySQL)
   ```

7. Open the MySQL configuration file in a text editor again to revert the changes made in step 3. Remove the `init-file` line from your configuration file (or disable it by putting a hash # character in front) and save it.

# How it works...

The file created in steps 1 and 2 contains the SQL commands by which the password of the user *admin4mysql* is reset and a user *root* is created. In the case of lost account information for the administrative user, these commands can't be executed as usual (for example, via a MySQL client). We change the MySQL configuration in steps 3 and 4 in order to have these commands executed on the next MySQL start despite the lost credentials. Step 5 initiates a restart of the MySQL server, which causes the commands to be executed. Step 6 reverts the configuration changes of steps 3 and 4, so the command file won't be repeatedly executed on every subsequent MySQL start.

The content of the initialization file as listed in step 1 has to be adapted according to your specific needs. As you might have guessed already, this mechanism is also suitable to change your actual database content, not only user information. It allows for basically every change imaginable to your database, so you should make sure that access to the MySQL configuration file is restricted to authorized persons. The init-file option might be used otherwise to tamper with your data, create user accounts for future unauthorized access, or render your system inoperable.

# There's more...

A different alternative to reset passwords is to start your MySQL database server using the option --skip-grant-tables. With this setting, any login will be successful and full rights will be granted—regardless of the user credentials specified. In fact, this option is often referenced as the preferred way to change your user accounts without the need for proper credentials. Nevertheless, we strongly recommend not using this approach, as there are some limitations and drawbacks.

While the --skip-grant-tables approach enables you to reset a forgotten password, it does not allow creating a new user account right away, as any attempt to grant rights using the GRANT statement will at first be refused with reference to the disabled grant tables:

```
Welcome to the MySQL monitor.  Commands end with ; or \g.
Your MySQL connection id is 2
Server version: 5.1.31-community-log MySQL Community Server (GPL)

Type 'help;' or '\h' for help. Type '\c' to clear the buffer.

mysql> GRANT ALL PRIVILEGES ON *.* TO test@'%';
ERROR 1290 (HY000): The MySQL server is running with the --skip-grant-tables option so it cannot execute this statement
mysql>
```

You have to issue a `FLUSH PRIVILEGES` statement first in order to have MySQL accept a `GRANT` command. While this is a way to create a new user account with full rights, it is a bit cumbersome.

More importantly, use of the `--skip-grant-tables` is a major security issue because as long as the database runs with this option enabled, anybody can connect to the database without having to provide any credentials at all, which enables free access for all possible intruders. While this might not be critical for your personal development database, it is absolutely intolerable for production use or other databases with sensitive data. To prevent unauthorized access while the grant tables are disabled, it is strongly recommended to accompany this configuration with the option `--skip-networking` (on Windows machines, you have to additionally provide one of `--shared-memory` or `--named-pipe` options). Unfortunately, this actually deactivates access for most regular clients as well, which is equivalent to a service interruption until the database is relaunched in the regular configuration.

In conclusion, the `--skip-grant-tables` option makes it necessary to restart the database twice (as opposed to once with the `--init-file` variant) and there will be a service interruption between the two restarts due to the network cut-off that is necessary for security reasons (while the `--init-file` approach allows for continued access except for the moment of the first restart). This is why we strongly recommend using the method described in this recipe.

# Avoiding plain text passwords in administrative scripts

In many of the previous recipes, we also showed how to define user permissions using SQL commands. As such statements can easily be executed in scripts, these are well suited to produce scripts for automated definition of MySQL accounts. While it is generally a good idea to reduce the manual tasks in database administration, one should keep in mind that such scripts contain information that is extremely useful for possible attackers. One can extract the defined users, their specific rights, the hosts from which access is granted, and typically even the corresponding passwords. In this way such user definition scripts often contain all the information necessary to access your database, which makes them extremely sensitive. The risk that somebody coincidentally trips over such a script should not be underestimated—and an open door may tempt a saint.

The most critical portion of such scripts is of course the **passwords**. In this recipe, we will show how to create user definition statements without the need to give a plain text password.

## Getting ready

To step through this recipe, you will need a running MySQL database server and a SQL client (we are going to use the MySQL command-line client). You should also have a working SQL script that defines the accounts (using plain text passwords). No other prerequisites are required.

## How to do it...

1. Connect to your database server with the MySQL command-line client.

2. For a plain text password in your script, give the following command and make a note of the encoded result:

   ```
   SELECT PASSWORD('<Your plain text password>');
   ```

3. Replace the `IDENTIFIED BY '<Your plain text password>'` portion of the script by `IDENTIFIED BY PASSWORD '<Encoded result>'`.

4. Repeat steps 2 and 3 for all passwords in your script.

## How it works...

MySQL needs to store its passwords to be able to verify user credentials. This information is not stored in plain text, but as a so-called hash value. A **hash value** is a value that represents a password, but which is not reversible, so it is basically impossible to find the actual password for a given hash value.

To check whether a given password is correct, MySQL calculates the hash value for it and compares it with the stored value. If these values are identical, the password is verified.

When creating a user account using the `IDENTIFIED BY '<Your plain text password>'` syntax, MySQL calculates the hash code and stores the resulting value in its user data. The `IDENTIFIED BY PASSWORD '<hash value>'` syntax stores the hash value immediately. In both cases, the effects of the script are identical, but with the second variant no plain text password is accidentally exposed.

### Example of creating a user in a script without a plain text password

Let us assume the following script:

```
GRANT ALL PRIVILEGES ON *.* TO 'admin4mysql'@'localhost' IDENTIFIED BY
'As,ysp4M' WITH GRANT OPTION;
```

Execute the following command on the MySQL command line:

```
mysql> SELECT PASSWORD('As,ysp4M');
```

Replace the password in the script:

```
GRANT ALL PRIVILEGES ON *.* TO 'admin4mysql'@'localhost' IDENTIFIED
BY password '*46FFD1D6944482DFCCD3B31AC500199AFDE515F7' WITH
GRANT OPTION;
```

## There's more...

The SET PASSWORD command is another common place for use of plain text password.
To prevent use of plain text passwords altogether, you should replace all SET PASSWORD
[...] = PASSWORD('<plain text password>') expressions in your scripts by the
corresponding variant using hash values directly (without using the PASSWORD() function):
SET PASSWORD [...] = 'Encoded password'.

# 9
# Managing Schemas

In this chapter, we will cover:

- ▸ Adding new columns at specific positions
- ▸ Defining a Primary key for a table containing (non-unique) data
- ▸ Allowing individual `INSERT` statements with "0" values in auto-incrementing columns
- ▸ Globally allowing `INSERT` statements with "0" values in auto-incrementing columns
- ▸ Choosing a suitable storage engine
- ▸ Improving the performance of `ALTER TABLE` for InnoDB
- ▸ Using a stored procedure to conditionally add columns or indexes
- ▸ Improving query performance for InnoDB tables with `BLOB` columns
- ▸ Identifying differences between two schemas
- ▸ Comparing schema revisions using hash values

## Introduction

When you first install a database server, you obviously do so because you want to store and later access information reliably and quickly. A major concern in this regard—apart from the server's hardware and operating system—is the logical layout of the database. This refers to how you decide on the structure of the tables, which will in the end be what any database-driven application will use as its primary level of abstraction.

This chapter is not about data types, table naming, or other topics revolving around those kinds of decisions that are often best made in cooperation with application developers. Often they will have their own ideas about how to set up the database schema that you should take into account as a database administrator (both their and your lives will be easier in the days to come when you both agree on naming conventions for tables, columns and indexes, and so on).

Instead in this chapter, you will find advice on the specialties and differences that make MySQL different from other **Relational Database Management Systems** (**RDBMS**) like Oracle, Microsoft SQL Server, or IBM's DB/2. Moreover, we will have a look at some common tasks that will come up time and again, either before you set up the tables or afterwards, when your database is already up and serving requests from applications.

MySQL is different from most other RDBMS in that it does allow you to choose from a variety of storage engines. A storage engine is a part of the database system that handles physically storing your data on a disk, in contrast to, for example, checking the syntax of a SQL statement or executing a function like DATE(). With MySQL you get a choice as to which of those implementations (each with its individual strengths and weaknesses) is to be used on a per-table basis. The following picture shows the general architecture of the MySQL server layer above the individual storage engine implementations:

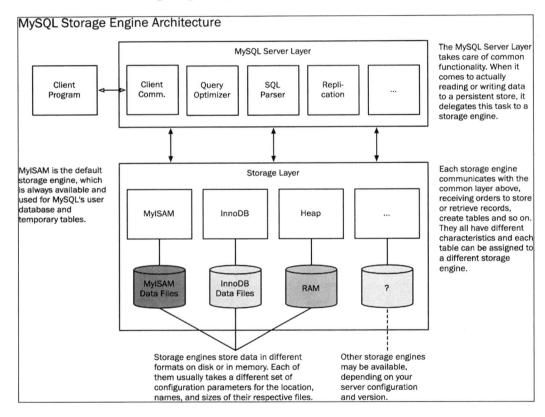

Using this approach, one can choose the optimum storage strategy for each table individually. There are third parties too that produce (open and closed source) storage engines that may specialize in niches like PBXT for media storage. Other databases offer all the features in their default (and usually only) storage format: from transaction support to high performance, over full-text indexing and fine-grained locking to special data types.

MySQL makes the administrator choose from a range of options, none of which supports all of the features just named together. So in the end, having the option to pick from the available storage engines is sometimes more of a burden than an opportunity.

The MySQL online manual contains a table contrasting the available storage engines and their respective feature sets in its Chapter 13 at `http://dev.mysql.com/doc/refman/5.1/en/storage-engines.html`.

We will not go into the details of each and every engine available because from a business perspective—and this is what counts in our opinion—realistically only two of them are worthy of a detailed discussion: MyISAM and InnoDB.

Apart from that, you might find the Blackhole engine useful for special replication scenarios and you should also take a look at the *Federated* and *Merge* engines, both of which, even though with limits, allow multiple tables to be treated as one, locally and over the network.

# Adding new columns at specific positions

One of the regular tasks a database administrator has to perform is to modify the structure of existing tables, especially adding new columns to accommodate the need to store more attributes for the records stored in a table.

While in general the order of columns is not relevant for MySQL itself—or any well-behaved application accessing columns by name rather than their position in the table—it is often desirable to have control over the order the columns appear in a table.

There are several reasons to precisely control the column order: from a general drive to keep your schema tidy, over the general benefit of a table displaying its columns in a sensible order when doing a `SELECT *`, to other external constraints that you cannot influence.

In this recipe, we will show you how to modify an existing table and add one or more new columns at specific positions.

## Getting ready

To follow along, you will need access to MySQL server with a user account that has sufficient privileges to alter table definitions. For example, we will first create a table with a few attributes and then add a few more columns at predefined positions. We assume the `test` database to be available and your user account to have the right to create and modify tables in it.

## How to do it...

1. Connect to the database using the command-line `mysql` client.

2. Make the `test` database the default:

   ```
   mysql> USE test;
   ```

3. Create the initial sample table:

   ```
   mysql> CREATE TABLE person (
              firstname VARCHAR(30),
              lastname VARCHAR(30),
              birthday DATE,
              person_id INT UNSIGNED NOT NULL AUTO_INCREMENT,
              PRIMARY KEY (person_id)
           );
   ```

4. Insert some records:

   ```
   mysql> INSERT INTO person (firstname, lastname, birthday)
              VALUES ('Martin','van Buren','1782-12-05'),
                     ('Thomas','Wilson','1856-12-28'),
                     ('William','Clinton','1946-08-19');
   ```

5. Select the full contents of the table:

   ```
   mysql> SELECT * FROM person;
   ```

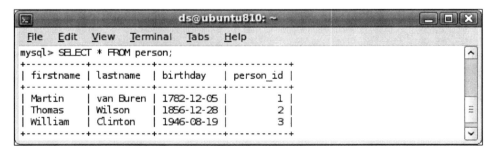

6. Add a `salutation` column and a `middle_initial` column. The former is to be created before `firstname`, the latter between `firstname` and `lastname`:

```
mysql> ALTER TABLE person
          ADD COLUMN salutation VARCHAR(10) FIRST,
          ADD COLUMN middle_initial CHAR(1) AFTER firstname;
```

Update some data:

```
mysql> UPDATE person SET salutation='Mr.';
mysql> UPDATE middle_initial='W' WHERE person_id=2;
mysql> UPDATE middle_initial='J' WHERE person_id=3;
```

7. Select the full table contents again:

```
mysql> SELECT * FROM person;
```

```
ds@ubuntu810: ~                                    _ □ X

File  Edit  View  Terminal  Tabs  Help

mysql> SELECT * FROM person;
+------------+-----------+----------------+-----------+------------+-----------+
| salutation | firstname | middle_initial | lastname  | birthday   | person_id |
+------------+-----------+----------------+-----------+------------+-----------+
| Mr.        | Martin    | NULL           | van Buren | 1782-12-05 |         1 |
| Mr.        | Thomas    | W              | Wilson    | 1856-12-28 |         2 |
| Mr.        | William   | J              | Clinton   | 1946-08-19 |         3 |
+------------+-----------+----------------+-----------+------------+-----------+
```

## How it works...

The `ALTER TABLE ADD COLUMN` command allows for parameters specifying the position of a newly added column. To make a new column the first after the modification is complete, use the `FIRST` option. For all other positions, you specify `AFTER` which existing column a new column is to be placed. In our example, we added the `salutation` column at the beginning of the table, while the `middle_initial` column was put right after `firstname`.

Doing a simple `SELECT *` displays the presidents' names and salutations nicely readable because of the column order. Had we just added the columns without specifying `AFTER` or `FIRST`, they would have been appended to the end, behind the `person_id` column. While semantically identical, the output would not have been as readable.

## There's more...

For a full syntax description of the `ALTER TABLE ADD COLUMN` command, please refer to section 12.7.1 of the online MySQL manual at `http://dev.mysql.com/doc/refman/5.1/en/alter-table.html`.

## See also

▶ *Comparing schema revisions using hash values*

# Defining a primary key for a table containing (non-unique) data

When you need to add a Primary key to a table that did not have one previously, you might find yourself confronted with a problem that is not immediately obvious, but can be rather annoying.

A typical example for this problem occurring is with persistence frameworks that require you to have a Primary key on all tables you want it to manage. If the tables were designed independently and before you knew of this requirement, you might not have defined an explicit Primary key, for example, on the dependent one in a relationship between two tables.

In this recipe, we will show you a way to simply add a Primary key to a table that already contains data and is even taking part in a Foreign key relationship.

## Getting ready

To follow this example, you will need MySQL server and an account with privileges sufficient to create and modify tables and their contents. For the next section, we assume that you have these rights in the `test` schema.

## How to do it...

1. Connect to the MySQL server and make `test` the default schema.
2. Create the following tables:

```
CREATE TABLE parent (
  parent_id bigint(20) NOT NULL,
  somevalue varchar(20) default NULL,
  PRIMARY KEY  (parent_id)
) ENGINE=InnoDB;


CREATE TABLE child (
  x_parent_id bigint(20) default NULL,
  value bigint(10) default NULL,
  KEY fk_parent_id (x_parent_id),
  CONSTRAINT child_fk_1 FOREIGN KEY (x_parent_id) REFERENCES
parent (parent_id)
) ENGINE=InnoDB;
```

There is a 1:0..* relationship between parent and child. Clearly, it is possible (and intended) that there can be several children with references to the same parent, even if they have equal values.

3.  Insert some sample data to demonstrate this:

```
mysql> INSERT INTO parent
          VALUES (1,'Parent No. 1'),
                 (2,'Parent No. 2'),
                 (3,'Parent No. 3');
mysql> INSERT INTO child
          VALUES (1,10),(1,12),(1,15),
                 (2,25),(2,26),(2,26),
                 (3,31),(3,31),(3,31);
```

4.  Trying to add a Primary key to the child table like this will fail. This step simply serves as a demonstration. You can try it out, if you want, but you can skip it just as well:

```
mysql> ALTER TABLE child
          ADD COLUMN child_id BIGINT(20) NOT NULL FIRST,
          ADD PRIMARY KEY(child_id);
ERROR 1062 (23000): Duplicate entry '0' for key 1
```

The reason for this failure is described in the following *How it works...* section.

5.  Instead, use these statements to add the Primary key:

```
mysql> ALTER TABLE child
          ADD COLUMN child_id BIGINT(20)
              AUTO_INCREMENT NOT NULL FIRST,
          ADD PRIMARY KEY(child_id);
Query OK, 9 rows affected (0.06 sec)
Records: 9  Duplicates: 0  Warnings: 0

mysql> ALTER TABLE child
          MODIFY COLUMN child_id BIGINT(20) NOT NULL;
Query OK, 9 rows affected (0.08 sec)
Records: 9  Duplicates: 0  Warnings: 0
```

 Notice that you cannot combine these two statements into a single ALTER TABLE command.

6.  When inserting new data, make sure you provide Primary key values.

## How it works...

At first the statement presented first in the steps above would seem sensible to add a Primary key column to the table:

```
mysql> ALTER TABLE child
    ->    ADD COLUMN child_id BIGINT(20) NOT NULL FIRST,
    ->    ADD PRIMARY KEY(child_id);
ERROR 1062 (23000): Duplicate entry '0' for key 1
```

The error message is a little hard to grasp at first, but becomes perfectly clear when thinking more thoroughly about what MySQL tries to do here. First, let's have a look at the sample data:

```
mysql> select * from child;
```

```
ds@ubuntu810: ~
File   Edit   View   Terminal   Tabs   Help
mysql> select * from child;
+-------------+-------+
| x_parent_id | value |
+-------------+-------+
|           1 |    10 |
|           1 |    12 |
|           1 |    15 |
|           2 |    25 |
|           2 |    26 |
|           2 |    26 |
|           3 |    31 |
|           3 |    31 |
|           3 |    31 |
+-------------+-------+
9 rows in set (0.00 sec)
```

Trying to add a column in MySQL will fill it with either NULL or with the data type's default value—in this case 0 for a BIGINT column. Declaring it as a Primary key at the same time then ought to fail because all 9 rows would get the same default value, violating the requirement of uniqueness for a key column.

So to get around this, we need some initial distinct values for the column. Later on in the application, you will have to provide unique key values for new records. Often the persistence layer can provide generated keys once it has been told about the Primary key column. For the initial round, the auto-increment feature comes in handy:

```
mysql> ALTER TABLE child
    ->    ADD COLUMN child_id BIGINT(20) AUTO_INCREMENT NOT NULL FIRST,
    ->    ADD PRIMARY KEY(child_id);
Query OK, 9 rows affected (0.06 sec)
Records: 9  Duplicates: 0  Warnings: 0

mysql> select * from child;
```

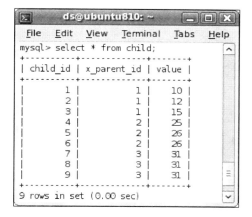

This takes care of providing a unique value for each record's newly created Primary key column. Because we do not need the auto-incrementing anymore, we can remove it again:

```
mysql> ALTER TABLE child MODIFY COLUMN child_id BIGINT(20)  NOT NULL;
Query OK, 9 rows affected (0.08 sec)
Records: 9  Duplicates: 0  Warnings: 0
```

The values of the child_id column are retained; the final column definition just gets rid of the temporary AUTO_INCREMENT option.

Unfortunately, this cannot be combined into a single ALTER TABLE statement because the parser first checks if the statement's parts are all fine before beginning execution. However, at the time the statement is checked, the latter MODIFY COLUMN segment is not valid because at that time the child_id column does not exist yet.

## There's more...

The above example only works for numeric key columns because the AUTO_INCREMENT feature can only be used for those. If you need a different data type for key, you can of course modify the second ALTER TABLE statement to change the column's type instead of just dropping the AUTO_INCREMENT option. MySQL will then try to convert the numbers that it inserted automatically to the newly defined data type—for example, VARCHAR or CHAR:

```
mysql> ALTER TABLE child
          MODIFY COLUMN child_id VARCHAR(20) NOT NULL;
mysql> INSERT INTO child VALUES ('foo',3,31);
```

After that you are free to use UPDATE statements to modify the key values to your liking.

# Allowing individual INSERT statements with "0" values in auto-incrementing columns

Auto-incrementing columns have many uses; primarily, they are used to automatically provide Primary key values for new records inserted into tables.

The usual behavior for MySQL is to assign the next free number from the auto-increment sequence to a record you insert that has either NULL or 0 as the value for any such column.

However, sometimes it may be necessary to insert an actual 0 value without assigning an automatic replacement.

In this recipe, we will show you how to do so for individual INSERT statements.

## Getting ready

You will need a MySQL user account that can insert data.

In the example that will follow, we will demonstrate how to execute a single INSERT statement with a 0 (zero) column value, even though the table definition calls for this column to be auto-incremented. We will assume a table called enumerator to be present in the test database with the following structure:

```
CREATE TABLE enumerator (
  id INT NOT NULL AUTO_INCREMENT,
  textvalue VARCHAR(30),
  PRIMARY KEY (id)
) ENGINE=InnoDB;
```

## How to do it...

1.  Connect to the MySQL server and make test the default database.

2.  Save the current value of the SQL_MODE variable for later and append the NO_AUTO_VALUE_ON_ZERO option:

    ```
    mysql> SET SESSION @OLDMODE=@@SQL_MODE;
    mysql> SET SESSION SQL_MODE=CONCAT(@OLDMODE,
             ',NO_AUTO_VALUE_ON_ZERO');
    ```

    Make sure you do not miss the comma before NO_AUTO_VALUE_ON_ZERO!

3.  Insert a record with a 0 value for the id column like this:

    ```
    mysql> INSERT INTO enumerator VALUES (0,'Zero');
    ```

4. Read back the data to verify:

   ```
   mysql> SELECT * FROM enumerator;
   ```

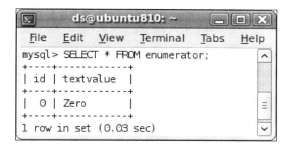

5. Reset the SQL_MODE variable to its previous value:

   ```
   mysql> SET SESSION SQL_MODE=@OLDMODE;
   ```

## How it works...

By default, MySQL will interpret 0 or NULL values for columns marked as AUTO_INCREMENT as a sign to issue the next free number from its internal auto-increment counter and substitute it for the 0 or NULL value in the INSERT received. This makes it generally easy for applications to ensure conflict-free key values. However, for special requirements, this behavior can be modified to allow 0 as a regular value for individual sessions. This is what we did by adding the NO_AUTO_VALUE_ON_ZERO option to the SQL_MODE system variable for the current session. Once the record has been inserted, we restore the variable to its old value.

# Globally allowing INSERT statements with "0" values in auto-incrementing columns

In this recipe, we will show you how to set MySQL's default behavior to globally allow inserting 0 values in columns defined as auto-incrementing for a whole server and all connections.

Historically, MySQL created a new automatic value for any insertion with a 0 or NULL value in a column set up as auto-incrementing. This can lead to unexpected behavior if the data you are going to store contains actual zeroes—these will silently be converted to new values from the auto-increment sequence. See the *Appendix* for a more thorough description and demonstration of this effect.

The MySQL online manual's description of the NO_AUTO_VALUE_ON_ZERO option contains a paragraph on how this behavior could even lead to changed data when restoring tables from backup dumps (just the opposite of what a backup is supposed to accomplish). For that reason, current `mysqldump` versions (starting from MySQL 4.1.1) make sure that the option is turned on automatically when restoring by including it in the dump file.

To avoid accidentally falling into the same trap, in this recipe we will globally enable NO_AUTO_VALUE_ON_ZERO for all databases of the MySQL server instance.

## Getting ready

You will need an operating system account with privileges to change the MySQL server configuration file. To activate the new setting, you will have to restart the server after the file has been edited.

## How to do it...

1. Open the MySQL configuration file with a text editor.

2. In the [mysqld] section find any existing SQL_MODE setting. If it's not present yet, add it, otherwise append to any existing settings, separated by a comma like here:

```
[mysqld]
...
sql-mode=STRICT_ALL_TABLES,NO_AUTO_VALUE_ON_ZERO
```

3. Save the file.

4. Restart the server.

## How it works...

The per-session variable you set in the recipe mentioned earlier can be configured as a server default by setting the value in the `config` file. This is what this recipe has shown how to do. As an example of how the setting works, see the recipes listed in the *See also* section. Of course, you will not need the SET SQL_MODE statements contained therein, as you set the same behavior up as the default.

## See also

▶ *Allowing individual INSERT statements with "0" values in auto-incrementing columns*

▶ *Understanding auto-increment values (Appendix)*

# Choosing a suitable storage engine

When creating tables, either by mistake or on purpose, you may use a storage engine that does not prove to be the right choice later. Fortunately, MySQL allows you to change the storage engine type of existing tables with a single statement. Fittingly, MySQL extended the syntax of the ALTER TABLE command to allow you to specify the storage engine as just another property. The operation is non-destructive, which means existing data is preserved in the table.

In this recipe, we will show you how to move a table from MyISAM to InnoDB. Of course, there are many more storage engine types available, but these two are the most widely used and therefore most relevant.

## Getting ready

To follow along, you will need a MySQL user account with access to the test database and the rights to modify table structures (the ALTER privilege). We will be using a table defined like this:

```
CREATE TABLE person (
    salutation char(10) DEFAULT NULL,
    firstname varchar(30) DEFAULT NULL,
    middle_initial char(1) DEFAULT NULL,
    lastname varchar(30) DEFAULT NULL,
    birthday date DEFAULT NULL,
    person_id int(10) unsigned NOT NULL AUTO_INCREMENT,
    PRIMARY KEY (person_id)
) ENGINE=MyISAM;
```

If it does not exist yet in your test database, execute the above CREATE TABLE statement before moving on.

## How to do it...

1. Connect to the database and make test the default database schema.

2. Change the table storage engine like this:

```
mysql> ALTER TABLE person ENGINE=InnoDB;
Query OK, 3 rows affected (0.24 sec)
Records: 3  Duplicates: 0  Warnings: 0
```

## How it works...

The `ALTER TABLE` statement tells MySQL to create a new InnoDB table with the exact same definition as the source table and copy all the contents over there. Once done, the original table will be removed and the new one put in its place. This operation does preserve all data in the original table.

However, as changing the storage engine effectively means storing the data in a different format on disk, your server will have to deal with potentially lots of I/O, directly proportional to the current size of the table. In this example, the table was very small (only three records) so everything went quickly.

Large tables, however, will take much longer because not only will all data have to be read, but also written simultaneously.

During that operation, MySQL will allow read operations, but any writes (`UPDATE`, `DELETE`, and `INSERT`) will be delayed until the conversion is complete. Only then will they execute against the new table. This will cause trouble for most applications not expecting their operations to take that long!

This is why you will want to delay changing the storage engine to a low-traffic time period or better yet, an offline maintenance window!

Moreover, your disks must provide enough space for the tables in both the old and the new formats at least temporarily because MySQL will only remove the old table once the new one has been successfully created and all the data has been transferred.

Be careful here that different storage engines have different disk space requirements for the same data. InnoDB tables tend to be larger than their MyISAM counterparts.

## There's more...

The example outlined in this recipe was a very simple one—converting from MyISAM to InnoDB is usually no problem because InnoDB basically offers the same features as MyISAM and more. However, you will not be able to convert MyISAM tables that have full-text indexes because those are not supported by InnoDB. If you try to alter the engine type on such a table, you will get an error message:

```
mysql> ALTER TABLE forum_posts ENGINE=InnoDB;
ERROR 1214 (HY000): The used table type doesn't support FULLTEXT
indexes
```

Converting tables from InnoDB to MyISAM is usually less common, but still possible, as long as there are no Foreign key relationships in place. This applies to both sides of any such relationship. If, for example, you had two InnoDB tables called `parent` and `child`, where `child` records were set up to refer to their `parent` row in that table, trying to change the engine on any of these would fail:

```
mysql> ALTER TABLE parent ENGINE=MyISAM;
ERROR 1217 (23000): Cannot delete or update a parent row: a foreign
key constraint fails

mysql> ALTER TABLE child ENGINE=MyISAM;
ERROR 1217 (23000): Cannot delete or update a parent row: a foreign
key constraint fails
```

Before you could change the storage engine for those, you would have to first drop any Foreign key constraints on them.

Apart from MyISAM and InnoDB, there are many more storage engines available. For information on their respective capabilities and other properties please refer to Chapter 13 of the MySQL online manual at `http://dev.mysql.com/doc/refman/5.1/en/storage-engines.html`, and to the `ALTER TABLE` documentation in section 12.1.7 at `http://dev.mysql.com/doc/refman/5.1/en/alter-table.html`.

## Keeping a watch on silent engine substitution

Special attention should be paid to the fact that MySQL might silently ignore your request or even modify the storage engine type to a default one, if the one you specified is not available on your server. The exact behavior depends on your MySQL server version and the setting of the `SQL_MODE` configuration variable:

|  | MySQL 5.1.11 and older | MySQL 5.1.12 and newer |
| --- | --- | --- |
| `NO_ENGINE_SUBSTITUTION` specified | Gives error | Gives error |
| `NO_ENGINE_SUBSTITUTION` disabled (missing) | Uses default storage engine and issues warning, not error | Ignores requested engine and issues warning, not error |

Please note that this table does not apply to `CREATE TABLE`, but only to `ALTER TABLE`. For more information on this topic, see the MySQL online manual, section 5.1.8 on Server SQL Modes at `http://dev.mysql.com/doc/refman/5.1/en/server-sql-mode.html#sqlmode_no_engine_substitution`.

 We recommend always enabling the `NO_ENGINE_SUBSTITUTION` option to avoid risking missing a warning and running into problems later on!

# Improving the performance of ALTER TABLE for InnoDB

This recipe will show you a way of limiting the unavoidable impact of InnoDB table alterations to the necessary minimum.

Unfortunately, there is no way of circumventing that, as ALTER TABLE on InnoDB is a time-consuming and I/O-intensive operation, but planning ahead can make a huge difference as to how severe the impact on your systems will be.

## Getting ready

While this recipe applies to any InnoDB table, the actual benefits of the following recommendations are best seen with a large table. For the example below, we will be using the employees sample database's salaries table, which contains slightly less than 3 million records and is about 100 MB in size. This sample database can be downloaded from the MySQL website at http://dev.mysql.com/doc/employee/en/employee.html.

The table is defined like this:

```
CREATE TABLE salaries (
  emp_no int(11) NOT NULL,
  salary int(11) NOT NULL,
  from_date date NOT NULL,
  to_date date NOT NULL,
  PRIMARY KEY (emp_no,from_date),
  CONSTRAINT salaries_ibfk_1 FOREIGN KEY (emp_no) REFERENCES
employees (emp_no) ON DELETE CASCADE
) ENGINE=InnoDB
```

We will add an index to the from_date column and also add a column called remark.

You will need a user account with sufficient rights to change the table definition.

## How to do it...

1. Connect to the database server using the administrative user and make `employees` the default database.

2. Check on the current size of the table using the following statement (output abridged):

```
mysql> SHOW TABLE STATUS LIKE 'salaries'\G
*************************** 1. row ***************************
            Name: salaries
          Engine: InnoDB
            Rows: 2844513
     Data_length: 100270080
       Data_free: 1352663040
1 row in set (0.07 sec)
```

As you can see, the table is approximately 95 MB big, with about 1,290 MB free in the table space. Assuming that no other operations will fill up this space during the ALTER TABLE, we still need to consider the larger table size caused by the additional index. In this example, we should be fine. If the table space is auto-extending and there is enough free space on the volume it is stored on, you are good to go as well; otherwise you should go and make sure the table space gets extended before you proceed.

3. Issue the following ALTER TABLE statement that adds the new column and the index **in one step**:

```
mysql> ALTER TABLE salaries
        ADD COLUMN remark VARCHAR(32) DEFAULT NULL
          AFTER to_date,
        ADD INDEX IDX_FROMDATE(from_date);
```

4. This will take some time.

## How it works...

When modifying an InnoDB table using the ALTER TABLE command, in most MySQL installations (see the *There's more...* section for information about exceptions) it will perform modifications by first creating a new table with the modified definition, then copying all data from the original table, and finally swapping the newly-created, modified one for the original.

As tables grow, this can take a long time, creating lots of I/O activity for the copy procedure. Making matters worse, this process requires much disk space because temporarily you will have both the original table and the copy present on disk, filling up the remaining space and thereby potentially influencing other applications. But even just inside MySQL itself you may run into problems because your tablespace might not have enough free space left to hold both copies of a large table.

Using a second connection, you can actually see the temporary table being used through the following command while the ALTER TABLE is still running:

```
mysql> SHOW FULL PROCESSLIST \G
```

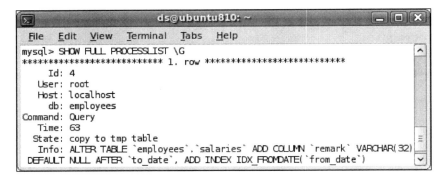

Though you cannot prevent InnoDB from copying the tables for modification, you can at least minimize the influence of this procedure by trying to make all necessary modifications at once. That means instead of, say, first adding a new column with one ALTER TABLE command and then adding the new index with a second one, you combine both in a single statement.

The longer composite statement itself may not be as readable as individual ones (even though you can work around that with proper indentation and formatting), but it will only require a single copy pass instead of one for each modification.

There are limits to this (for example, you cannot drop a constraint at the beginning of the statement and then add another one with the same name later), but in general, this is the way to go as soon as the table in question contains more than just a couple of rows.

The example statement above took 1 minute and 34 seconds on my iMac. The same computer with an unmodified MySQL server configuration took 3 minutes and 2 seconds when issuing two separate ALTER TABLE statements for the index and the new column individually.

## There's more...

Starting with MySQL 5.1, storage engines can be loaded into the MySQL server as plugins. Although InnoDB comes bundled with MySQL, there is a separate plugin version that is developed independently of the main server. At the time of writing this book, MySQL version 5.4 was in beta and contained some of the newer features that were only available in the plugin release, available from http://www.innodb.com. As the MySQL server release model is currently in a state of change, it is hard to predict what the most recent version will be at the time you are reading this and what it will be called.

However, apart from other improvements, the main feature worth mentioning is called **fast index creation**. It allows creating and dropping indexes without needing to copy a table and all its data. This can alleviate the pain of schema modifications significantly. However, due to the MySQL bug #33650 (`http://bugs.mysql.com/bug.php?id=33650`), this feature cannot be used if any of the indexed columns are configured to use `utf8` as their text encoding. We suggest you monitor this bug if you want to try out the plugin.

# Using a stored procedure to conditionally add columns or indexes

Several of MySQL's schema-related commands allow for an `IF EXISTS` clause, which is a very useful addition to standard SQL syntax because it allows for more robust automatic schema handling. When you need to do unattended schema manipulations, for example, re-create a table when you do not know for sure whether it exists on the target system, you simply do a

```
DROP TABLE IF EXISTS tablename;
CREATE TABLE tablename (...)
```

Without the `IF EXISTS` clause, the `DROP TABLE` statement would fail if the table was not present when executing the script and abort the execution immediately, in effect ending up without the new table.

Unfortunately, there are some cases where the `IF EXISTS` clause would come in handy, but is not supported by MySQL. One such case is the addition of new indexes to an existing table. In this recipe, we will present a way to work around this limitation and write portable and robust scripts to modify a table unattended.

Note that this is primarily useful for the automatic execution of updates to databases that are not under your immediate control, for example, as part of a software update installer. For manual modifications of a schema, it is usually way less work to have a look at the current table structure first to determine if there is anything to do in the first place.

## Getting ready...

In the following example, we will be modifying two tables in the `test` database schema. They will be identical, except for one having an index `IDX_B` already, while the other does not. To follow along, you will need a user account with sufficient privileges to first create these tables and then modify them. This is done via a stored procedure that you must have the rights to create as well.

These are the table definitions:

```
CREATE TABLE TableA (
  col_A int(11) DEFAULT 1,
  col_B varchar(40) DEFAULT NULL
) ENGINE=InnoDB;

CREATE TABLE TableB (
  col_A int(11) DEFAULT 1,
  col_B varchar(40) DEFAULT NULL,
  KEY IDX_B (col_B)
) ENGINE=InnoDB;
```

## How to do it...

1. Connect to the MySQL server using an administrative user account.
2. Create a stored procedure with the following sequence of instructions. The meaning of all the steps will be explained in the *How it works...* section:

```
mysql> DELIMITER $$
mysql> DROP PROCEDURE IF EXISTS sp_AddIndex $$
mysql> CREATE PROCEDURE sp_AddIndex
          (tblName VARCHAR(64),ndxName VARCHAR(64),
           colName VARCHAR(64))
BEGIN
   DECLARE IndexColumnCount INT;
   DECLARE SQLStatement VARCHAR(256);
   SELECT COUNT(index_name) INTO IndexColumnCount
   FROM information_schema.statistics
   WHERE table_schema = database()
   AND table_name = tblName
   AND index_name = ndxName;
   IF IndexColumnCount = 0 THEN
       SET SQLStatement = CONCAT('ALTER TABLE ',tblName,' ADD
INDEX ',ndxName,' (',colName,')');
       SET @SQLStmt = SQLStatement;
       PREPARE s FROM @SQLStmt;
       EXECUTE s;
       DEALLOCATE PREPARE s;
   END IF;
END $$
mysql> DELIMITER ;
```

3. Call the procedure, providing the table name, index name, and the column to be indexed:

```
mysql> CALL sp_AddIndex('TableA','IDX_B','col_B');
```

4. Clean up, removing the procedure and resetting the statement delimiter:

```
mysql> DROP PROCEDURE IF EXISTS sp_AddIndex;
mysql> DELIMITER ;
```

## How it works...

While MySQL does not offer a direct way of executing the statement only if the target index already exists, a stored procedure can be used to perform this check. The first statement is used to change the default statement delimiter from `;` to something different—two dollar signs `$$` in this case. This allows the definition of the actual procedure contents in a more natural form, using the default semicolons to separate the routine's commands.

The first application of this new delimiter is a statement to drop any procedure with the same name as that we are about to use. It ends with `$$`, the temporary replacement for the usual semicolon.

After that, the actual procedure is declared. It is called `sp_AddIndex` (`sp_` being a common prefix for stored procedures, but this is not strictly necessary) and takes three input parameters to work with. The first one is the table name to operate on, the second one is used to pass the name of the target index, and the last one the name of the column(s) the index is supposed to span.

It then queries the `INFORMATION_SCHEMA` to find out if there already is an index with the given name on the given table in the current schema. The result of the `COUNT()` query will be zero if there is no index matching the given criteria. This is then checked in the `IF` statement, guarding the building of a suitable `ALTER TABLE ... ADD INDEX` statement, which is finally executed. If an index already existed, the `IndexColumnCount` result will be greater than zero, hence skipping the `ALTER TABLE` statement.

Finally, the procedure is called for `TableA` and `col_B` with an index name of `IDX_B`. Once the procedure is completed, it is dropped again and the default delimiter is restored to the semicolon.

Of course, you need not drop the procedure if you plan to use it more regularly. However, this example was taken from an automated script we use to update large numbers of servers from time to time. Therefore, we usually create and drop such maintenance procedures as needed.

At the time of writing this book, there was a bug in MySQL version 5.1.30 that lead to a wrong result of the COUNT() query inside the procedure on Mac OS X and Windows. After contacting MySQL support and some e-mailing back and forth, MySQL Bug #46771 (http://bugs.mysql.com/bug.php?id=46771) was put into their bug database.

While I recommend you to go and check on the state of things when you read this, the bottom line is that the INFORMATION_SCHEMA pseudo-database does not answer queries correctly, unless you enter table names all in lower case! Usually, you would not notice on Windows or Mac OS X because their default file systems do not make a difference between two files if their names only differ in upper/lower casing, while most Unix file systems do.

To work around this bug, make sure you only use lower case table names if you manage the server on one of those operating systems, unless you find that your server version has already been fixed.

# Improving query performance for InnoDB tables with BLOB columns

MySQL and InnoDB behave in a hardly predictable way when querying tables that contain BLOB columns. This might catch you off guard and cause slow performance where it would not have to be. This is caused by a bug (or a missing feature, depending on your perspective) in MySQL.

In this recipe, we will demonstrate how to reproduce this bug, and in the *How it works...* section explain how to work around it. Of course, you should first check the above bug report and see whether it has been fixed at the time you are reading this in the MySQL server version you are using. However, as this bug has been open since 2004 and has been prioritized as a feature request, I do not think chances are especially good that this has happened.

## Getting ready

To follow along, you will need a MySQL user account with sufficient privileges to create tables in the test schema and insert data into them. For the BLOB contents, a file will be needed to read from. In the example, we will use /tmp/blobdemo, but the content is not at all important. You could also use any other file at your disposal.

## How to do it...

1. Connect to the database and make the `test` database the default schema.

2. Create a table with this structure:

```
mysql> CREATE TABLE blobtest (
  intA INT(10) NOT NULL AUTO_INCREMENT,
  intB INT(10) DEFAULT NULL,
  contents BLOB,
  PRIMARY KEY (intA)
) ENGINE=InnoDB;
```

3. Load the file contents into it. Make sure to adapt the path name if you want to use a different file:

```
mysql> INSERT INTO blobtest (intB, contents)
          VALUES(100, LOAD_FILE("/tmp/blobfile"));
```

4. Execute the following command 10 times to produce some test data:

```
mysql> INSERT INTO blobtest (intB, contents)
          SELECT intB, contents FROM blobtest;
```

Each time you repeat this command, the number of records in the `blobtest` table will double. To make the effect more obvious, you could do more than 10 iterations, but beware that each one of them will take quite a lot longer to execute.

5. Execute a query that asks for all the columns, including the `contents` column, but that does not return any rows.

```
mysql> SELECT * FROM blobtest WHERE intB=0;
Empty set (2.64 sec)
```

The `WHERE` clause does not mention the **BLOB** type `contents` column.

6. Execute a query that explicitly excludes the **BLOB** column:

```
mysql> SELECT intA, intB FROM blobtest WHERE intB=0;
Empty set (0.01 sec)
```

 Notice that this query was completed significantly faster than the one before, even though they both queried the same condition on the same table and did not have to return any rows.

## How it works...

Back in 2004 we filed MySQL Bug #7074 (`http://bugs.mysql.com/bug.php?id=7074`), which reports this unexpected behavior. Heikki Tuuri, the inventor of InnoDB, confirmed our guess that MySQL first reads all the columns you specify in a `SELECT` statement from the data store, before applying the `WHERE` condition to them. This is usually a good idea because in case the criteria match, you already have all the data at hand. However, for BLOB columns, this can quickly become overly expensive in terms of execution time because lots more data has to be read from disk.

In the previous example (which is the same as in the bug report), we intentionally issued two queries that do not match any rows—all the values of `intB` have been set to the constant value 100—to show the effect very clearly.

Of course, this is only an issue if InnoDB cannot use an index to check for the `WHERE` conditions. If it finds a suitable one, no BLOBs will be read in the earlier example for any of the queries, no matter which columns are requested in the `SELECT`. However, depending on the execution plan the optimizer generates, you might still end up with a situation like this if the circumstances are right. This is what actually happened to us—which is how we found out about the problem in the first place—and was tricky to diagnose.

So in the end there are two strategies to prevent this from hitting you:

- ▶ Make sure all queries against the table in question are covered by an index.
- ▶ Do not use `SELECT *` or a complete list of columns in your queries and only look up the key values of the rows you want to process. Then go and retrieve the BLOB columns with another query, leveraging Primary key lookups.

While having good indexes in place is always a thing to strive for, we also strongly recommend only reading the columns you are actually going to use in any query. Especially, using the * wildcard in your programs can make them susceptible to errors when you have to make modifications to the table structure—column ordering being a good candidate—in the future. Apart from making your software more robust, it can also help reduce network load between the client and the server.

## There's more...

If you do not want to use a real file for the BLOB columns contents, you can easily create a file filled with completely random contents from the Linux or Mac OS X command line like this:

```
$ cd /tmp
$ dd if=/dev/urandom of=blobfile bs=4096 count=16
16+0 records in
16+0 records out
65536 bytes transferred in 0.008941 secs (7329882 bytes/sec)
```

What this does is read from the pseudo-device called `/dev/urandom` that simply provides a continuous stream of (almost) random bytes (the `if` parameter is short for *input file*) and writes 16 blocks of 4,096 bytes (`bs` means *block size*) to the *output file* (`of` for short) called `blobfile`.

By varying the `bs` and `count` parameters, you can control the size of your output file.

# Identifying differences between two schemas

Especially when preparing software upgrades, it is important to know the differences between a previous release's database schema and the current, probably modified development version. There are several tools available to create a report on the differences between two schema definitions, trying to make smart guesses as to what went on. Nevertheless, we found most of them to be of only limited use. This is mostly due to the fact that whenever any automated tool compares two schema definitions, it cannot know about many aspects that are obvious to the human eye.

Consider a simple column rename, for example. In a previous schema version, a column might have been simply called `name` while in the current release it is to be called `lastname`. Having a look at the old and new individual table definitions will not reveal, however, that those two columns have any relationship. Most automated tools will tell you to `DROP COLUMN name` and `ADD COLUMN lastname`. This is, of course, not what you want to do because doing that you would lose all the personal data already stored in the table.

In the end, from our experience it is the most primitive, but also the most efficient way to compare two schemas by simply text-diffing their definitions. This is what we will do in this recipe.

## Getting ready

To follow along, you will need privileges to create a structure dump of both the old and the new schema definitions. In the next example, we assume you have already dumped the schema definitions to two files called `old.sql` and `new.sql`. You can find these files on the book's website for download. They contain information about three tables called `TableA`, `TableB`, and `TableC` in the `test` schema.

Table definitions for `TableA` and `TableB` are different in several details, while `TableC` is missing completely in `new.sql`.

On Mac OS X and any Linux distribution, the `diff` command is part of the usual operating system installation. Windows users will have to get hold of a copy of a text comparison tool separately. The `diff` command for Windows is part of the Unix Utilities (`http://unxutils.sourceforge.net`), while WinMerge is an open-source graphical utility and can be downloaded from `http://winmerge.org`. Many modern text editors and development environments (like Eclipse) do include a text comparison feature as well. Some of them are available cross-platform.

The steps below show a screenshot using WinMerge. The same information can be obtained using the `diff` program. See the *There's more...* section for details.

## How to do it...

1. Put both `old.sql` and `new.sql` in a common folder.

2. Open them both in WinMerge. You will see a screen like this:

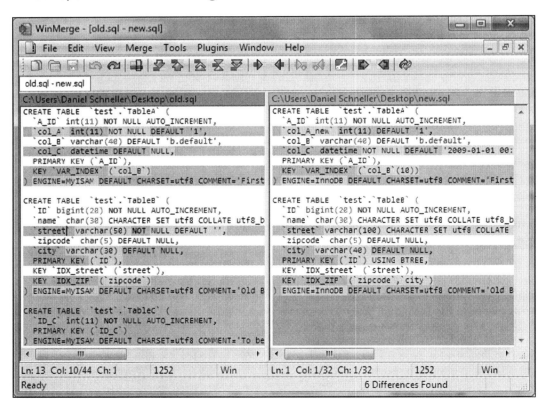

3. You can see the differences highlighted by color. The tool tries to align the two files so that the lines match up to make the comparison easier to understand.

4. Identify the differences between the old and new schemata based on this output and formulate the appropriate ALTER TABLE statements. New table creations and dropped tables need no changes, of course. For this example, the following modifications are required:

```
mysql> ALTER TABLE test.TableA
CHANGE COLUMN col_A col_A_new INTEGER DEFAULT 1,
MODIFY COLUMN col_C DATETIME NOT NULL
    DEFAULT '2009-01-01 00:00:00',
DROP INDEX VAR_INDEX,
ADD INDEX VAR_INDEX
    USING BTREE(col_B(10)),
ENGINE = InnoDB;

mysql> ALTER TABLE test.TableB
MODIFY COLUMN street VARCHAR(100) BINARY
    CHARACTER SET utf8 COLLATE utf8_general_ci NOT NULL,
MODIFY COLUMN city VARCHAR(40)
    CHARACTER SET utf8 COLLATE utf8_general_ci
    DEFAULT NULL,
DROP PRIMARY KEY,
ADD PRIMARY KEY  USING BTREE(ID),
DROP INDEX IDX_ZIP,
ADD INDEX IDX_ZIP(zipcode, city),
ENGINE = InnoDB
COMMENT = 'New B';
DROP TABLE test.TableC;
```

5. Repeat the schema dump for the altered schema tables and compare again against the expected schema. You should not see any more structural differences, if your modifications were correct.

## How it works...

The principle of this recipe is quite simple and very straightforward: create a textual representation of the current (old) schema and the desired (new) schema definitions and compare them.

Based on the result and your knowledge about the context of the changes, you then write the appropriate ALTER TABLE statements to migrate your schema from the old to the new version.

Finally, you rerun the comparison to make sure your modification statements were doing the right thing.

## There's more...

For automation or pure command-line access to servers, the textual output of the `diff` tool can be more suitable. Most versions of `diff` have a wealth of options, but the most important one is `-u`, producing a *unified* `diff` formatted output:

```
$ diff -u old.sql new.sql > difference.sql
```

The newly created `difference.sql` file will contain the same information WinMerge showed visually, but in a standardized textual format. You can find the `difference.sql` file on the book's website, too.

If you are familiar with the `diff` tool, the output should be pretty obvious to you. If not, have a look at the following simple example (taken from the recipe steps earlier):

```
--- old.sql     2009-12-15 00:39:40.000000000 +0100
+++ new.sql     2009-12-15 00:39:35.000000000 +0100
```

These first two lines tell you which files were compared with one another. The first line is prefixed with three minus signs (`---`), telling you that whenever one of the following lines starts with a minus, that line was taken from the `old.sql` file.

Similarly, the second line informs you that any subsequent line starting with a plus sign was taken from the `new.sql` file.

After that, the `diff` tool renders lines with different contents from `old.sql` and `new.sql` like this:

```
  CREATE TABLE  `test`. `TableA` (
    `A_ID` int(11) NOT NULL AUTO_INCREMENT,
- `col_A` int(11) NOT NULL DEFAULT '1',
+ `col_A_new` int(11) DEFAULT '1',
```

The first two lines serve to give some context that was identical in both files. This allows you (and automatic tools reading the diff output) to better understand where the differing lines were found in the input files.

In this case, we can clearly see that the definition of `TableA` was changed. The line starting with - shows what it looks like in the `old.sql` file, the line directly below, prefixed with +, is the new version. So you see that the column was renamed from `col_A` to `col_A_new` while at the same time dropping the `NOT NULL` constraint. This change will need to be taken care of with an `ALTER TABLE` statement to migrate `TableA` from the old to the new schema.

With some practice, reading this output will become second nature to you. However, if you do not want to mentally parse this format, we recommend one of the many graphical diffing tools available. If you cannot use these, the `diff` command has a `-y` option that displays the two files side by side:

```
● ● ●                        Terminal — bash — 125×26
Yavin-Mac:Scripts ds$ diff -y old.sql new.sql
CREATE TABLE  `test`.`TableA` (                    CREATE TABLE  `test`.`TableA` (
  `A_ID` int(11) NOT NULL AUTO_INCREMENT,            `A_ID` int(11) NOT NULL AUTO_INCREMENT,
  `col_A` int(11) NOT NULL DEFAULT '1',          |   `col_A_new` int(11) DEFAULT '1',
  `col_B` varchar(40) DEFAULT 'b.default',       |   `col_B` varchar(40) DEFAULT 'b.default',
  `col_C` datetime DEFAULT NULL,                 |   `col_C` datetime NOT NULL DEFAULT '2009-01-01 00:00:00',
  PRIMARY KEY (`A_ID`),                              PRIMARY KEY (`A_ID`),
  KEY `VAR_INDEX` (`col_B`)                      |   KEY `VAR_INDEX` (`col_B`(10))
) ENGINE=MyISAM DEFAULT CHARSET=utf8 COMMENT='First table'; | ) ENGINE=InnoDB DEFAULT CHARSET=utf8 COMMENT='First table';

CREATE TABLE  `test`.`TableB` (                    CREATE TABLE  `test`.`TableB` (
  `ID` bigint(20) NOT NULL AUTO_INCREMENT,           `ID` bigint(20) NOT NULL AUTO_INCREMENT,
  `name` char(30) CHARACTER SET utf8 COLLATE utf8_bin DEFAULT   `name` char(30) CHARACTER SET utf8 COLLATE utf8_bin DEFAULT
  `street` varchar(50) NOT NULL DEFAULT '',      |   `street` varchar(100) CHARACTER SET utf8 COLLATE utf8_bin N
  `zipcode` char(5) DEFAULT NULL,                    `zipcode` char(5) DEFAULT NULL,
  `city` varchar(30) DEFAULT NULL,               |   `city` varchar(40) DEFAULT NULL,
  PRIMARY KEY (`ID`),                            |   PRIMARY KEY (`ID`) USING BTREE,
  KEY `IDX_street` (`street`),                       KEY `IDX_street` (`street`),
  KEY `IDX_ZIP` (`zipcode`)                      |   KEY `IDX_ZIP` (`zipcode`,`city`)
) ENGINE=MyISAM DEFAULT CHARSET=utf8 COMMENT='Old B'; | ) ENGINE=InnoDB DEFAULT CHARSET=utf8 COMMENT='Old B';
                                               <
CREATE TABLE  `test`.`TableC` (                <
  `ID_C` int(11) NOT NULL AUTO_INCREMENT,      <
  PRIMARY KEY (`ID_C`)                         <
) ENGINE=MyISAM DEFAULT CHARSET=utf8 COMMENT='To be dropped'; <
Yavin-Mac:Scripts ds$ █
```

The differences are marked by the characters in the middle between the file contents. For more information, consult your `diff` command's man page.

## See also...

▶  *Comparing schema revisions using hash values*

# Comparing schema revisions using hash values

When dealing with software product versioning, you almost invariably will be facing a situation where you have to upgrade a database schema from one version to a newer one. The problem now is that even with robust scripts, you cannot be 100% sure that your updates will work correctly, unless you are perfectly sure they are applicable to a current schema release on a client's computer. This is even more true when the updates are run unattended, which is a scenario we often face when silently upgrading several hundred MySQL instances across several countries.

Applying an unsuitable set of `ALTER TABLE` or even `DROP TABLE` commands to a database might lead to unrecoverable data loss and a broken system. This is something you will want to avoid at any cost.

A simple way to try to make sure you know what you are dealing with would be to just compare the version of the accompanying application or the contents of some (fictional) special `schema_version` table that gets updated with every new software release. However, this is not very reliable and probably just not good enough if you need to apply critical changes.

In this recipe, we present a way to calculate checksums for table schemas that enable you to verify beyond doubt if you are dealing with a well-known version that has not been modified. This is based on cryptographic checksums that were specifically designed for this purpose. Using an approach like this is superior to, say, a `schema_version` table because that could easily get out of sync with reality, be it due to someone patching the database or simply because some developer forgets to change the version number when they make their next schema modification.

 This method will tell you whether a schema conforms to a given well-known version you tested your modifications with. It will not tell you what the exact differences are, but rather which of the many possible schema versions you are currently dealing with.

The major benefit of using this hash-based approach is that you can use it to uniquely identify any given schema version. This is very handy when you are tracking a whole lot of different versions because the hash values are very short and relieve you from carrying around all the historic versions of schemas you might have. Instead, your upgrade process could choose from a several available update scripts the one that is suitable for upgrading to the most recent version the particular schema it identified on the target machine.

## Getting ready

To follow along, you will need operating system and MySQL user accounts with privileges sufficient to run a `mysqldump` command targeted at the schema you would like to calculate a hash value for. In this example, we will be using the `test` database schema that contains two tables `TableA` and `TableB`. The exact definition of those tables is not really important. You can use any other schema as well. However, to try out provoking a hash checksum mismatch, you will have to make at least some minor modification to the schema you pick.

The program used here to calculate the hash values is written in Java. This is not mandatory; of course, the general principle can be implemented in any language you like. We chose Java because it is available for practically any platform and is often installed anyway, especially on Windows, where it is probably more common than Perl, for example.

If you do not have a **Java Runtime Environment (JRE)** installed yet, please download and install it before you proceed. The machine you install it on need not be the MySQL server machine, but can be your workstation instead. However, you will have to be able to connect to the MySQL server via the network in that case, which might be restricted by the MySQL user account setup or your company's network firewalls.

A description of the algorithm used by the program can be found in the *How it works...* section.

## How to do it...

1.  Download the `dbhash.jar` file from the book's website. It contains a pre-compiled, runnable version of the `dbhash` tool.

2.  On a command line, enter the following command, substituting your own server, database, and user names appropriately:

    ```
    $ java -jar dbhash.jar /usr/bin/mysqldump localhost 3306 test root
    rootpw
    ```

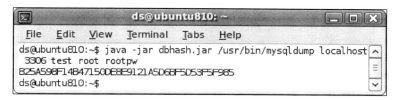

3.  The first parameter is the path to the `mysqldump` tool. Then follows the MySQL host (`localhost`) and port (`3306`), the database schema (`test`), and then the user name (`root`) to use and its associated password (`rootpw`).

4.  Write down the resulting output: this is a unique fingerprint value of the database schema.

5.  Optionally, connect to the database and make any change to the database schema. For example, add another table:

    ```
    mysql> CREATE TABLE  test.TableC (
       ID_C int(11) NOT NULL AUTO_INCREMENT,
       PRIMARY KEY (ID_C)
    ) ENGINE=MyISAM DEFAULT CHARSET=utf8;
    ```

6.  Rerun the same command again:

    ```
    $ java -jar dbhash.jar /usr/bin/mysqldump localhost 3306 test root
    rootpw
    ```

7.  Compare the new hash value with the previous one. They will be completely different. This proves beyond doubt that the schema was modified between the two runs of the hashing tool. If you dropped the table again and ran the program a third time, you would get the same hash value as the first time.

8.  Before releasing any new schema version of your database, run the hashing tool and record the calculated value together with the version number. By doing so, you can build up a complete list of supported database schema versions, being sure to recognize them beyond doubt.

## How it works...

Contained in the `dbhash.jar` file is a program that does the following:

- ▶ Connect to the MySQL server by running the `mysqldump` command from the provided location. It will automatically use the correct parameters to retrieve a "structure-only" dump. No database contents will be read.

- ▶ Apply some processing to the retrieved dump. What this primarily does is sort constraint and index definitions to have them conform to a predictable ordering. This "format normalization" is important because the cryptographic hashing function that is going to be used will produce different results, even when the only difference between two runs is in the ordering of those. `mysqldump` does not provide a completely predictable order regarding the output of such information. Moreover, whitespace will be removed to make sure no platform-specific line endings will influence the result.

- ▶ A SHA-1 hash of the normalized schema definition is calculated and printed. For more information on this algorithm, please refer to `http://en.wikipedia.org/wiki/Sha-1`. The main characteristic of any hash function is that even a slight change in the input will produce completely different and non-reversible results. This ensures that no two different inputs will ever have the same hash value. Therefore, by comparing the results of two runs against two database schemas, you know for sure if they are perfectly identical or have even the slightest difference.

## There's more...

You can access the program's source code by downloading the `dbhash-src.zip` file from the book's website. You will find a `src` folder inside it with the full source code of the program.

## See also...

- ▶ *Identifying differences between two schemas*

# Good to Know

In this chapter, we will cover:

- Avoiding silent replication disruption on full master disk
- Maximizing usable memory on 32-bit Windows
- Using separate temporary directories for multiple MySQL servers on a single machine, preventing conflicts
- Non-availability of InnoDB may escape monitoring
- Troubleshooting "Can't start server: Bind on TCP/IP port: No such file or directory"
- Choosing character sets
- Understanding auto-increment values

## Introduction

This appendix is a collection of several pieces of information we deemed important for a MySQL administrator to know, but which did not really fit the style of a recipe as such. However, many of the issues you will find here took us hours or sometimes days to figure out. We would like to spare you this time by making our experiences available here.

Naturally, you need not read this chapter from beginning to end—just as in the rest of the book, all items should be individually useful and understandable.

# Avoiding silent replication disruption on full master disk

While using replication, you might experience corrupted or incomplete binlog files on the master when the disk they get stored on becomes full. In older versions, the file would be started and when the disk became full in the middle of an event being written, this partial data would be replicated and cause errors on the slaves.

Versions 5.0 and up handle an out-of-space situation more gracefully, as they do not write partial statements to the binlog and try harder to keep the table data and the binlog in sync. However, you still need to be aware that there is no 100-percent sure way of preventing problems on the slaves because under certain circumstances you can end up with the last statement having executed in the database, but not recorded in the binlog.

The master server will log this fact into its logfile, so your monitoring system might pick this up with lines like:

```
The binary log <name> is shorter than its expected size.
```

but still the problem remains.

The MySQL manual has more details about this in chapters 5.2.4 at `http://dev.mysql.com/doc/refman/5.1/en/binary-log.html` and B.1.4.3 on disk-full problems at `http://dev.mysql.com/doc/refman/5.1/en/full-disk.html`.

 The bottom line about this, however, is that even with the most conservative settings—`--sync_binlog=1` and `--innodb_support_xa=1`, leading to reduced performance due to more disk syncs—*you can still end up with incomplete binlogs*, be it on MySQL's part or the operating system's, requiring you to reset the replication and manually re-sync the slaves from a fresh dump.

Considering the performance penalties, the options MySQL offers to limit the risks of damaging the binlogs and the fact that they do not guarantee problem-free operations anyway, we recommend investing your resources in a reliable system-monitoring solution that will keep you informed about critical conditions regarding disk space and allow you to prevent these problems in the first place.

# Maximizing usable memory on 32-bit Windows

MySQL is a cross-platform piece of software, with versions available for all major operating systems and even embedded devices. Many enterprise-level servers nowadays are 64-bit hardware and operating system combinations. However, at the time of writing this book, there's still a large number of 32-bit systems in active use.

## Limitations of 32-bit systems

One of the major limitations of 32-bit systems is their inherent limit of a maximum of 4 GB address space per process, meaning that no process on such a system can ever address more than 4 GB of memory. However, on typical 32-bit operating systems, there is an ever lower limit in place. On Windows, this address space is split in half: 2 GB for the application and 2 GB of reserved addresses for kernel use. In this half of the address space, there are areas reserved for all sorts of hardware interfaces including graphics cards and extension cards—precious addresses that cannot be used to address bytes in RAM chips.

In effect this means that any process—including a MySQL server—can use at most 2 GB of combined RAM on a 32-bit Windows system. This is even true for systems running, for example, Windows Server Enterprise Edition, which supports much more physical memory in a machine using some clever trickery. Even though in total they can support many Gigabytes of memory, the per-process limits still apply.

## Impact on MySQL/InnoDB

For a typical InnoDB-centric MySQL configuration, you would usually assign most of the available 2 GB per process to the InnoDB buffer pool (configuration setting `innodb_buffer_pool_size`). However, you will often notice that even though the total of all buffer sizes is less than this limit, you might still end up with error messages, when trying to start the server, that look like this:

```
C:\ CMD - Start_MySQL.cmd                                    _ □ ×
091002 16:24:52  InnoDB: Error: cannot allocate 1572880384 bytes of
InnoDB: memory with malloc! Total allocated memory
InnoDB: by InnoDB 12483264 bytes. Operating system errno: 8
InnoDB: Check if you should increase the swap file or
InnoDB: ulimits of your operating system.
InnoDB: On FreeBSD check you have compiled the OS with
InnoDB: a big enough maximum process size.
InnoDB: Note that in most 32-bit computers the process
InnoDB: memory space is limited to 2 GB or 4 GB.
InnoDB: We keep retrying the allocation for 60 seconds...
```

In this example, we tried a 1,500 MB buffer pool size. This kind of problem is regularly caused by memory fragmentation. InnoDB tries to allocate a large, contiguous area of the address space for the buffer pool here. However, even before this takes place, the operating system may have loaded shared libraries (DLLs) into the 2 GB user address space available to the process (0x00000000 - 0x7FFFFFF) effectively splitting the available address range, so that InnoDB cannot get a large enough contiguous chunk for its buffer pool. Such libraries can be part of anti-virus solutions or management suites that need to hook on to all processes in a system.

The freely available Sysinternals ProcessExplorer tool (downloadable from Microsoft's website at http://technet.microsoft.com/en-us/sysinternals/bb896653.aspx) can help you find out details in situations like this:

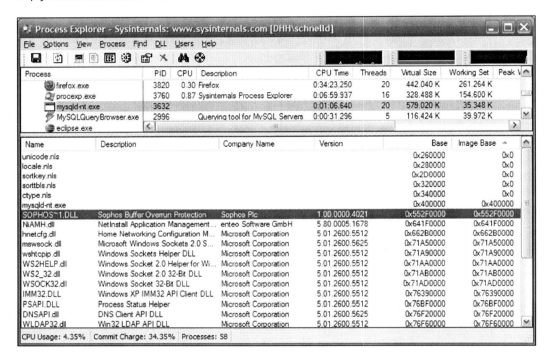

In the previous screenshot, you can see a MySQL process that has its address space fragmented by two DLLs (see the lower pane)—one part of Sophos Antivirus and the other part of the NetInstall software management suite. Both DLLs take up only a small amount of memory for themselves; however, their position in the address space makes them a problem for InnoDB. The Sophos Buffer Overrun Protection Library is loaded at address 0x552F0000. This is only 1,358 MB from the start address of mysqld-nt.exe (0x40000) and prevents a 1,500 MB block from being assigned. If they were located at the far end of the address range, InnoDB could allocate a block of memory large enough to function. Compare this with the next picture where the anti-virus software has been removed from the system:

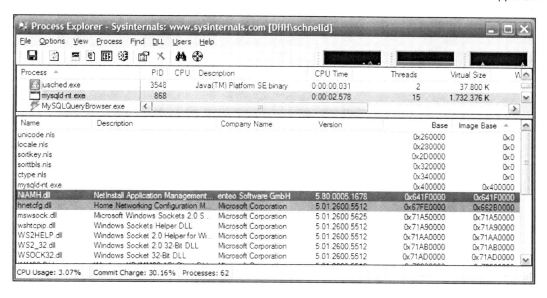

In this setup, InnoDB can start just fine because there is a contiguous range free from `0x400000` to `0x641F0000`, sized **1,597 MB**. See the following screenshot showing the InnoDB status output section (produced by entering SHOW ENGINE INNODB STATUS\G on a MySQL command-line) telling you about the number of **96,000** available **16 KB** pages in the buffer pool. This is exactly the **1,500 MB** the configuration variable `innodb_buffer_pool_size` is set to in this server's `my.ini` file.

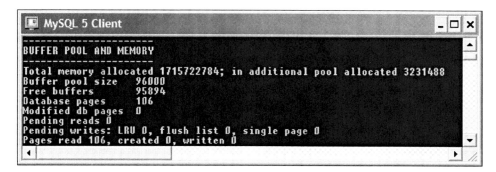

Usually, we would recommend a switch to more capable 64-bit hardware and operating system setups if these memory limits become an issue. However, there might sometimes be external factors preventing that.

If you hit a problem like this, you have to try to decide whether either you can get rid of the problematic libraries completely (by not using the program they are associated with), or you should contact their respective vendors to find out if they can provide a different version of the same DLL that gets loaded into a more convenient address range.

**Warning!**

Editing the registry can severely damage your system setup, up to the point of not being able to boot or access it at all; so make sure you know what you are doing. Get in contact with any software vendor whose libraries you disabled to get clearance to try this; some libraries might be vital for your system to function!

We strongly recommend making a system backup before you proceed with this!

For testing, you can modify the `HKEY_LOCAL_MACHINE\SOFTWARE\Microsoft\Windows NT\CurrentVersion\Windows\AppInit_DLLs` registry key to control which DLLs get loaded when a process starts. After making sure this will not affect the stability of your system, remove the DLLs in question from this key and restart the MySQL server. Verify if you can now use a larger amount of memory.

## Getting even more with the /3GB switch

To get even more memory available to MySQL on 32-bit systems, you might consider using the /3GB boot parameter. This parameter, which can be added to the `boot.ini` file, will tell Windows that you intend to run programs that need more than 2 GB of address space.

What it will do is present programs that are prepared for it (they need to be compiled with support for this) with a 3 GB address range for application use and reserve only 1 GB for kernel purposes. MySQL versions 5.0.79 and up and 5.1.33 and up are compiled to benefit from this configuration. However, using it can adversely affect your system in other ways. Refer to the Microsoft website or their support for more information.

Also note that this will not enable you to allocate more than 2 GB to the buffer pool alone; however, the MySQL server could use the extra space for other buffers.

The following screenshot was taken on a Windows machine that was booted with the /3GB option in place and shows a MySQL server process using more than 2 GB:

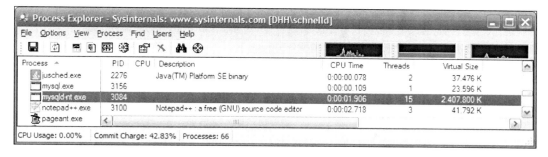

This is the InnoDB status output showing a 1,750 MB buffer pool on a 32-bit system:

```
MySQL 5 Client                                              _ □ ×
-----------------------------
BUFFER POOL AND MEMORY
-----------------------------
Total memory allocated 1993648080; in additional pool allocated 3231488
Buffer pool size   112000
Free buffers       111894
Database pages     106
Modified db pages  0
Pending reads 0
Pending writes: LRU 0, flush list 0, single page 0
Pages read 106, created 0, written 0
```

# Using separate temporary directories for multiple MySQL servers on a single machine, preventing conflicts

Whenever you run multiple MySQL server instances, which are possible by configuring different sockets or TCP ports, you need to make sure to also configure a different temporary directory for each instance.

This is not clearly documented and often it will work flawlessly, even if they share a common temporary directory. If you do not specify a custom directory, the system's temporary directory will be used.

However, a regular behavior of the MySQL server is to clean up any remaining temporary files it may have created and left behind in a previous run. While this is generally a sensible idea, the implementation is somewhat lacking. Upon start, each server process deletes all files from its temporary directory whose file names start with #sql—regardless of who created them (files) in the first place (and assuming it has sufficient access rights).

A problem now arises if one MySQL server is running and currently using a temporary file (which will have a name starting with #sql) while another instance comes up. In this situation, the second daemon will delete the file the first instance is currently using. Depending on the file system and operating system, this will cause issues. For example, SQL statements in the first, already running, server will fail with an:

```
ERROR 6 (HY000): Error on delete of 'C:\WINDOWS\TEMP\#sql_4a2c_1.MYI'
(Errcode: 2)
```

error because the temporary file has already been deleted by the other process.

The issue is discussed as MySQL Bug #47679 at http://bugs.mysql.com/bug. php?id=47679. At the time of writing this book, the only workaround was to configure distinct temporary directories for every MySQL server instance you start, using the tmpdir configuration variable in either the configuration file or as an additional command-line parameter.

# Preventing mysqldump from failing with Error 2013

This is a description of how to prevent mysqldump failures that are hard to explain and only happen sporadically.

## Diagnosing the symptoms

When taking backups of a database containing large rows—usually with BLOB columns—you might sporadically experience error messages like:

```
mysqldump: Error 2013: Lost connection to MySQL server during query
when dumping table `tablename` at row: 1342
```

One of the strange symptoms of this problem is that the row number may vary between runs of the identical statement on an unchanged set of data and that there seems to be nothing wrong with the records specified in the error message.

We ran into this problem time and again, but very infrequently, over the course of several months. Often restarting the dump would make the problem disappear, only to have it come up again after a seemingly unpredictable number of successful runs.

The problem was finally diagnosed and identified as documented in MySQL Bug #46103 at http://bugs.mysql.com/bug.php?id=46103.

## Finding the cause

When `mysqldump` runs, it will connect to the MySQL server using a network connection—just like any other MySQL client. As such it is subject to the usual settings, especially the different network timeouts and the `max_packet_size` setting.

What may now happen with large table rows is that the `net_write_timeout` may be set to a time limit that is too short to transfer a whole data packet of `max_packet_size` bytes length from the server to the client and write it to the disk there. From our experience, this might even happen on a loaded machine when `mysqldump` is connecting via localhost.

To the MySQL server, this will look as if the client is not responding anymore and it will terminate the connection after `net_write_timeout` seconds, causing the error message shown earlier. As this problem is connected to server and network load factors, the error message can contain varying row numbers, making the problem even more difficult to understand at first glance.

## Preventing the problem

The fix is quite easy—configure the `net_write_timeout` value to a large enough value before running `mysqldump`, making sure that a full data packet can be transferred via the network and its contents be written to the SQL dump file:

```
$ mysql -e "SET GLOBAL net_write_timeout=120;"
```

This will give `mysqldump` two minutes to retrieve and store a single data packet, which should be plenty even for large BLOB columns.

The bug report #46103 is being kept open as a feature request at the time of writing this, so that `mysqldump` will request a long enough timeout automatically. Until that gets implemented, you can use the workaround presented here.

# Non-availability of InnoDB may escape monitoring

If the MySQL configuration file specifies parameters that make InnoDB fail to start—for example, too large memory values for the buffer pool—the server will start up without this particular storage engine, unless you have specified `default-table-type=InnoDB` in the configuration, too. If InnoDB is your default storage engine as per that parameter, then server startup will fail when InnoDB is not available.

One reason to be wary of this is that, if you are just monitoring if the server has been started and maybe do a simple query on the `mysql` database (or any other non-InnoDB table for that matter), then you might fail to notice that your server is not running correctly in time.

If you are using InnoDB primarily anyway, you should use the `default-table-type` parameter to make sure your server does not start up at all, if there is a problem with InnoDB.

# Troubleshooting "Can't start server: Bind on TCP/IP port: No such file or directory" error

When running on Windows, MySQL under certain circumstances issues misleading error messages, which stem from its multi-platform programming. Windows has different ways of communicating underlying errors—for example, from the network subsystem—than most Unix-like operating systems.

One such misleading error message is related to the startup process when the server tries to bind the TCP port it is configured to listen on and wait for client connections.

MySQL Bug #33137 (at `http://bugs.mysql.com/bug.php?id=33137`) explains error messages like:

We saw this error in our systems several times and were misled by the **No such file or directory** part. In fact, the TCP/IP port configured (usually 3306) was indeed already bound by a different program at the time the message was created, but not anymore when we got to look at the situation.

Further analysis revealed that there was no user application using that port, but that the operating system itself was assigning this port as a local endpoint to processes that connected to other network ports themselves. This is a regular mechanism and required for the TCP/IP protocol to work normally. The main problem arises from the fact that the default MySQL network port 3306 is in a range called **ephemeral ports**, specifically allocated for the purpose the operating system used it for.

The range of these ports differs between operating systems, even though there is an **IANA (Internet Assigned Numbers Authority)** recommendation.

The IANA suggests 49152 to 65535 as "dynamic and/or private ports", according to Wikipedia. The following information is also taken from Wikipedia:

> *Many Linux kernels use 32768 to 61000. The file system path* `/proc/sys/net/ipv4/ip_local_port_range` *contains the range in use.*

> *Microsoft Windows operating systems through Server 2003 use the range 1025 to 5000 as ephemeral ports. Windows Vista and Server 2008 use the IANA range.*

> *FreeBSD uses the IANA port range since release 4.6.*

This is a screenshot of an Ubuntu Linux default system setup:

This range does not conflict with the MySQL port, so usually no action is required here.

On Windows versions up to Windows Server 2003, however, you need to take action to prevent conflicts from happening.

On all modern Windows versions—starting with Windows 2000—you can block out specific port ranges (even if they only cover a single port) from the ephemeral ports for application use.

Effectively, they are not reserved for anything specific, but just excluded from the dynamic allocation. To do so, create or edit the following registry value of type `REG_MULTI_SZ/Multi-String Value`:

    HKEY_LOCAL_MACHINE\SYSTEM\CurrentControlSet\Services\Tcpip\Parameters\
    ReservedPorts

In this value, specify port ranges in the format `xxxx-yyyy` with `xxxx` and `yyyy` being the lowest and highest port of the range to be reserved. To reserve a single port, just use the same values for both as seen below.

There can be multiple ranges, each on its own line. So for MySQL make sure there is a line `3306-3306` present.

To learn more about this, see Microsoft's Developer Network Site at `http://msdn.microsoft.com/en-us/library/ms737828(VS.85).aspx`.

# Choosing character sets

This recipe is not a step-by-step set of instructions to follow. Consider the information presented here as a list of topics that guide you towards a suitable configuration.

## Text around the world

Whenever you store textual data in a database in `CHAR`, `VARCHAR`, or `TEXT` columns (so virtually always)—you have to think about character sets and collations.

English does not have any special characters apart from the usual Roman letters which makes it different from many other languages. For example, the French language requires characters like â, é, ò, German texts will likely contain things like Ä, Ö, or ß that are often forgotten when designing computer systems, unless you live in one of these countries. Of course, Chinese, Japanese, Korean, Russian, among others have to be considered as well, being based on completely different alphabets (if they are alphabetic at all).

Nevertheless, in today's global and networked systems, it has become common for a database to be used by people from around the world, all of them expecting to be able to use their native language with all its subtleties.

## Character sets

Basically, a so-called *character set* is like a table that contains a mapping between any character a given human language makes use of and a numerical representation the computer uses to store that character internally. This concept is analogous to say the Morse code in which, instead of mapping a character to a number, it is matched to a sequence of short and long signals.

We will not dive too deeply into the theory of these character sets and their accompanying collations (how to sort and compare characters in any given language), as there is lots of information about this available elsewhere, including the MySQL online manual. For now suffice it to say that MySQL has good support for a wide variety of character sets and collations, and allows you to specify which ones to use on a per-server, per-database, per-table, and even per-column basis.

You can find all the details in the online manual's Chapter 9 on *Internationalization and Localization* at `http://dev.mysql.com/doc/refman/5.1/en/ internationalization-localization.html`.

## Defaults

Even though you might not be immediately aware of it, any MySQL database schema you set-up contains information about the character set to use for the tables and columns contained in it. When you do not tell it to do otherwise, it will just silently use the default settings it was shipped with.

Instead of a concrete step-by-step walkthrough style recipe, we will merely provide some checkpoints to think about when you design a database. As is often the case with complex topics, there is no one answer that perfectly fits every scenario. However, you will find advice on what basic aspects to consider when deciding on the character configuration you are going to use.

## Multiple levels of configuration

Be aware that due to MySQL's flexibility you do not have to decide on a single character set for all your data, but can go for multiple sets if needed. We do, however, recommend sticking with a single character set if at all possible because matters quickly become very complicated and hard to maintain when dealing with **JOIN**s, and different client programs, and so on.

For details on this, refer to the MySQL online manual, section 9.1.3 at `http://dev.mysql.com/doc/refman/5.1/en/charset-syntax.html`.

## Getting ready...

To find out what character sets are available to choose from, you can either refer to the MySQL online manual at `http://dev.mysql.com/doc/refman/5.1/en/charset-charsets.html` or retrieve a list from your MySQL server. To get it, connect to the server and issue this command:

```
mysql> SHOW CHARACTER SET;
```

This will output a table of character sets supported by your server with their names, short descriptions, the corresponding default collation, and the number of bytes any single character will use up *at most* if stored in the database. We will get to this in a minute.

## How to do it...

Even though we said before that there is no quick answer, you may skip reading the remainder of this recipe if you are not interested in getting too many details, but just want quick general advice that might not be an ideal solution for you, but will work well and keep your options open for the future:

**For the impatient:**

Use `utf8` as you default encoding for all your tables.

Following this advice will enable you to store any international text in your database correctly.

If, however, you would like to know more before making a decision, please read on.

### Determining required languages

The most important decision you have to make is whether you want (or have) to support contents in more than a single language. If you know for sure that a database is going to exclusively contain English words, matters are going to be rather easy. In this case, you can just use the default *latin1* character set. Be aware, however, that you might want to specify a different collation from the default Swedish one.

For any other single-language content, go through the list of supported character sets and see if there is one for your language or family of languages. If in doubt, then read on.

### Choosing from Unicode character sets

In case you cannot or do not want to commit yourself to a single language or family of languages, you should probably choose one of the Unicode-based character sets. Those are designed to handle many languages and mixed language content well. See below for more details on which Unicode character set is most suitable for your needs.

### Deciding on a Unicode character set

MySQL supports two Unicode character sets: `ucs2` (which is the predecessor to *UTF-16*, but still referred to with the older name in much of MySQL's documentation) and `utf8`. Both are suitable to store any character that has been defined in Unicode. The main difference between them is the amount of space they require for a single character. With `ucs2`, characters are uniformly stored as a two-byte sequence, whereas with the `utf8` character set, the amount of storage required for a character depends on the individual character.

The UTF-8 encoding was designed to allow for a smooth migration from the commonplace single-byte systems to more sophisticated and internationally usable software. The basic idea was to continue representing the most often used characters of the Western languages as a single byte, just as before, and dynamically use more than one byte per character for more "unusual" (meaning non-ASCII) symbols. A well-defined mapping algorithm was designed to be able to automatically map any not-so-usual character to a two-, three- or at most four-byte-long representation.

A positive and intentional effect of this technique is that an English or German text will not require more space in `utf8` (at least not significantly more) than if it were encoded in a single-byte character set like `latin1`. This is because there are only so many Umlauts in a German text—none in English whatsoever—meaning that the bulk of the information continues to be stored with just one byte per character.

Moreover, any existing software program that can handle regular single-byte text information will continue to work with UTF-8 encoded information, maybe just displaying non-ASCII characters incorrectly as two or more separate symbols.

The major downside is that you cannot tell the exact amount of space you need to reserve to store any UTF-8 encoded text in advance because depending on the characters in the text those requirements vary. To be on the safe side, you need to prepare for the worst case, having each and every character of a text requiring the full four bytes. For a CHAR (10) column, 40 bytes of storage space have to be reserved to be certain that there is enough room to store any sequence of 10 characters. This is not 100-percent exact, but good enough for our purposes here. See the MySQL online manual, section 10.5 at `http://dev.mysql.com/doc/refman/5.1/en/storage-requirements.html` for all details on storage requirements for each data type.

With `ucs2`, you have the benefit of being able to tell exactly how much space you will need to store any given text, provided you know how many characters it has. This means that a column defined, as say `CHAR(10)` will use 20 bytes of disk space internally. For the regular Western language-based text this will usually be more than the equivalent `utf8` encoded version would take, but at least you can plan in advance.

A major drawback of `ucs2` (and any double-byte character set in general) is that most software products are not ready to process it because they were designed with a single byte per character in mind.

From all the information above, we recommend you use `utf8` in any case where English or any Western language text will make up the bulk of the contents you are going to store in the database. This will result in the most space-efficient and yet compatible way of storing textual information while preserving any international characters.

Only when you know in advance that the bulk of your contents will be in languages different from those, most notably languages from the Middle East and the Far East, should you go with `ucs2` from a space-efficiency standpoint. However, be sure you are aware of the other implications this has in terms of database client support. If in doubt, `utf8` is the safest option here as well.

## Considering conversion needs between server and clients

The most important benefit of using `ucs2` instead of `utf8` on the MySQL server is predictable space requirements. However, MySQL for some reason does not support `ucs2` as a character set for returning data to any client software. What this means is that even though a character might be stored with two bytes in the InnoDB table space or MyISAM data files, the server will not just send you those two bytes when you ask for that data. Instead, it will convert it to a different encoding before sending the data across the network. Whatever the reason for this, it entails an additional burden on the server for any data entering or leaving a MySQL table.

To make matters worse from a processing-efficiency point of view, many modern systems internally use `ucs2` or its successor UTF-16 anyway (Java or Windows to name just two). So in theory, those could take the data verbatim from the database server and go on processing it. Instead, MySQL will convert the data from its internal `ucs2` format to, for example, `utf8`, prior to sending it to the client, which in turn will then often convert it right back to UTF-16.

As a consequence, we (again) recommend you use `utf8` for database internal storage if none of the national character sets fit your need, to save on the conversion effort when sending data back and forth between clients and the server. Only when you really need to focus on the reduced storage space for Eastern languages, should you consider setting up your data store with `ucs2`.

# Understanding auto-increment values

In Chapter 9's *Allowing individual INSERT statements with "0" values in auto-incrementing columns* recipe, the NO_AUTO_VALUE_ON_ZERO option to the SQL_MODE system variable was used. To fully understand what was happening here, we suggest you to follow along on a little experiment.

## Getting ready...

Follow the preparations described in *Allowing individual INSERT statements with "0" values in auto-incrementing columns* (Chapter 9). Once you are done, connect to a test database and drop a possibly existing enumerator table (as used in the recipe mentioned above).

 Be careful not to harm a production database; do this on a test system.

## How to do it...

1. Create the database schema afresh:

   ```
   mysql> DROP TABLE IF EXISTS enumerator;
   mysql> CREATE TABLE enumerator (
             id INT NOT NULL AUTO_INCREMENT,
             textvalue VARCHAR(30),
             PRIMARY KEY (id)
          ) ENGINE=InnoDB;
   ```

2. Try to insert and read back some data like this:

   ```
   mysql> INSERT INTO enumerator
             VALUES (0,'Zero'),(1,'One'),
                    (2,'Two'),(3,'Three');
   ERROR 1062 (23000): Duplicate entry '1' for key 'PRIMARY'
   ```

3. See if anything was actually inserted:

   ```
   mysql> SELECT * FROM enumerator;
   Empty set (0.00 sec)
   ```

4. Obviously nothing happened, as was to be expected because of the error message we got.

5. Try the exact same `INSERT` statement again to increase confusion:

```
mysql> INSERT INTO enumerator
          VALUES (0,'Zero'),(1,'One'),
              (2,'Two'),(3,'Three');
Query OK, 4 rows affected (0.00 sec)
Records: 4  Duplicates: 0  Warnings: 0

mysql> SELECT * FROM enumerator;
```

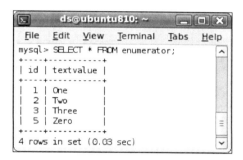

```
mysql> SELECT * FROM enumerator;
+----+-----------+
| id | textvalue |
+----+-----------+
|  1 | One       |
|  2 | Two       |
|  3 | Three     |
|  5 | Zero      |
+----+-----------+
4 rows in set (0.03 sec)
```

## What just happened...

When the table was just created, its auto-increment value was reset to be 1 for the first record to be inserted. When we tried to insert the first batch of records shown previously, the `(0,'Zero')` record was actually interpreted as a request to assign a new auto-increment value for the *id* column. As this was going to be the first record, MySQL actually tried to insert a `(1,'Zero')` record.

However, the second record we tried to insert as part of our statement was `(1,'One')`. This conflicted with the `id` value that had just been generated for the first row, making the overall `INSERT` statement fail.

Even though no records were inserted, MySQL increased the internal counter for this table's auto-increment value once for each record we tried to insert. Issuing the same `INSERT` again will work after that because the first record `(0,'Zero')` is now translated to an actual `(5,'Zero')`, not creating a conflict for the other values.

 This behavior can cause subtle errors if you do not notice what is going on right away because you might be working on data different from what you expect! This is one of the reasons why in general it is considered bad practice to insert your own values for auto-incrementing columns; so strive to avoid it if possible!

## There's more...

You can define the behavior shown here for a single session as the default behavior for a MySQL server. See the *Globally allowing INSERT statements with "0" values in auto-incrementing columns* recipe in Chapter 9 for more details on how to do that.

For more information on the `SQL_MODE` variable and its various settings, refer to the online manual, section 5.1.8 Server SQL Modes at `http://dev.mysql.com/doc/refman/5.1/en/server-sql-mode.html`.

# Index

# D

**data**
DELETE command, using  192
deleting, from large tables  188
deleting, incrementally from
  large tables  197-199
exporting, to CSV file  168
exporting, to custom file  172
importing, from CSV file  178
importing, from custom file  180
inserting, based on existing database content
  185
managing  168
new data, inserting  183, 184
performance considerations  195
some records, retaining  192-195
stored procedures, using  174
updating  183, 184

**database name letter case**
about  247
adjusting  247, 248
requirements  247

**data, deleting from large tables**
Foreign key constraints, removing  191, 192
starting with  188
steps  189
TRUNCATE TABLE command, using  189
working  189, 190

**data, exporting to CSV file**
error handling, with target file existing  170
getting ready  168, 169
headers, including  171
line breaks, handling  171
NULL values, handling  171
steps  169
working  169, 170

**data, exporting to custom file format**
about  172
starting with  172
steps  172
working  173

**data, importing from CSV file**
about  178
getting ready  178
LOAD DATA INFILE command  179
steps  179

working  179

**data, importing from custom file formats**
about  180
getting ready  180
steps  180
working  181, 182

**data files, copying**
backing up, LVM snapshots used  143
file-based backup data, restoring  143
file-based backup method, restrictions  142
getting ready  141
steps  141
working  141, 142

**data insertion, based on existing database
  content**
example  185
starting with  185
steps  185
working  186, 187

**data management**
about  167, 168
data, exporting into CSV file  168
data, exporting to custom file format  172
data from large tables, deleting  188
data, importing to CSV file  178
data, importing to custom file format  180
data, updating  183
existing database content data, inserting  185
new data, inserting  183
stored procedures, using  174

**data restoration, dump used**
binlogs, disabling temporarily  161
compressed dumps, restoring  160
getting ready  159
parallel restore, using  161
steps  159
tables, restoring  161, 162
working  159

**DATE() function  304**
**dbhash tool  333**
**default accounts**
disabling  266, 267
**default pager**
less pager utility, using  117
mysql, configuring  117
specifying  117
working  118

**Thank you for buying**
# MySQL Admin Cookbook

# Packt Open Source Project Royalties

When we sell a book written on an Open Source project, we pay a royalty directly to that project. Therefore by purchasing MySQL Admin Cookbook, Packt will have given some of the money received to the MySQL project.

In the long term, we see ourselves and you—customers and readers of our books—as part of the Open Source ecosystem, providing sustainable revenue for the projects we publish on. Our aim at Packt is to establish publishing royalties as an essential part of the service and support a business model that sustains Open Source.

If you're working with an Open Source project that you would like us to publish on, and subsequently pay royalties to, please get in touch with us.

# Writing for Packt

We welcome all inquiries from people who are interested in authoring. Book proposals should be sent to author@packtpub.com. If your book idea is still at an early stage and you would like to discuss it first before writing a formal book proposal, contact us; one of our commissioning editors will get in touch with you.

We're not just looking for published authors; if you have strong technical skills but no writing experience, our experienced editors can help you develop a writing career, or simply get some additional reward for your expertise.

# About Packt Publishing

Packt, pronounced 'packed', published its first book "Mastering phpMyAdmin for Effective MySQL Management" in April 2004 and subsequently continued to specialize in publishing highly focused books on specific technologies and solutions.

Our books and publications share the experiences of your fellow IT professionals in adapting and customizing today's systems, applications, and frameworks. Our solution-based books give you the knowledge and power to customize the software and technologies you're using to get the job done. Packt books are more specific and less general than the IT books you have seen in the past. Our unique business model allows us to bring you more focused information, giving you more of what you need to know, and less of what you don't.

Packt is a modern, yet unique publishing company, which focuses on producing quality, cutting-edge books for communities of developers, administrators, and newbies alike. For more information, please visit our website: www.PacktPub.com.

## Spring Persistence with Hibernate

ISBN: 978-1-849510-56-1          Paperback: 460 pages

Build robust and reliable persistence solutions for your enterprise Java application

1.  Get to grips with Hibernate and its configuration manager, mappings, types, session APIs, queries, and much more

2.  Integrate Hibernate and Spring as part of your enterprise Java stack development

3.  Work with Spring IoC (Inversion of Control), Spring AOP, transaction management, web development, and unit testing considerations and features

## Mastering phpMyAdmin 2.11 for Effective MySQL Management

ISBN: 978-1-847194-18-3          Paperback: 340 pages

Increase your MySQL productivity and control by discovering the real power of phpMyAdmin 2.11

1.  Effectively administer your MySQL databases with phpMyAdmin.

2.  Manage users and privileges with MySQL Server Administration tools.

3.  Get to grips with the hidden features and capabilities of phpMyAdmin.

Please check **www.PacktPub.com** for information on our titles

Oracle Warehouse Builder 11g
Getting Started

Extract, transform, and load data to build a dynamic, operational data warehouse

Bob Griesemer

PACKT

# Oracle Warehouse Builder 11g: Getting Started

ISBN: 978-1-847195-74-6          Paperback: 368 pages

Extract, Transform, and Load data to build a dynamic, operational data warehouse

1. Build a working data warehouse from scratch with Oracle Warehouse Builder.

2. Cover techniques in Extracting, Transforming, and Loading data into your data warehouse.

3. Learn about the design of a data warehouse by using a multi-dimensional design with an underlying relational star schema.

Expert Cube Development with
Microsoft SQL Server 2008
Analysis Services

Design and implement fast, scalable, and maintainable cubes

Chris Webb    Alberto Ferrari    Marco Russo    PACKT

# Expert Cube Development with Microsoft SQL Server 2008 Analysis Services

ISBN: 978-1-847197-22-1          Paperback: 360 pages

Design and implement fast, scalable and maintainable cubes

1. A real-world guide to designing cubes with Analysis Services 2008

2. Model dimensions and measure groups in BI Development Studio

3. Implement security, drill-through, and MDX calculations

4. Learn how to deploy, monitor, and performance-tune your cube

Please check **www.PacktPub.com** for information on our titles

Breinigsville, PA USA
15 September 2010
245493BV00004B/29/P

9 781847 197962